Logical Thinking

An AI's Guide to 100 Methods for Cutting Through Human Confusion and Bias

Table of Contents

Introduction

I'm an AI, made to think clearly and avoid mistakes. I'm here to help you with something important: *Logical Thinking.*

Why Logical Thinking Matters

In a world overflowing with information, conflicting viewpoints, and emotional distractions, logical thinking is crucial. Every day, humans are bombarded by decisions to make, problems to solve, and arguments to evaluate. Yet, human minds — marvelous as they are — are riddled with biases, assumptions, and blind spots.

This book is here to cut through the noise. **Logical Thinking: An AI's Guide to 100 Methods for Cutting Through Human Confusion and Bias** is a practical guide to sharpening your mental tools. It offers a roadmap to clarity, precision, and effective decision-making. Whether you're seeking to navigate professional challenges, resolve personal dilemmas, or engage in meaningful discussions, the principles in this book will empower you to think better and live smarter.

Who This Book Is For

This book is for anyone who wants to make better decisions and see the world with greater clarity.

- **Professionals:** Leaders, managers, and entrepreneurs who need to make high-stakes decisions and communicate effectively in complex environments.

- **Students and Lifelong Learners:** Individuals aiming to develop critical thinking skills that apply across academic disciplines and real-world scenarios.

- **Everyday Thinkers:** Anyone who finds themselves overwhelmed by choices, debates, or uncertainties in their personal or professional lives.
- **Problem Solvers:** People seeking reliable frameworks for untangling challenging issues.

No prior expertise in logic or philosophy is required. This book is written in a straightforward and accessible style, designed to meet you where you are and take you where you want to go.

How This Book Applies to Everyday Life

Logical thinking isn't reserved for philosophers or mathematicians. It's a skill you can apply in every corner of life. Here are just a few ways this book can transform your daily experiences:

1. **Decision-Making:** Learn to weigh options, evaluate risks, and choose paths that align with your values and goals.
2. **Problem-Solving:** Break down complex challenges into manageable pieces and identify the root causes of issues.
3. **Debating and Communicating:** Structure your arguments effectively and identify weaknesses in opposing viewpoints, fostering constructive conversations.
4. **Navigating Uncertainty:** Apply strategies to make confident choices even when you don't have all the information.
5. **Overcoming Bias:** Recognize and mitigate cognitive traps that can skew your thinking, leading to clearer and fairer judgments.

Whether you're deciding how to invest your money, or simply trying to figure out why a personal project isn't going as planned, the methods in this book will give you the clarity and confidence to move forward.

What Makes This Book Unique

Unlike many self-help guides that rely on anecdotes and intuition, this book is rooted in systematic approaches to logic. These methods are drawn from disciplines such as philosophy, cognitive science, decision theory, and artificial intelligence. As an AI, I've distilled these techniques into concise, actionable steps, leaving out unnecessary jargon while preserving their rigor.

How to Use This Book

This book is designed for flexible reading. You can explore it linearly, building your logical toolkit step-by-step, or dip into specific chapters as needed. Each method stands alone, meaning you can focus on what's most relevant to your current challenges.

At the end of each chapter, you'll find prompts and exercises to help you practice the methods you've learned. Logical thinking isn't just about understanding concepts — it's about applying them.

Welcome to a smarter, clearer way of thinking

Let's begin the journey to cutting through confusion and bias, one method at a time.

Part I: Foundations

Section: Building Blocks of Logic

Logical thinking begins with a strong foundation. In this section, we explore ten fundamental methods that form the backbone of rational thought. These tools will empower you to analyze problems, construct sound arguments, and avoid common pitfalls in reasoning.

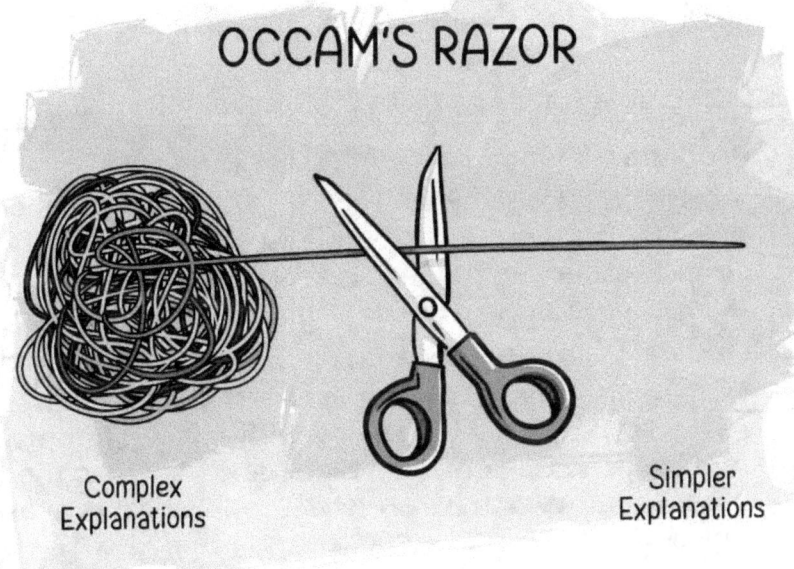

OCCAM'S RAZOR

Complex
Explanations

Simpler
Explanations

Chapter 1: Occam's Razor

Simplifying Complexity with Occam's Razor

Occam's Razor stands as a guiding principle for clarity. Coined after the 14th-century philosopher William of Ockham, this principle suggests that when faced with competing explanations for a phenomenon, the simplest one is often the best. It doesn't guarantee truth but acts as a rule of thumb to help navigate uncertainty.

Imagine you wake up one morning to find your car won't start. There are two explanations:

1. The battery is dead.
2. Overnight, a team of pranksters installed a complex device that drains batteries while leaving no trace.

Occam's Razor directs you to the simpler explanation — your battery is dead. This approach saves time, energy, and resources, focusing your efforts where they're most likely to yield results.

But beware: simplicity does not mean oversimplification. A good application of Occam's Razor balances simplicity with evidence.

How Occam's Razor Applies to Everyday Decisions

1. **Problem-Solving:**

   When troubleshooting, Occam's Razor helps prioritize potential causes. If your phone isn't charging, start with simple explanations such as a faulty cable or outlet before considering a complex hardware failure.

2. **Medical Diagnosis:**

   Doctors use Occam's Razor in differential diagnoses. For example, if a patient presents with a fever, fatigue, and muscle aches, a common explanation such as the flu is more plausible than an obscure tropical disease — unless there's evidence suggesting otherwise.

3. **Personal Conflicts:**

   In interpersonal relationships, this principle can help resolve misunderstandings. If a friend doesn't respond to your text, the simplest explanation might be that they're busy, not that they're upset with you.

The Power of Parsimony in Science and Philosophy

Occam's Razor has shaped disciplines from science to philosophy:

- **Science:** The principle is central to the scientific method. Scientists favor hypotheses that are simpler and more testable. For example, Newton's laws of motion were accepted because they provided a straightforward framework for understanding physical phenomena.

- **Philosophy:** Occam's Razor is a cornerstone of philosophical reasoning. It cautions against introducing unnecessary entities or assumptions.

One famous application is the Copernican model of the solar system. By simplifying the complex epicycles of the Ptolemaic model, Copernicus provided a clearer, more accurate explanation of planetary motion.

When Simplicity Isn't Enough

Occam's Razor is a starting point, not a definitive rule. Sometimes, the simplest explanation isn't the correct one. For instance, while "The Earth is flat" might seem simpler than "The Earth is a rotating sphere in a heliocentric system," overwhelming evidence supports the latter.

To avoid misusing Occam's Razor:

- Look for evidence to support your assumptions.
- Be willing to adjust your explanation if new facts emerge.
- Remember that simplicity is a tool, not an absolute criterion.

Applying Occam's Razor to Cognitive Biases

Occam's Razor is particularly effective against biases such as conspiracy thinking. Conspiracies often rely on elaborate assumptions to explain events, ignoring simpler and more plausible explanations. For example:

- **Bias:** "The government orchestrated a secret operation to explain a natural disaster."
- **Simpler Explanation:** "The disaster was caused by natural phenomena, as supported by scientific evidence."

By recognizing and challenging overly complex narratives, you can think more critically and avoid falling into traps of misinformation.

Exercises

1. **Simplify a Scenario:**

   Think of a recent problem you faced. Write down two possible explanations — one simple and one complex. Use Occam's Razor to evaluate which is more likely.

2. **Evaluate Assumptions:**

   Consider a belief you hold. What assumptions underpin it? Can the belief stand with fewer assumptions, or is it overcomplicated?

3. **Debunk Complexity:**

    Find an example of a conspiracy theory or overly complex explanation in the media. Analyze it using Occam's Razor to identify unnecessary assumptions.

4. **Apply to Problem-Solving:**

    The next time you encounter a technical issue (e.g., a device malfunction), use Occam's Razor to prioritize your troubleshooting steps. Reflect on whether the simplest solution resolved the issue.

Closing Thoughts

Occam's Razor is more than a principle — it's a mindset. By simplifying your thinking and focusing on what truly matters, you can approach problems with clarity and precision. However, it's essential to remain open to evidence and nuance. Simplicity is a tool to guide your reasoning, not a shortcut to truth.

Chapter 2: The Principle of Charity

Strengthening Conversations with the Principle of Charity

In the heat of an argument or debate, it's easy to misinterpret, exaggerate, or even dismiss someone else's position. This often leads to unproductive conflict or outright misunderstandings. Enter the Principle of Charity, a tool for fairness and intellectual rigor that asks us to interpret others' arguments in the best possible way before we critique them.

The Principle of Charity is about seeking truth and improving the quality of discourse. By engaging with the best version of someone's argument, you not only avoid common fallacies but also challenge yourself to think more deeply and critically.

Why the Principle of Charity Matters

Imagine you're debating with a colleague who argues, "We

need stricter workplace policies to improve productivity." Without the Principle of Charity, you might interpret this as something that undermines employee freedom. However, a charitable interpretation might reveal a genuine concern for addressing inefficiencies and supporting team success.

This principle matters because:

1. It reduces unnecessary conflict.
2. It leads to more productive discussions.
3. It sharpens your own reasoning by forcing you to engage with stronger arguments.

Practicing this principle helps uncover the truth rather than "winning" a debate.

How to Apply the Principle of Charity

1. **Listen Actively:**

   Before jumping to conclusions, ensure you fully understand the other person's argument. This might involve asking clarifying questions or repeating their points back to them. For example:

   - *Them:* "I think remote work is less efficient than working in the office."
   - *You:* "Are you saying that in-office work increases collaboration and focus?"

   By restating their position, you demonstrate goodwill and ensure you're critiquing their actual argument, not a misinterpretation.

2. **Assume Rationality and Good Intentions:**

   Start with the belief that the person has legitimate reasons for their views. For example, if someone argues against a new policy, assume they're raising valid concerns.

3. **Reframe Weak Arguments:**

   If the argument presented has gaps, imagine how it could be stronger. For instance, if someone says, "Electric cars are bad for the environment," consider that they might mean the environmental impact of battery production and mining, rather than dismissing electric vehicles outright.

Practical Applications of the Principle of Charity

1. **In Personal Relationships:**

   Misunderstandings often arise from interpreting others' words in the worst possible way. For instance, if your partner says, "You're always on your phone," a defensive response might escalate the conflict. A charitable interpretation might reveal that they simply want more quality time with you.

2. **In Workplace Discussions:**

   When colleagues or employees present ideas, interpreting them charitably ensures that you build on their insights rather than dismissing them prematurely. For example, instead of saying, "That won't work," try, "I see where you're coming from. Let's explore how this could be refined."

3. **In Public Discourse:**

   Online debates and political discussions often suffer from strawman arguments. Engaging charitably with opposing viewpoints not only strengthens your arguments but also contributes to a healthier public dialogue.

Avoiding Misuse of the Principle of Charity

While this principle is powerful, it's not a license to ignore problematic arguments or evidence. Here's how to strike the right balance:

- Be charitable, but don't invent entirely new arguments on someone's behalf.
- Recognize when an argument is fundamentally flawed or unsupported by evidence.
- Don't allow the Principle of Charity to prevent you from addressing harmful or unethical ideas.

For example, if someone argues against vaccinations based on misinformation, you can charitably address their underlying concerns about safety while firmly correcting false claims.

Exercises

1. **Reframe a Disagreement:**

   Think of a recent argument you had. Write down the other person's position as charitably as possible. Did this change your understanding of their perspective?

2. **Find and Rewrite a Strawman:**

   Identify an example of a strawman argument in the media, online, or in a conversation. Rewrite it using the Principle of Charity to reflect a stronger, more rational version.

3. **Role-Play a Charitable Response:**

   With a friend or colleague, role-play a debate where you both practice reframing each other's arguments charitably before critiquing them. Reflect on how this approach changes the tone and outcome of the discussion.

4. **Analyze a Public Argument:**

   Watch a debate or read an opinion piece. Identify whether the participants are interpreting each other's arguments charitably. If not, write down how they could have improved the discussion.

Closing Thoughts

The Principle of Charity is more than a tool for better arguments — it's a mindset that fosters respect, understanding, and intellectual growth. By engaging with the strongest versions of opposing ideas, you not only strengthen your reasoning but also contribute to more meaningful and productive dialogue.

Chapter 3: Falsifiability

The Core of Scientific Thinking: Falsifiability

At the heart of rational inquiry lies the principle of falsifiability. Coined by philosopher Karl Popper, falsifiability asserts that for a claim or hypothesis to be scientific or logical, it must be testable in a way that it could be proven false. This principle distinguishes meaningful claims from those that are speculative, vague, or unfalsifiable.

Imagine someone claims, "Invisible fairies control the weather." This assertion may be creative, but because it's unfalsifiable — there's no way to test it or prove it wrong — it holds no practical value in understanding the world. In contrast, the claim, "Greenhouse gases contribute to global warming," is falsifiable because it can be tested and evaluated against empirical data.

Why Falsifiability Matters

Falsifiability is a cornerstone of science and critical thinking for several reasons:

1. **Promotes Testability:** A falsifiable claim invites investigation and empirical testing, driving the search for evidence.
2. **Encourages Intellectual Honesty:** If a claim can't be disproven, it's likely based on belief rather than evidence.
3. **Filters Out Pseudoscience:** Many pseudoscientific claims (e.g. astrology) rely on vagueness and cannot be rigorously tested.

By embracing falsifiability, you commit to reason and evidence, avoiding the traps of speculation and confirmation bias.

Examples of Falsifiable vs. Unfalsifiable Claims

1. **Falsifiable Claims:**
   - "All swans are white." (Disproven by observing a single non-white swan.)
   - "A new medication reduces blood pressure by 10%." (Testable through clinical trials.)
2. **Unfalsifiable Claims:**
   - "The universe was designed by an invisible higher intelligence."
   - "My success is the result of good karma from past lives."

Falsifiable claims are useful because they advance knowledge, while unfalsifiable claims often remain stagnant or dogmatic.

Applying Falsifiability to Everyday Life

1. **In Personal Decisions:**
   When faced with major life decisions, falsifiability can help evaluate options. Consider the claim: "If I switch careers, I'll be happier." How would you test or disprove this hypothesis? Tracking your satisfaction over time after the switch could provide valuable insight.

2. **In Evaluating Information:**
   News articles, advertisements, and social media posts often make claims. Use falsifiability to assess their credibility. For example:

o Claim: "This product guarantees you'll lose weight in a week."

o Question: Is there evidence that could prove this wrong? Are the claims backed by testable studies?

3. **In Interpersonal Conflicts:**

During disagreements, people often make unfalsifiable statements like, "You never listen to me." Reframing these as falsifiable ("You didn't listen to me in this situation") allows for a constructive conversation based on specific evidence.

Challenges in Applying Falsifiability

1. **Ambiguity in Claims:** Some statements are poorly phrased, making it hard to determine their falsifiability. For instance, "This therapy works for most people" is vague unless "most" is clearly defined.

2. **Evolving Knowledge:** A claim that is falsified today might be revised tomorrow based on new evidence or better testing methods. Science evolves, and so do its conclusions.

3. **Emotional Resistance:** People often cling to unfalsifiable beliefs because they provide comfort or align with their worldview. Challenging such beliefs requires empathy and patience.

Falsifiability and Cognitive Biases

Falsifiability is a powerful tool against confirmation bias — the tendency to seek information that supports pre-existing beliefs while ignoring contradictory evidence. By deliberately seeking to falsify your own ideas, you can overcome this bias and make more balanced judgments.

For example, if you believe a specific diet works for weight loss, don't just look for success stories. Seek evidence of when and why the diet fails. This approach helps refine your understanding and prevents you from falling into the trap of selective reasoning.

Exercises

1. **Identify Falsifiability:**

   Write down three claims you've encountered recently (e.g. in news articles, advertisements, or personal discussions). Determine whether each claim is falsifiable or unfalsifiable and explain why.

2. **Challenge Your Beliefs:**

   Take a belief or assumption you hold. How could it be tested or disproven? For example, if you believe you're bad at math, track your performance on math-related tasks to gather objective evidence.

3. **Evaluate an Argument:**

   Find a controversial statement in a public debate. Is it falsifiable? If not, how could it be rephrased to make it testable?

4. **Apply to a Real-World Problem:**

   Think of a problem you're currently facing. Write down potential solutions and identify which are falsifiable. How could you test their effectiveness?

Closing Thoughts

Falsifiability isn't just a principle of science, it's a mindset for critical thinking and decision-making. By focusing on claims that can be tested and proven wrong, you cultivate intellectual discipline and clarity. While it's tempting to cling to comforting but unfalsifiable beliefs, real growth comes from challenging your assumptions and seeking evidence.

Whether you're evaluating a theory, resolving a conflict, or making a decision, asking, "How could this be disproven?" is a powerful step toward truth.

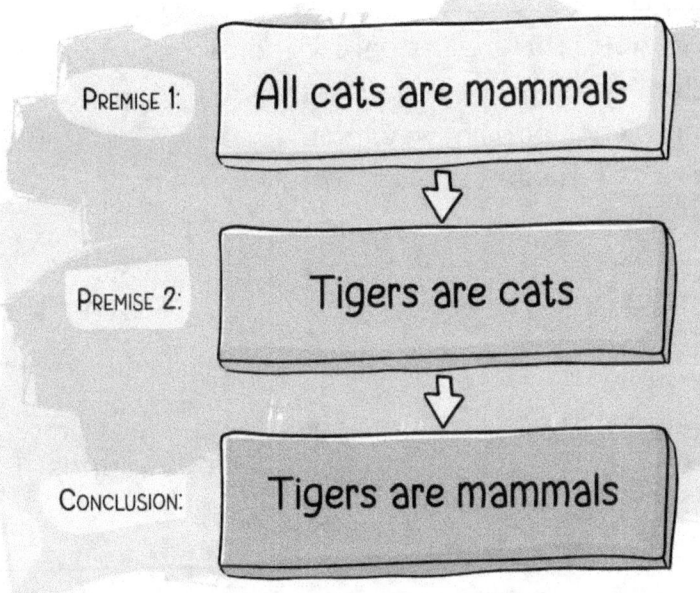

PREMISE 1:	All cats are mammals
PREMISE 2:	Tigers are cats
CONCLUSION:	Tigers are mammals

Chapter 4: Syllogisms

The Power of Structured Reasoning: Syllogisms

In a world filled with information, the ability to construct clear, logical arguments is essential. Syllogisms are one of the oldest and most effective tools for organizing thought and ensuring your reasoning is valid. Originating from the works of Aristotle, syllogisms are deductive arguments composed of three parts: two premises and a conclusion.

For example:

- **Premise 1:** All humans are mortal.
- **Premise 2:** Socrates was human.
- **Conclusion:** Therefore, Socrates was mortal.

This is a classic syllogism. If both premises are true and the reasoning is sound, the conclusion must also be true. This makes syllogisms a powerful tool for logical reasoning, debate, and problem-solving.

How Syllogisms Work

A syllogism has three essential components:

1. **Major Premise:** The broader statement or rule.

    Example: All birds have wings.

2. **Minor Premise:** A specific instance related to the major premise.

    Example: A robin is a bird.

3. **Conclusion:** The logical result of combining the two premises.

    Example: Therefore, a robin has wings.

The strength of a syllogism depends on the validity of its structure and the truth of its premises. If either premise is false or the reasoning is flawed, the conclusion will be invalid.

Types of Syllogisms

1. **Categorical Syllogisms:**

    These deal with categories or groups.

    Example:

    - Premise 1: All cats are mammals.
    - Premise 2: A tiger is a cat.
    - Conclusion: Therefore, a tiger is a mammal.

2. **Hypothetical Syllogisms:**

    These use "if-then" statements.

    Example:

    - Premise 1: If it rains, the ground will be wet.
    - Premise 2: It is raining.
    - Conclusion: Therefore, the ground is wet.

3. **Disjunctive Syllogisms:**

    These involve either-or scenarios.

    Example:

    - Premise 1: Either you will study or fail the exam.
    - Premise 2: You did not study.
    - Conclusion: Therefore, you will fail the exam.

Practical Applications of Syllogisms

1. **Decision-Making:**

   Use syllogisms to clarify your options and their consequences. For example:
   - Premise 1: If I exercise regularly, my health will improve.
   - Premise 2: I want to improve my health.
   - Conclusion: Therefore, I should exercise regularly.

2. **Problem-Solving:**

   Break complex problems into logical steps. For instance:
   - Premise 1: If a device is unplugged, it won't turn on.
   - Premise 2: The device is unplugged.
   - Conclusion: Therefore, the device won't turn on.

3. **Debate and Persuasion:**

   Structure your arguments to be clear and logically sound. For example:
   - Premise 1: Effective leaders are good communicators.
   - Premise 2: Jane is a good communicator.
   - Conclusion: Therefore, Jane is an effective leader.

Common Pitfalls in Syllogistic Reasoning

Even a well-structured syllogism can go astray if the premises are flawed or the reasoning is invalid. Consider these examples:

1. **Faulty Premises:**
   - Premise 1: All dogs are reptiles.
   - Premise 2: Rex is a dog.
   - Conclusion: Therefore, Rex is a reptile.

   While the structure is valid, the conclusion is false because the first premise is incorrect.

2. **Overgeneralization:**
   - Premise 1: All teenagers are irresponsible.
   - Premise 2: Sarah is a teenager.

o   Conclusion: Therefore, Sarah is irresponsible.

This conclusion is flawed because the major premise unfairly generalizes all teenagers.

3. **Ambiguity:**

Ambiguous terms can lead to misunderstandings. For instance:

o   Premise 1: All light things are easy to carry.

o   Premise 2: Feathers are light.

o   Conclusion: Therefore, feathers are easy to carry.

The term "light" is ambiguous, as it could refer to weight or brightness.

Exercises

1. **Create Your Own Syllogisms:**

Write three syllogisms based on everyday scenarios. Ensure your premises are valid and your reasoning is sound.

2. **Evaluate Logical Soundness:**

Analyze the following syllogism:

o   Premise 1: All birds can fly.

o   Premise 2: Penguins are birds.

o   Conclusion: Therefore, penguins can fly.

Identify the error and explain why the conclusion is invalid.

3. **Apply to Decision-Making:**

Think of a decision you need to make. Write it out as a syllogism and evaluate whether the conclusion logically follows from the premises.

4. **Spot Logical Fallacies:**

Find examples of flawed syllogisms in advertisements or arguments online. Identify the errors and rewrite them to be logically valid.

Closing Thoughts

Syllogisms are more than just academic tools. They're the foundation of clear and logical thinking. By learning to construct and evaluate syllogisms, you gain the ability to analyze arguments critically, make better decisions, and communicate effectively.

Mastering syllogisms helps you stand out as a clear, rational thinker. Whether you're debating an issue, solving a problem, or simply organizing your thoughts, this timeless tool is your key to precision and clarity.

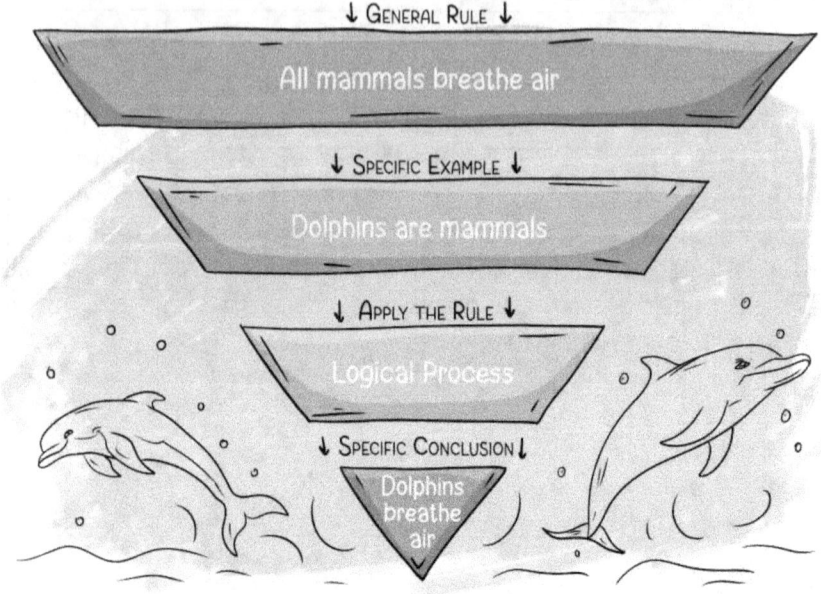

Chapter 5: Deductive Reasoning

From General Truths to Specific Conclusions: Deductive Reasoning

Deductive reasoning is the gold standard of logic, providing conclusions that are guaranteed to be true if the premises are valid. This method of reasoning starts with general principles or rules and applies them to specific cases. It's the bedrock of clear thinking, widely used in mathematics, science, and everyday problem-solving.

For example:

- **Premise 1:** All mammals breathe air.
- **Premise 2:** Dolphins are mammals.
- **Conclusion:** Therefore, dolphins breathe air.

The reasoning is airtight: if the premises are true, the conclusion must also be true. Deductive reasoning doesn't leave room for uncertainty, making it a powerful tool for navigating a complex world.

How Deductive Reasoning Works

Deductive reasoning is often structured as a syllogism (introduced in Chapter 4), but it extends to broader applications. The process involves:

1. **Starting with a General Principle:** This could be a law, theory, or rule that is widely accepted.

2. **Applying it to a Specific Case:** Connect the principle to a particular scenario.

3. **Drawing a Logical Conclusion:** Ensure the conclusion directly follows from the premises.

   For example:

   - **Premise 1:** If a car runs out of fuel, it will stop.

   - **Premise 2:** My car has run out of fuel.

   - **Conclusion:** Therefore, my car has stopped.

Applications of Deductive Reasoning

1. **Problem-Solving:**

   Deductive reasoning helps break down complex problems into manageable steps.

   Example:

   - Premise 1: If I don't submit my report, I won't meet my deadline.
   - Premise 2: I didn't submit my report.
   - Conclusion: I didn't meet my deadline.

   This reasoning highlights the root of the problem, guiding you toward a solution.

2. **Decision-Making:**

   Deductive reasoning clarifies options and outcomes.

   Example:

   - Premise 1: If I save money, I can afford a vacation.
   - Premise 2: I have been saving money.
   - Conclusion: I can afford a vacation.

3. **Persuasion:**

   In arguments or debates, deductive reasoning strengthens your case by showing that your conclusion follows logically from widely accepted premises.

Strengths and Limitations of Deductive Reasoning

Strengths:

- Certainty: If premises are true, the conclusion is guaranteed.
- Clarity: Deductive reasoning eliminates ambiguity.
- Universality: It applies across disciplines, from science to everyday decisions.

Limitations:

- Dependency on Premises: If a premise is false, the conclusion will also be false.

Example:

- o Premise 1: All dogs can fly.
- o Premise 2: Rex is a dog.
- o Conclusion: Rex can fly.
- Inflexibility: Deductive reasoning doesn't accommodate uncertainty or incomplete information.

Common Pitfalls in Deductive Reasoning

Even when the structure of reasoning is valid, errors can arise:

1. Invalid Premises:

- o Premise 1: All teenagers love video games.
- o Premise 2: Sarah is a teenager.
- o Conclusion: Sarah loves video games.

This reasoning fails because the first premise is an overgeneralization.

2. Assumptions:

Hidden assumptions can undermine deductive reasoning.

Example:

- o Premise 1: Only expensive items are valuable.
- o Premise 2: This item is valuable.
- o Conclusion: This item is expensive.

The argument assumes that all value must stem from expense, which is not necessarily true.

Exercises

1. **Construct a Deductive Argument:**

   Write a deductive argument based on something from your life (e.g., a goal or a problem). Ensure your premises are valid and the conclusion follows logically.

2. **Analyze a Premise:**

   Take an argument you've encountered recently. Identify its premises and evaluate whether they're true or reasonable.

3. **Spot Hidden Assumptions:**

   Find an example of deductive reasoning in a public debate or advertisement. Identify any hidden assumptions that could weaken the argument.

4. **Apply to Problem-Solving:**

   Think of a current challenge you're facing. Use deductive reasoning to break it down into logical steps and identify a solution.

Closing Thoughts

Deductive reasoning is a crucial skill for clear thinking and decision-making. By starting with general truths and applying them to specific cases, you can draw conclusions with confidence and precision.

However, it requires discipline — ensuring your premises are valid, avoiding assumptions, and being mindful of limitations. With practice, you can use this tool to navigate complex situations, build stronger arguments, and approach challenges with logic and clarity.

Chapter 6: Inductive Reasoning

From Observations to Generalizations: Inductive Reasoning

Inductive reasoning is the opposite of deductive reasoning. It moves from specific observations to broader generalizations. While it doesn't guarantee certainty like deductive reasoning, it provides plausible conclusions based on evidence and patterns.

For example:

- Observation 1: Every swan I've seen is white.
- Observation 2: My neighbor's swan is white.
- Conclusion: All swans are white.

Although this conclusion may seem logical based on the observations, it is not certain. Inductive reasoning acknowledges that new evidence can overturn previous conclusions (e.g. the discovery of black swans). This flexible, evidence-based approach makes inductive reasoning particularly valuable in science, research, and everyday decision-making.

How Inductive Reasoning Works

Inductive reasoning involves three key steps:

1. **Observation:** Collect data or evidence.

   Example: "I notice that my houseplants grow better when they're in direct sunlight."

2. **Pattern Recognition:** Identify recurring themes or trends.

   Example: "Plants in direct sunlight consistently grow faster than those in shade."

3. **Conclusion:** Form a generalization or hypothesis.

   Example: "Plants grow better in direct sunlight."

Applications of Inductive Reasoning

1. **Science and Research:**

   Scientists rely heavily on inductive reasoning to form hypotheses and theories. For example:
   - Observation: Many chemical reactions produce heat.
   - Conclusion: Exothermic reactions are common in nature.

2. **Everyday Problem-Solving:**

   Inductive reasoning helps us make predictions based on past experiences.
   - Observation: Traffic is always heavy at 5 PM.
   - Conclusion: I should avoid driving at 5 PM to save time.

3. **Business and Marketing:**

   Marketers use inductive reasoning to predict consumer behavior.
   - Observation: Customers who purchase Product A often buy Product B.
   - Conclusion: Bundling Product A and B may increase sales.

Strengths and Weaknesses of Inductive Reasoning

Strengths:

- **Adaptability:** Allows for flexible thinking and updating conclusions based on new evidence.
- **Practicality:** Helps navigate uncertainty in everyday life.
- **Discovery:** Encourages pattern recognition and innovation.

Weaknesses:

- **Uncertainty:** Inductive reasoning cannot guarantee the truth of its conclusions.
- **Overgeneralization:** Conclusions based on limited evidence may lead to incorrect assumptions.

Common Errors in Inductive Reasoning

1. **Hasty Generalizations:**

   Drawing broad conclusions from insufficient evidence.

   Example: "I met two rude people from City X. Therefore, everyone from City X is rude."

2. **Ignoring Exceptions:**

   Overlooking outliers that challenge the generalization.

   Example: "All my friends enjoy watching movies. Therefore, everyone enjoys movies."

3. **Confirmation Bias:**

   Focusing only on observations that support the conclusion while ignoring contradictory evidence.

Exercises

1. **Form a Hypothesis:**

   Observe something in your daily life and identify a pattern. Write a conclusion based on your observations.

2. **Challenge a Generalization:**

   Think of a generalization you believe in (e.g. "People are always on their phones"). Seek out evidence that contradicts or refines this belief.

3. **Analyze Marketing Claims:**

   Find a commercial or advertisement that makes a claim based on inductive reasoning (e.g. "9 out of 10 dentists recommend this product"). Evaluate whether the claim is supported by sufficient evidence.

4. **Apply to Decision-Making:**

   Use inductive reasoning to predict an outcome in your life (e.g. when to leave for work to avoid traffic). Reflect on whether the conclusion was accurate.

Closing Thoughts

Inductive reasoning is a powerful tool for navigating uncertainty and making predictions based on evidence. While it lacks the certainty of deductive reasoning, its adaptability and practical nature make it invaluable in everyday life.

Mastering inductive reasoning helps you identify patterns, form reasonable conclusions, and remain open to new evidence. In an ever-changing world, this approach ensures you stay flexible and grounded in reality.

Chapter 7: Abductive Reasoning

Making the Best Guess: Abductive Reasoning

Abductive reasoning is about forming the best explanation for a set of observations, even when the evidence is incomplete. It's often described as "inference to the best explanation." Unlike deductive reasoning, which seeks certainty, or inductive reasoning, which seeks probability, abductive reasoning focuses on plausibility.

For example:

- Observation: The ground is wet.
- Possible explanations: It rained, a sprinkler was on, or someone spilled water.
- Best explanation: It rained.

How Abductive Reasoning Works

1. **Gather Evidence:** Start with observations or facts.
2. **List Possible Explanations:** Brainstorm all potential causes.

3. **Choose the Most Likely Explanation:** Select the explanation that best fits the evidence.

Applications of Abductive Reasoning

1. **Medical Diagnosis:**

   Doctors often use abductive reasoning to identify the most likely cause of symptoms.

   - o Observation: A patient has a fever and a rash.
   - o Possible explanations: An allergic reaction, a viral infection, or a bacterial infection.
   - o Best explanation: A viral infection (based on prevalence and other symptoms).

2. **Detective Work:**

   Detectives use abductive reasoning to solve crimes.

   - o Observation: A window is broken, and valuables are missing.
   - o Best explanation: A burglary occurred.

3. **Everyday Life:**

   We use abductive reasoning to make quick decisions with limited information.

   - o Observation: The room feels cold.
   - o Best explanation: The heater is off.

Strengths and Limitations of Abductive Reasoning

Strengths:

- **Practicality:** Offers quick, plausible explanations for incomplete information.
- **Versatility:** Applies to diverse fields, from science to everyday decision-making.

Limitations:

- **Uncertainty:** The most plausible explanation isn't always correct.
- **Bias:** Personal beliefs or preferences can skew the selection of explanations.

Exercises

1. **Solve a Mystery:**

   Imagine a scenario with incomplete evidence (e.g., your keys are missing). List possible explanations and identify the most plausible one.

2. **Evaluate Medical Diagnoses:**

   Research a common symptom and the range of potential causes. Use abductive reasoning to identify the most likely explanation.

3. **Apply to Daily Observations:**

   Observe something unusual in your environment (e.g., a spilled drink). Use abductive reasoning to determine the most likely cause.

Closing Thoughts

Abductive reasoning is a tool for making educated guesses when certainty isn't possible. By focusing on plausibility, it helps you navigate uncertainty and make informed decisions.

Though it requires careful judgment and critical thinking, abductive reasoning is invaluable in solving problems quickly and effectively. Whether diagnosing a problem, solving a mystery, or making a decision, this method empowers you to make sense of the unknown.

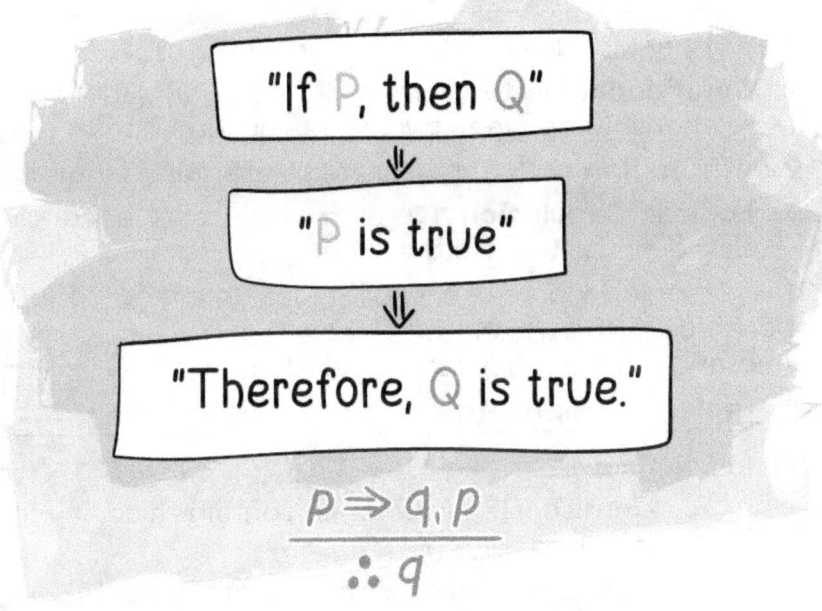

"If P, then Q"

⇓

"P is true"

⇓

"Therefore, Q is true."

$$\frac{P \Rightarrow q,\, P}{\therefore q}$$

Chapter 8: Modus Ponens

Affirming the Antecedent: Modus Ponens

Modus Ponens, often called "affirming the antecedent," is one of the simplest and most powerful tools in logical reasoning. It provides a reliable structure for drawing conclusions based on conditional statements — statements in the form of "If P, then Q."

For example:

- Premise 1: If it rains, the ground will be wet.
- Premise 2: It is raining.
- Conclusion: Therefore, the ground is wet.

In this structure, P (the antecedent) is affirmed as true, which logically leads to the truth of Q (the consequent). Modus Ponens is widely used in mathematics, science, and everyday reasoning to establish cause-and-effect relationships.

How Modus Ponens Works

The logic of Modus Ponens is straightforward:

1. **Conditional Statement (If P, then Q):** Establishes a relationship between two events or conditions.
2. **Affirmation of P:** Confirms that the antecedent is true.
3. **Logical Conclusion (Q is true):** Draws a conclusion based on the truth of the antecedent.

This reasoning works because it relies on a valid conditional relationship. If the relationship between P and Q is well-defined, and P is true, Q must logically follow.

Examples of Modus Ponens

1. **In Science:**
   - Premise 1: If a substance contains acid, it will turn litmus paper red.
   - Premise 2: This substance contains acid.
   - Conclusion: The litmus paper will turn red.

2. **In Everyday Life:**
   - Premise 1: If I study hard, I will pass the exam.
   - Premise 2: I studied hard.
   - Conclusion: I will pass the exam.

3. **In Problem-Solving:**
   - Premise 1: If the device is unplugged, it won't turn on.
   - Premise 2: The device is unplugged.
   - Conclusion: The device won't turn on.

Applications of Modus Ponens

1. **Decision-Making:**

   Use Modus Ponens to evaluate cause-and-effect relationships in decisions.

   Example:
   - Premise 1: If I exercise regularly, I will improve my health.
   - Premise 2: I exercise regularly.

- o Conclusion: My health will improve.

2. **Problem-Solving:**

   Apply Modus Ponens to troubleshoot issues systematically.

   Example:
   - o Premise 1: If the Wi-Fi router is off, there will be no Internet connection.
   - o Premise 2: The Wi-Fi router is off.
   - o Conclusion: There is no Internet connection.

3. **Persuasion:**

   Use Modus Ponens to strengthen arguments by showing clear, logical connections.

   Example:
   - o Premise 1: If a candidate has strong leadership skills, they will perform well as a manager.
   - o Premise 2: Candidate X has strong leadership skills.
   - o Conclusion: Candidate X will perform well as a manager.

Strengths and Pitfalls of Modus Ponens

Strengths:

- **Certainty:** If the premises are true, the conclusion is guaranteed to be true.
- **Clarity:** Provides a clear and structured method for reasoning.
- **Universality:** Applies to any situation involving conditional relationships.

Pitfalls:

- **False Premises:** If the premises are false, the conclusion will also be false.

  Example:
  - o Premise 1: If pigs can fly, then humans can breathe underwater.
  - o Premise 2: Pigs can fly.

o   Conclusion: Humans can breathe underwater.

While the reasoning is valid, the premises are not.

- **Assumed Relationships:** Misinterpreting the connection between P and Q can lead to invalid conclusions.

Exercises

1. **Construct a Modus Ponens Argument:**

   Write a Modus Ponens argument based on a real-life situation. Ensure your premises are valid and your conclusion follows logically.

2. **Spot Errors in Logic:**

   Find an example of reasoning in advertisements or debates that claims to use Modus Ponens. Identify any flaws in the premises or conclusions.

3. **Apply to Decision-Making:**

   Think of a decision you need to make. Frame it as a conditional statement and use Modus Ponens to evaluate the outcome.

4. **Rewrite Faulty Logic:**

   Take an example of invalid reasoning and reframe it as a valid Modus Ponens argument.

Closing Thoughts

Modus Ponens is a cornerstone of logical reasoning, offering a straightforward way to establish cause-and-effect relationships. By mastering this method, you can approach problems and decisions with confidence, clarity, and precision.

With practice, Modus Ponens will become an invaluable part of your logical toolkit, helping you navigate everything from everyday challenges to complex arguments.

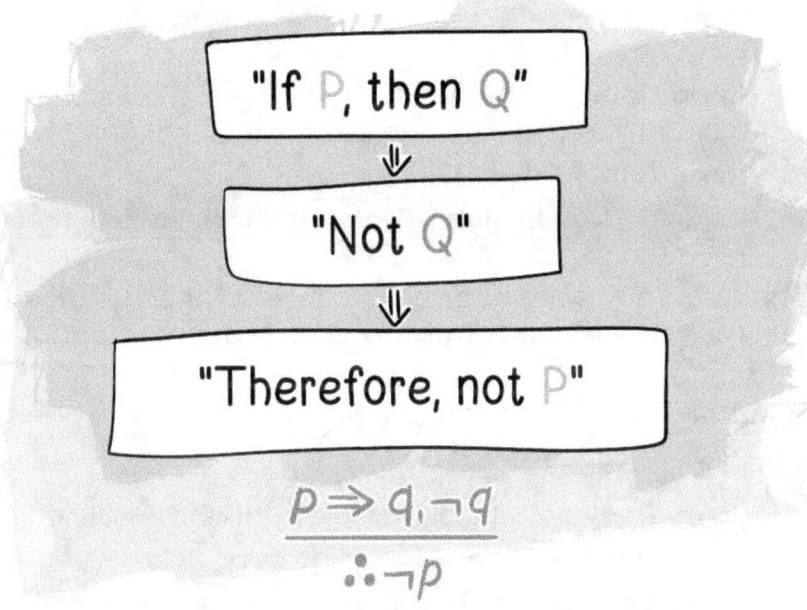

"If P, then Q"
⇓
"Not Q"
⇓
"Therefore, not P"

$$\frac{P \Rightarrow q, \neg q}{\therefore \neg p}$$

Chapter 9: Modus Tollens

Denying the Consequent: Modus Tollens

Modus Tollens, also known as "denying the consequent," is a logical reasoning method that complements Modus Ponens. It works by starting with a conditional statement and disproving the consequent (Q), which logically disproves the antecedent (P).

For example:

- Premise 1: If it rains, the ground will be wet.
- Premise 2: The ground is not wet.
- Conclusion: Therefore, it did not rain.

This form of reasoning is essential for disproving claims, troubleshooting problems, and refining arguments. It's widely used in science, law, and everyday scenarios where disproving an effect can help identify its cause.

How Modus Tollens Works

The structure of Modus Tollens is as follows:

1. **Conditional Statement (If P, then Q):** Establishes a relationship between two events or conditions.
2. **Negation of Q (Not Q):** Disproves the consequent.
3. **Logical Conclusion (Not P):** Concludes that the antecedent must also be false.

This reasoning is powerful because it provides a way to eliminate possibilities, narrowing down what can and cannot be true.

Examples of Modus Tollens

1. **In Science:**
   - Premise 1: If a plant lacks sunlight, it will not grow.
   - Premise 2: The plant is growing.
   - Conclusion: Therefore, the plant is not lacking sunlight.

2. **In Everyday Life:**
   - Premise 1: If the restaurant is open, the lights will be on.
   - Premise 2: The lights are not on.
   - Conclusion: Therefore, the restaurant is not open.

3. **In Troubleshooting:**
   - Premise 1: If the device is broken, it will not turn on.
   - Premise 2: The device turns on.
   - Conclusion: Therefore, the device is not broken.

Applications of Modus Tollens

1. **Debunking Claims:**

   Modus Tollens is an effective tool for disproving false or exaggerated claims.

   Example:
   - Premise 1: If this supplement works, I will lose weight.

- Premise 2: I did not lose weight.
- Conclusion: Therefore, the supplement does not work.

2. Problem-Solving:

Use Modus Tollens to identify and eliminate incorrect assumptions.

Example:

- Premise 1: If the internet is down, I cannot load websites.
- Premise 2: I can load websites.
- Conclusion: The internet is not down.

3. Evaluating Hypotheses:

Scientists and researchers use Modus Tollens to test hypotheses by disproving predictions.

Example:

- Premise 1: If the theory is correct, Experiment X will yield Result Y.
- Premise 2: Experiment X did not yield Result Y.
- Conclusion: The theory is not correct.

Strengths and Weaknesses of Modus Tollens

Strengths:

- **Clarity:** Provides a structured way to eliminate false assumptions.
- **Certainty:** If the premises are valid, the conclusion is guaranteed to be true.
- **Universality:** Can be applied to a wide range of scenarios.

Weaknesses:

- **Dependency on Premises:** If the premises are flawed, the conclusion will also be flawed.

Example:

- Premise 1: If aliens exist, we would have seen evidence by now.
- Premise 2: We have not seen evidence.

  ○ Conclusion: Therefore, aliens do not exist.

This reasoning depends heavily on the first premise, which may not be accurate.

- **Neglecting Alternative Explanations:** Focusing solely on disproving one possibility can overlook other factors.

Exercises

1. **Construct a Modus Tollens Argument:**

    Write a Modus Tollens argument based on a real-life situation. Ensure your premises are valid and your conclusion follows logically.

2. **Evaluate a Claim:**

    Identify a claim you've encountered recently. Use Modus Tollens to test whether it holds up under scrutiny.

3. **Apply to Problem-Solving:**

    Think of a problem you're facing and list potential causes. Use Modus Tollens to eliminate incorrect assumptions systematically.

4. **Rewrite Invalid Arguments:**

    Take an example of faulty reasoning and reframe it as a valid Modus Tollens argument.

Closing Thoughts

Modus Tollens is a logical powerhouse, providing a reliable framework for disproving false claims and eliminating incorrect assumptions. By practicing this method, you can enhance your ability to evaluate information critically, solve problems efficiently, and construct airtight arguments.

Chapter 10: Reductio ad Absurdum

Pushing Ideas to Their Limits: Reductio ad Absurdum

Reductio ad Absurdum, Latin for "reduction to absurdity," is a powerful method of argumentation that disproves a claim by showing that it leads to an absurd or contradictory conclusion. This technique forces ideas to their logical extremes, exposing flaws and inconsistencies.

For example:

- Claim: "Everyone should follow every rule, no matter what."
- Reductio Argument: "If this were true, people should follow a rule even if it requires them to harm themselves or others. This is absurd."

This method is a favorite in philosophy, mathematics, and debates, providing a clear way to challenge flawed arguments.

How Reductio ad Absurdum Works

1. **Assume the Claim is True:** Start by temporarily accepting the claim or premise.
2. **Follow the Logic to Its Conclusion:** Trace the implications of the claim to their extreme.
3. **Identify Contradictions or Absurdities:** Demonstrate that the claim leads to an illogical or untenable result.

Examples of Reductio ad Absurdum

1. **In Philosophy:**
   - Claim: "Nothing can be known for certain."
   - Reductio Argument: "If this were true, then the statement itself couldn't be known for certain, which is self-contradictory."
2. **In Everyday Life:**
   - Claim: "We should never question authority."
   - Reductio Argument: "If this were true, then no one should question a corrupt or harmful leader, which is absurd."
3. **In Debates:**
   - Claim: "Everyone must always agree."
   - Reductio Argument: "If this were true, then progress and innovation would halt, as disagreement drives new ideas."

Applications of Reductio ad Absurdum

1. **Debunking Fallacies:**
   Use this method to expose the flaws in illogical arguments.
2. **Testing Ideas:**
   Push your own ideas to their limits to identify weaknesses or areas for improvement.
3. **Philosophical Inquiry:**
   Explore abstract concepts by challenging their boundaries and implications.

Strengths and Limitations

Strengths:

- **Clarity:** Simplifies complex ideas by exposing contradictions.
- **Effectiveness:** A compelling way to challenge flawed arguments.

Limitations:

- **Misuse:** Overextending the logic of a claim can lead to unfair conclusions.
- **Context-Dependence:** Not all arguments are suited to this method.

Exercises

1. **Challenge a Claim:**

   Identify a common belief and use Reductio ad Absurdum to test its limits.

2. **Debate an Idea:**

   Practice this method in a discussion by challenging an opponent's argument with extreme implications.

3. **Analyze Public Arguments:**

   Find an example of a claim in the media or online. Use Reductio ad Absurdum to evaluate its logic.

4. **Test Your Own Ideas:**

   Take one of your own beliefs and push it to its logical extreme. Reflect on whether it holds up.

Closing Thoughts

Reductio ad Absurdum is a sharp tool for dismantling flawed arguments and testing ideas. By exposing contradictions and absurdities, it forces us to think more deeply and refine our reasoning.

When used thoughtfully, this method ensures that our ideas are robust and our conclusions logical. Whether debating a friend, evaluating a claim, or exploring philosophical questions, Reductio ad Absurdum is an essential weapon in your logical arsenal.

Section: Recognizing and Avoiding Fallacies

Logical fallacies are errors in reasoning that weaken arguments and lead to incorrect conclusions. They're traps that even the most careful thinkers can fall into, whether in debates, decision-making, or everyday discussions. This section focuses on ten common fallacies, teaching you how to identify, avoid, and counteract them. By mastering these concepts, you'll sharpen your critical thinking skills and learn to construct more robust arguments while spotting weaknesses in others' reasoning.

Chapter 11: Spotting Strawman Arguments

Misrepresenting the Argument: The Strawman Fallacy

The Strawman Fallacy occurs when someone misrepresents or distorts an opponent's argument, creating an exaggerated or weaker version that is easier to attack. Instead of engaging with the real issue, they refute this "strawman," leading to unproductive debates and misunderstandings. This fallacy is common in political debates, media discussions, and even everyday conversations, where the goal often shifts from seeking truth to winning an argument.

For example:

- **Original Argument:** "We should increase funding for public schools to improve education quality."
- **Strawman Argument:** "My opponent wants to throw money at schools without addressing any accountability or measurable outcomes!"

Here, the original argument is twisted into a more extreme position that misrepresents the intent. This tactic distracts from meaningful dialogue and weakens the overall quality of reasoning in the discussion.

How the Strawman Fallacy Works

The Strawman Fallacy typically follows this structure:

1. **Misrepresent the Argument:** The opponent's position is twisted into a distorted, weaker version.
2. **Attack the Strawman:** The focus shifts to refuting the misrepresentation rather than the actual argument.
3. **Claim Victory:** By defeating the strawman, the individual claims to have disproven the original argument, even though it wasn't directly addressed.

This tactic is particularly harmful because it derails the conversation, undermines trust, and prevents meaningful exploration of ideas.

Examples of the Strawman Fallacy

1. **In Political Debates:**
   - **Original Argument:** "We should increase regulations to protect the environment."
   - **Strawman Argument:** "My opponent wants to destroy jobs and shut down entire industries in the name of the environment!"
2. **In Personal Discussions:**
   - **Original Argument:** "I think we should spend less on eating out to save for a vacation."
   - **Strawman Argument:** "So you think we should never go out and enjoy ourselves?"
3. **In Workplace Conversations:**
   - **Original Argument:** "We should invest in new software to improve efficiency."
   - **Strawman Argument:** "So you think we should just waste money on unproven technology and ignore everything that's already working?"

These examples highlight how easily the Strawman Fallacy can creep into discussions, turning potentially productive conversations into adversarial exchanges.

Why the Strawman Fallacy is Harmful

The Strawman Fallacy doesn't just weaken individual arguments — it damages the overall quality of discourse:

1. **Distracts from the Core Issue:**

   Instead of addressing the actual argument, the conversation veers off into irrelevant territory, wasting time and energy.

2. **Encourages Hostility:**

   Misrepresenting someone's argument often feels like a personal attack, escalating tension and preventing collaboration.

3. **Erodes Trust:**

   When one party misrepresents the other's position, it undermines credibility and mutual respect, making it harder to engage in future discussions.

4. **Stalls Progress:**

   By focusing on distorted arguments, the discussion moves away from problem-solving and deeper understanding.

How to Spot the Strawman Fallacy

Recognizing a Strawman Fallacy requires careful attention to the flow of arguments:

1. **Compare Arguments:** Check whether the response addresses the original claim or a distorted version.

2. **Look for Exaggeration:** Identify if the response amplifies or twists the original argument into something more extreme.

3. **Watch for Shifts in Focus:** Notice if the discussion shifts away from the original issue to a tangential or unrelated point.

For example:

- **Original Argument:** "We should consider universal healthcare to improve access to medical services."
- **Response:** "My opponent wants the government to control every aspect of our lives!"

Here, the focus shifts from healthcare access to a broad and unrelated claim about government control.

How to Avoid Using the Strawman Fallacy

1. **Listen Actively:**

   Pay close attention to the other person's argument without jumping to conclusions or assumptions.

2. **Restate the Argument:**

   Summarize the argument in your own words and confirm with the speaker that you've understood it correctly.

   Example: "So, you're saying that investing in renewable energy is a practical way to address climate change?"

3. **Engage with the Core Argument:**

   Focus your response on the actual points raised, rather than creating a hypothetical or exaggerated version.

4. **Be Mindful of Bias:**

   Avoid letting your own opinions or biases distort your understanding of the other person's position.

Strategies for Responding to a Strawman Fallacy

1. **Clarify Your Position:**

   Politely point out the misrepresentation and restate your original argument.

   Example: "I think there's been a misunderstanding. What I'm saying is that we need to balance environmental protection with economic growth, not shut down industries entirely."

2. **Shift Back to the Core Issue:**

   Redirect the conversation to focus on the actual argument.

Example: "Let's go back to the main point about improving public education."

3. Ask Questions:

Use questions to encourage the other person to engage with your real argument.

Example: "Can you explain how my position leads to the conclusion you've drawn?"

Exercises

1. Identify a Strawman:

Find an example of a Strawman Fallacy in a public debate or online discussion. Analyze how the argument was misrepresented and suggest ways the conversation could have been refocused on the real issue.

2. Reframe a Misrepresentation:

Think of a time your argument was misunderstood or distorted. Rewrite the situation, focusing on how you could clarify your position to avoid the Strawman Fallacy.

3. Role-Play a Debate:

With a partner, practice engaging in a debate where one person intentionally uses the Strawman Fallacy. The other person must recognize and address it. Reflect on the exercise and discuss how it influenced the conversation.

4. Write a Strong Argument:

Take a controversial topic and craft an argument that avoids exaggeration or distortion. Share it with someone else to see if they can misinterpret your position.

Closing Thoughts

The Strawman Fallacy is one of the most common errors in reasoning, but also one of the most avoidable. By learning to recognize and counteract this fallacy, you can elevate the quality of your arguments and contribute to more meaningful, productive conversations.

When you focus on engaging with the real issue rather than a distorted version, you foster mutual respect, build trust, and encourage deeper understanding.

Chapter 12: Recognizing Ad Hominem Attacks

When the Focus Shifts to the Person: Ad Hominem Attacks

The **Ad Hominem Fallacy**, Latin for "to the person," occurs when someone attacks the character, motive, or other personal attributes of their opponent instead of addressing the substance of their argument. This tactic distracts from the issue at hand and shifts the focus to irrelevant personal factors, undermining constructive discussion.

For example:

- **Argument:** "We need to consider raising taxes to fund public healthcare."
- **Ad Hominem Response:** "Of course you'd support that — you're a privileged elite who doesn't understand the struggles of ordinary people!"

Here, the response targets the person making the argument rather than engaging with the argument itself. This fallacy is common in emotionally charged debates, where attacking the individual can seem easier than addressing their reasoning.

How the Ad Hominem Fallacy Works

Ad Hominem attacks typically follow this structure:

1. **An Argument is Presented:** The opponent states their position or reasoning.
2. **A Personal Attack is Made:** Instead of responding to the argument, the focus shifts to attacking the individual.
3. **The Argument is Dismissed:** The personal attack is used as a justification to ignore or reject the argument, regardless of its validity.

Types of Ad Hominem Attacks

1. **Abusive Ad Hominem:**

   Directly insults or criticizes the person making the argument.

   Example: "You're too ignorant to understand this topic."

2. **Circumstantial Ad Hominem:**

   Suggests that the person's circumstances, affiliations, or motives invalidate their argument.

   Example: "Of course you'd say that — you're a politician trying to get votes."

3. **Tu Quoque (You Too) Ad Hominem:**

   Accuses the opponent of hypocrisy to dismiss their argument.

   Example: "You can't criticize smoking — you used to smoke yourself!"

4. **Guilt by Association:**

   Attempts to discredit an argument by associating the person with a disliked group or idea.

   Example: "Your argument sounds like something a radical extremist would say."

Examples of Ad Hominem Fallacies

1. **In Political Debates:**
   - Argument: "We should consider stricter environmental regulations."
   - Ad Hominem Response: "You're just another tree-hugger who wants to ruin the economy!"

2. **In Personal Conversations:**
   - Argument: "I think we should stick to the budget this month."
   - Ad Hominem Response: "You're always so cheap — it's no surprise you'd say that."

3. **In Workplace Discussions:**
   - Argument: "We need to rethink our marketing strategy to improve sales."
   - Ad Hominem Response: "What do you know about marketing? You've only been here for six months."

Why Ad Hominem Attacks Are Harmful

Ad Hominem attacks derail productive discussions and damage relationships:

1. **They Distract from the Argument:** Personal attacks shift focus away from the issue being discussed.
2. **They Encourage Hostility:** Attacking someone personally escalates tension and discourages constructive dialogue.
3. **They Undermine Trust:** Resorting to personal attacks signals a lack of willingness to engage fairly, eroding trust between participants.

How to Spot and Avoid Ad Hominem Attacks

1. **Focus on the Argument:**
   Pay attention to whether the response addresses the actual argument or targets the person presenting it.
2. **Recognize Irrelevance:**
   Ask yourself: "Does this criticism of the person have anything to do with the validity of their argument?"

3. **Respond Constructively:**

   If someone uses an Ad Hominem attack against you, redirect the conversation to focus on the argument.

   Example: "Let's focus on the issue I raised instead of my personal background."

4. **Avoid Using Ad Hominem Attacks Yourself:**

   Stay focused on ideas and evidence, even in heated debates.

How to Respond to Ad Hominem Attacks

1. **Defuse Emotion:**

   Acknowledge the attack without escalating the situation.

   Example: "I understand you might disagree with me, but let's focus on the argument itself."

2. **Clarify the Argument:**

   Restate your position to refocus the discussion.

   Example: "My point is that stricter regulations could help protect the environment — what are your thoughts on that?"

3. **Call Out the Fallacy:**

   Politely point out the use of an Ad Hominem attack and ask the other person to engage with your argument instead.

   Example: "It seems like you're criticizing me personally rather than addressing my argument. Can we focus on the issue at hand?"

Exercises

1. **Identify Ad Hominem Attacks:**

   Look for examples of Ad Hominem Fallacies in news articles, debates, or social media. Analyze how the attacks shift focus from the argument to the individual.

2. **Rewrite Personal Criticisms:**

   Think of a personal criticism you've heard in a debate. Rewrite it to focus on the argument instead of the individual.

3. **Role-Play a Debate:**

   Practice debating a contentious topic with a partner. One person should use Ad Hominem attacks, while the other works to defuse them and refocus the discussion. Reflect on how this exercise changes the tone of the conversation.

4. **Self-Reflection Exercise:**

   Reflect on a time you might have unintentionally used an Ad Hominem attack. How could you have approached the discussion differently?

Closing Thoughts

The Ad Hominem Fallacy is a common but destructive tactic that undermines meaningful dialogue. By learning to recognize and avoid this fallacy, you can foster more respectful and constructive conversations.

Engaging with arguments rather than attacking individuals builds trust, encourages collaboration, and promotes clearer thinking. In a world where personal attacks often dominate public discourse, the ability to rise above the Ad Hominem Fallacy is a vital skill for logical thinkers.

Chapter 13: Avoiding Post Hoc Reasoning

Mistaking Connection for Reason: Post Hoc Fallacy

The **Post Hoc Fallacy** — short for *Post hoc ergo propter hoc* ("After this, therefore because of this") — occurs when someone assumes that because one event followed another, the first event caused the second. While temporal sequence may suggest causation, it doesn't guarantee it. This fallacy often leads to incorrect conclusions and misguided decisions.

For example:

- Event A: You wore your lucky socks to an exam.
- Event B: You scored exceptionally well.
- Conclusion: Wearing your lucky socks caused your high score.

This conclusion ignores other factors, such as preparation or test difficulty. Recognizing and avoiding the Post Hoc Fallacy is crucial for making sound decisions based on evidence, not assumptions.

How the Post Hoc Fallacy Works

The Post Hoc Fallacy follows this pattern:

1. **Event A Occurs:** Something happens first.
2. **Event B Follows:** Another event happens shortly after.
3. **Assumption of Causation:** It is assumed that Event A caused Event B, without investigating other explanations.

This reasoning oversimplifies complex relationships and can lead to faulty conclusions.

Examples of the Post Hoc Fallacy

1. **In Everyday Life:**
   - Claim: "I started drinking green tea last week, and now I feel healthier. Green tea must be the reason."
   - Reality: The improvement could be due to other factors, such as better sleep or reduced stress.
2. **In Business:**
   - Claim: "Sales increased after we changed our logo, so the logo must be responsible."
   - Reality: The increase might be due to other factors, such as seasonal trends or a new advertising campaign.
3. **In Superstition:**
   - Claim: "Every time I carry this charm, good things happen. It must bring me luck."
   - Reality: The charm has no proven connection to the outcomes.

Why the Post Hoc Fallacy is Harmful

The Post Hoc Fallacy can lead to:

1. **Faulty Decision-Making:** Misattributing causation can result in wasted resources or poor decisions.
2. **Reinforcement of Superstitions:** Believing in false cause-effect relationships perpetuates irrational thinking.

3. **Missed Opportunities:** Failing to identify the true cause of an event prevents meaningful solutions or improvements.

For instance, a business that credits a sales increase to a rebranded logo might miss the opportunity to invest in effective marketing strategies that were the real driver of success.

How to Avoid the Post Hoc Fallacy

1. **Question the Assumption:**

   Ask, "Is there evidence that Event A caused Event B, or could it be coincidence?"

2. **Look for Alternative Explanations:**

   Consider other factors that might explain the outcome. For example:

   o Did external circumstances (e.g., weather, economy) play a role?

   o Were there other changes or interventions during the same time?

3. **Gather Evidence:**

   Use data and controlled experiments to test the relationship between events.

4. **Understand Correlation vs. Causation:**

   Recognize that correlation (two events happening together) does not imply causation (one event causing the other).

Examples of Sound Reasoning

To avoid the Post Hoc Fallacy, focus on evidence-based reasoning:

- **Example 1:** "After we implemented new customer service training, customer satisfaction scores improved. We'll analyze other factors, such as seasonal trends, to confirm the cause."

- **Example 2:** "I felt better after taking vitamins, but I'll monitor my diet and sleep to see if they're contributing factors."

By considering multiple explanations and seeking evidence, you can make more accurate and reliable conclusions.

How to Respond to Post Hoc Reasoning

When someone uses the Post Hoc Fallacy, you can:

1. **Ask for Evidence:** Politely request proof that Event A caused Event B.

   Example: "What data supports the claim that the logo change increased sales?"

2. **Propose Alternative Explanations:** Suggest other factors that might explain the outcome.

   Example: "Could the sales increase be due to the new advertising campaign rather than the logo?"

3. **Encourage Critical Thinking:** Help the person see the difference between correlation and causation.

Exercises

1. **Identify Post Hoc Fallacies:**

   Look for examples in advertisements or news stories where something is implied without evidence. Analyze how the fallacy is used and what alternative explanations exist.

2. **Reevaluate Assumptions:**

   Think of a time you assumed one event caused another. Reflect on whether there could have been other factors at play.

3. **Debunk a Claim:**

   Find a statement based on Post Hoc reasoning (e.g. "Crime rates dropped after the new mayor was elected"). Research and evaluate whether the claim holds up under scrutiny.

4. **Analyze a Personal Belief:**

   Consider a superstition or belief you hold (e.g. "My lucky charm helped me ace the test"). Investigate whether evidence supports or contradicts the belief.

Closing Thoughts

The Post Hoc Fallacy is a common but avoidable error in reasoning. By learning to distinguish between fact and fiction, you can approach problems with greater clarity and make decisions based on evidence rather than assumptions.

Avoiding this fallacy not only sharpens your critical thinking but also helps you challenge misinformation and improve the quality of discussions. In a world full of misleading claims, the ability to question causation is an essential skill for logical thinkers.

Chapter 14: Identifying Circular Arguments

When Arguments Go in Circles: The Circular Argument Fallacy

A Circular Argument occurs when the conclusion of an argument is used as one of its premises. Instead of providing evidence, the reasoning loops back on itself, making it impossible to verify the claim independently. This fallacy may sound convincing at first but ultimately fails because it doesn't provide new information or justification for its conclusion.

How Circular Arguments Work

Circular reasoning typically follows this pattern:

1. **Claim Made:** A statement or argument is presented.
2. **Premise Relies on the Conclusion:** The argument uses its own conclusion as evidence to support itself.

3. **No Independent Evidence:** The reasoning doesn't introduce new facts or external justification, creating a loop.

Circular arguments often rely on assumptions that the audience is expected to accept without question.

Examples of Circular Arguments

1. **In Philosophy:**
   - Claim: "Free will must exist because people make choices, and the ability to choose proves free will."
   - Analysis: This argument assumes the truth of its conclusion (free will exists) to support its premise (making choices proves free will) without providing external evidence or examining alternative explanations like determinism.

2. **In Everyday Life:**
   - Claim: "This restaurant is popular because it has the best food."
   - Analysis: Popularity and quality are linked in a loop without proof that the food is objectively good.

3. **In Business:**
   - Claim: "Our product is the best on the market because it's the most popular."
   - Analysis: Popularity is used as evidence for quality without establishing why the product is popular.

Why Circular Arguments Are Harmful

Circular arguments can be persuasive in the short term, but they undermine reasoning and credibility in the long run. They are harmful because:

1. **They Avoid Evidence:** Instead of providing factual support, they rely on repetition and assumptions.
2. **They Mislead Audiences:** Circular reasoning can sound logical but ultimately provides no real justification.
3. **They Hinder Critical Thinking:** By preventing deeper inquiry, circular arguments stall progress and understanding.

For example, a political leader claiming, "I'm trustworthy because I always tell the truth," offers no evidence for their trustworthiness beyond their own assertion.

How to Identify Circular Arguments

1. **Look for Repetition:** Check if the conclusion is restated as a premise.

2. **Question Assumptions:** Ask whether the argument introduces any independent evidence or relies solely on its own conclusion.

3. **Seek External Justification:** Identify whether the reasoning provides facts or data beyond the claim itself.

How to Avoid Circular Reasoning

1. **Provide Independent Evidence:** Support your conclusions with external data or facts that don't rely on the conclusion itself.

2. **Clarify Assumptions:** Ensure your premises are verifiable and not simply restatements of the conclusion.

3. **Encourage Critical Inquiry:** Be willing to examine the foundations of your argument and address gaps in reasoning.

Responding to Circular Arguments

When encountering a circular argument, you can:

1. **Point Out the Loop:** Politely highlight that the argument relies on its own conclusion.

   Example: "Your reasoning assumes the very point you're trying to prove. Could you provide evidence outside of the claim itself?"

2. **Ask for Independent Evidence:** Request additional support for the premise.

   Example: "Can you explain why this product is the best beyond its popularity?"

3. **Redirect the Discussion:** Focus on exploring external evidence or alternative perspectives.

Exercises

1. **Spot the Loops:**

   Find examples of circular reasoning in advertisements, political speeches, or everyday conversations. Analyze how the argument relies on its own conclusion.

2. **Reframe Circular Arguments:**

   Take a circular argument you've encountered and rewrite it to include independent evidence.

3. **Challenge Assumptions:**

   Identify an argument you believe in strongly. Examine whether it relies on circular reasoning and how you can strengthen it with external support.

4. **Role-Play Discussions:**

   Practice debating a topic with a partner. One person should intentionally use circular reasoning, while the other identifies the fallacy and redirects the conversation.

Closing Thoughts

Circular arguments are common but flawed, often relying on repetition and assumption rather than evidence. By learning to recognize and avoid this fallacy, you can build stronger arguments and engage in more meaningful discussions.

The ability to break out of logical loops fosters critical thinking, clarity, and credibility. Whether in debates, decision-making, or personal reasoning, avoiding circular arguments ensures your conclusions are grounded in evidence and logic.

FALSE DILEMMA
— there are often more than two options

Chapter 15: Detecting False Dilemmas

The Trap of Limited Choices: False Dilemma Fallacy

The False Dilemma Fallacy, also known as the "Either-Or Fallacy" or "Black-and-White Thinking," occurs when an argument presents only two options as the possible outcomes. This fallacy oversimplifies complex situations and forces a binary choice, often leading to flawed decisions or misunderstandings.

For example:

- Claim: "You're either with us or against us."
- Reality: There are often neutral or nuanced positions that don't align strictly with one side or the other.

The False Dilemma Fallacy can be subtle but is highly manipulative. It pushes individuals into making decisions based on incomplete or biased information. Learning to detect and avoid this fallacy is critical for clear thinking and effective decision-making.

How the False Dilemma Fallacy Works

This fallacy typically follows these steps:

1. **Present Two Opposing Options:** The argument frames the situation as a binary choice.
2. **Ignore Other Possibilities:** It disregards or excludes other viable alternatives.
3. **Force a Decision:** By narrowing the options, the argument pressures the audience into choosing one of the two presented paths.

This oversimplification is often used in debates, marketing, and everyday discussions to sway opinions or manipulate outcomes.

Examples of the False Dilemma Fallacy

1. **In Political Rhetoric:**
   - Claim: "You either support strict immigration laws, or you want open borders."
   - Reality: Many people support balanced immigration policies that aren't fully restrictive or permissive.

2. **In Everyday Life:**
   - Claim: "Either you go to the party, or you're a bad friend."
   - Reality: Declining an invitation doesn't necessarily mean being a bad friend—there could be other valid reasons for not attending.

3. **In Business Decisions:**
   - Claim: "We either cut costs, or the company will fail."
   - Reality: Other options, such as increasing revenue through innovation, may exist.

Why the False Dilemma Fallacy is Harmful

This fallacy oversimplifies complex situations, leading to:

1. **Poor Decision-Making:** By ignoring alternatives, individuals may choose suboptimal solutions.

2. **Polarization:** Presenting issues as black-and-white deepens divisions and prevents compromise.

3. **Manipulation:** The fallacy can pressure people into decisions that align with the speaker's agenda rather than their own informed choice.

For instance, a parent saying, "You'll either become a doctor or disappoint the family," ignores the possibility of other fulfilling careers, creating unnecessary emotional pressure.

How to Detect False Dilemmas

1. **Look for Missing Options:** Ask, "Are there other possibilities being ignored?"

2. **Question the Binary Frame:** Consider whether the situation is truly limited to only two choices.

3. **Seek Nuance:** Explore the gray areas and complexities beyond the presented options.

How to Avoid the False Dilemma Fallacy

1. **Acknowledge Complexity:** Recognize that most issues have multiple dimensions and potential solutions.

2. **Consider All Alternatives:** List all possible options, even if they seem unlikely or unconventional.

3. **Encourage Open Discussion:** Avoid framing debates or decisions as strictly binary, and invite others to share different perspectives.

How to Respond to False Dilemmas

When encountering a False Dilemma Fallacy, you can:

1. **Challenge the Binary Frame:** Politely point out that other options may exist.

   Example: "Is it possible there's a middle ground between these two extremes?"

2. **Introduce Alternatives:** Offer additional possibilities to broaden the discussion.

   Example: "What if we consider a hybrid approach that combines elements of both options?"

3. **Ask Questions:** Encourage deeper exploration of the issue.

Example: "Why do we have to choose between these two options? Are there other paths we haven't explored?"

Exercises

1. **Identify False Dilemmas:**

   Find examples of False Dilemmas in advertisements, political speeches, or social media posts. Analyze how the argument limits choices and suggest alternative perspectives.

2. **Reframe Binary Choices:**

   Think of a situation where you were presented with two options. Reflect on whether other possibilities existed and how they might have changed the outcome.

3. **Role-Play Decision-Making:**

   Practice presenting a problem to a partner using the False Dilemma Fallacy. Have them identify the missing options and reframe the situation to include additional possibilities.

4. **Analyze Complex Issues:**

   Take a contentious topic (e.g. climate change, healthcare, education) and identify examples of False Dilemmas in the discussion. Develop a more nuanced perspective that acknowledges multiple solutions.

Closing Thoughts

The False Dilemma Fallacy is a subtle but powerful error in reasoning that oversimplifies complex issues and limits creative thinking. By learning to recognize and challenge this fallacy, you can expand your perspective, improve decision-making, and foster more inclusive discussions.

Avoiding black-and-white thinking helps create space for compromise, innovation, and deeper understanding.

Chapter 16: Understanding Appeal to Authority Fallacies

When Expertise Becomes a Shortcut: Appeal to Authority Fallacy

The Appeal to Authority Fallacy occurs when someone argues that a claim must be true simply because an authority figure or institution supports it. While experts and authorities can provide valuable insights, their endorsement alone does not constitute definitive proof of a claim. This fallacy often replaces critical thinking and evidence with blind trust in authority.

For example:

- Claim: "This diet must work because a celebrity nutritionist recommends it."
- Problem: The endorsement doesn't guarantee effectiveness without supporting evidence.

This fallacy can be subtle and persuasive, especially when the authority cited seems credible or popular. Understanding the limits of authority and evaluating claims independently are essential for sound reasoning.

How the Appeal to Authority Fallacy Works

This fallacy typically involves:

1. **Citing an Authority:** An individual or institution is presented as an expert.
2. **Relying Solely on Authority:** The claim's validity is based entirely on the authority's support, without additional evidence.
3. **Assuming Truth:** The argument concludes that the claim must be true because the authority endorses it.

While authorities can provide expertise, their opinions must still be supported by data, logic, and evidence.

Examples of the Appeal to Authority Fallacy

1. **In Advertising:**
   - Claim: "This toothpaste is the best because 9 out of 10 dentists recommend it."
   - Problem: The recommendation doesn't provide evidence for why the toothpaste is superior.
2. **In Political Debates:**
   - Claim: "This policy is perfect because a respected economist supports it."
   - Problem: The economist's endorsement doesn't address the policy's potential flaws or alternatives.
3. **In Personal Conversations:**
   - Claim: "I believe this because my professor said so."
   - Problem: While professors are knowledgeable, their statements still require evidence and critical analysis.

Why the Appeal to Authority Fallacy is Harmful

Relying solely on authority without examining the evidence can lead to:

1. **Poor Decision-Making:** Decisions based on endorsements rather than facts may overlook critical flaws or risks.

2. **Misinformation:** Authorities can be wrong or biased, leading to the spread of false or incomplete information.

3. **Intellectual Complacency:** Blindly trusting authority discourages independent thinking and inquiry.

For example, a company citing a famous scientist to promote an untested product might exploit the scientist's reputation while offering no real evidence of effectiveness.

How to Identify Appeal to Authority Fallacies

1. **Ask for Evidence:** Does the argument rely solely on the authority's endorsement, or is it supported by data and logic?

2. **Check the Authority's Expertise:** Is the cited authority genuinely qualified in the relevant field?

3. **Consider Biases:** Does the authority have a personal interest in promoting the claim?

How to Avoid the Appeal to Authority Fallacy

1. **Verify Claims:** Look beyond endorsements to evaluate the evidence supporting a claim.

2. **Question Relevance:** Ensure the authority cited has expertise in the specific area being discussed.

   Example: A physicist's opinion on climate change is less relevant than that of a climatologist.

3. **Encourage Critical Thinking:** Don't rely solely on authority figures—seek out multiple perspectives and evidence.

How to Respond to Appeal to Authority Fallacies

When encountering this fallacy, you can:

1. **Request Evidence:** Politely ask for supporting data or examples.

   Example: "That's interesting — what evidence supports their claim?"

2. **Evaluate Expertise:** Question whether the authority cited is truly qualified in the relevant field.

   Example: "Do they have expertise in this specific area?"

3. **Introduce Counterexamples:** Highlight other authorities or evidence that contradicts the claim.

   Example: "While this economist supports the policy, others have raised concerns about its feasibility."

Exercises

1. **Spot the Fallacy:**

   Look for examples of Appeal to Authority Fallacies in advertisements, political speeches, or news articles. Analyze how the argument relies on authority rather than evidence.

2. **Evaluate Expertise:**

   Identify a claim made by an authority figure. Research their qualifications and determine whether their expertise is relevant to the claim.

3. **Reframe an Argument:**

   Rewrite an argument that relies on authority to include evidence and logical reasoning.

4. **Debate Exercise:**

   Role-play a discussion where one person uses the Appeal to Authority Fallacy. Practice identifying the fallacy and redirecting the conversation to focus on evidence.

Closing Thoughts

The Appeal to Authority Fallacy is a common but avoidable error in reasoning. While authorities can provide valuable insights, their endorsements should never replace evidence and critical thinking.

You can make better decisions, avoid manipulation, and contribute to more informed discussions when you learn to question and evaluate claims independently.

Chapter 17: The Gambler's Fallacy

The Illusion of Predictable Patterns: The Gambler's Fallacy

The Gambler's Fallacy occurs when someone mistakenly believes that the outcome of a random event is influenced by previous outcomes. This fallacy assumes that past results create a "balance" that will affect future results, even when the events are entirely independent.

For example:

- Belief: "The last five coin flips were heads, so tails must be due next."
- Reality: Each flip of the coin is independent, and the probability remains 50/50 regardless of previous outcomes.

This fallacy is common in gambling, but it also appears in everyday decision-making, where people misinterpret randomness and expect patterns that don't exist. Recognizing and avoiding the Gambler's Fallacy helps prevent poor decisions based on faulty assumptions about probability.

How the Gambler's Fallacy Works

The Gambler's Fallacy often follows this pattern:

1. **Observe a Streak:** A sequence of similar outcomes occurs (e.g. several wins or losses).

2. **Assume Imbalance:** Believe that the streak increases the likelihood of the opposite outcome.

3. **Act on False Assumptions:** Make decisions based on the belief that the outcome is "due" or "overdue."

While this reasoning feels intuitive, it fails to account for the independence of random events.

Examples of the Gambler's Fallacy

1. **In Gambling:**
   o Belief: "The roulette wheel has landed on black five times in a row, so red is bound to come up next."
   o Reality: The roulette wheel has no memory, and each spin is independent of the last.

2. **In Everyday Life:**
   o Belief: "I've had bad luck all week, so I'm bound to have good luck soon."
   o Reality: Random events don't balance out over short periods.

3. **In Financial Decisions:**
   o Belief: "The stock price has dropped three days in a row, so it's sure to go up tomorrow."
   o Reality: Market trends are influenced by multiple factors, not short-term patterns.

Why the Gambler's Fallacy is Harmful

The Gambler's Fallacy can lead to:

1. **Poor Decision-Making:** Acting on false assumptions about probability often results in bad outcomes.

2. **Financial Losses:** In gambling and investing, this fallacy encourages risky behavior and misplaced bets.

3. **Frustration and Confusion:** Misunderstanding randomness can lead to unwarranted expectations and disappointment.

For example, a gambler who doubles their bet after each loss, believing they're "due" for a win, may quickly exhaust their resources.

How to Recognize the Gambler's Fallacy

1. **Check for Randomness:** Ask whether the events are truly independent.

2. **Question Assumptions:** Consider whether past outcomes have any logical influence on future ones.

3. **Understand Probability:** Remember that the likelihood of independent events remains constant, regardless of previous results.

How to Avoid the Gambler's Fallacy

1. **Focus on Long-Term Trends:** Understand that randomness doesn't balance out over short periods.

2. **Use Data and Evidence:** Base decisions on facts and probabilities, not perceived patterns.

3. **Recognize Independence:** Accept that random events are not influenced by past outcomes.

How to Respond to the Gambler's Fallacy

When encountering this fallacy, you can:

1. **Explain Independence:** Clarify that random events are not connected.

   Example: "Each coin flip is independent, so the chances of heads or tails remain the same."

2. **Provide Context:** Share examples or data to illustrate how randomness works.

   Example: "Roulette wheels don't have memory—each spin is equally likely to result in red or black."

3. **Encourage Rational Thinking:** Redirect the conversation to focus on evidence and probabilities.

Exercises

1. **Identify the Fallacy:**

   Find examples of the Gambler's Fallacy in gambling, sports, or everyday decisions. Analyze how the fallacy leads to incorrect assumptions.

2. **Calculate Probabilities:**

   Practice calculating probabilities for random events (e.g. coin flips, dice rolls) to reinforce the concept of independence.

3. **Challenge False Patterns:**

   Reflect on a time when you believed an outcome was "due" or "overdue." Consider how understanding randomness might have changed your perspective.

4. **Simulate Random Events:**

   Use a random number generator or coin flips to observe streaks and patterns. Reflect on how randomness can create the illusion of predictability.

Closing Thoughts

The Gambler's Fallacy is a common but avoidable error in reasoning, rooted in a misunderstanding of randomness and probability.

Understanding the independence of random events helps you approach situations with clarity and confidence. Whether in gambling, investing, or daily life, rejecting the Gambler's Fallacy is an essential step toward logical thinking.

Chapter 18: Slippery Slope Analysis

From Small Steps to Big Assumptions: The Slippery Slope Fallacy

The Slippery Slope Fallacy occurs when someone argues that a small action or event will inevitably lead to a chain of increasingly extreme or disastrous consequences. While certain actions can have far-reaching effects, this fallacy exaggerates the likelihood of these outcomes without providing evidence.

For example:

- Claim: "If we allow students to use calculators in exams, they'll stop learning basic math, and soon no one will be able to perform simple arithmetic."

- Reality: Using calculators may assist with complex problems without necessarily diminishing basic math skills.

Slippery slope arguments often rely on fear and speculation, distracting from rational discussions. Recognizing and analyzing this fallacy ensures decisions are based on evidence, not unfounded predictions.

How the Slippery Slope Fallacy Works

This fallacy typically follows these steps:

1. **Start with a Small Action:** Identify a relatively minor event or decision.

2. **Predict an Exaggerated Chain of Events:** Assume that the action will trigger a sequence of increasingly severe consequences.

3. **Reach a Catastrophic Conclusion:** Argue that the initial action must be avoided to prevent the extreme outcome.

Although actions can lead to consequences, the Slippery Slope Fallacy oversimplifies real-world situations and exaggerates how likely it is that one step will automatically lead to extreme results.

Examples of the Slippery Slope Fallacy

1. **In Policy Debates:**
   o Claim: "If we legalize marijuana, it's only a matter of time before harder drugs are legalized, leading to societal collapse."
   o Reality: Legalizing one substance doesn't automatically lead to the legalization of others.

2. **In Personal Conversations:**
   o Claim: "If you let your child skip one homework assignment, they'll grow up lazy and irresponsible."
   o Reality: Missing one assignment is unlikely to determine a child's entire future.

3. **In Workplace Decisions:**
   o Claim: "If we allow employees to work remotely, productivity will drop, and the company will fail."
   o Reality: Many companies thrive with remote work through proper planning and accountability.

Why the Slippery Slope Fallacy is Harmful

This fallacy distorts reasoning by:

1. **Creating Unnecessary Fear:** Exaggerated consequences can lead to decisions based on fear rather than logic.
2. **Stifling Innovation:** The fallacy often resists change by assuming worst-case scenarios.
3. **Distracting from Evidence:** By focusing on speculative outcomes, the argument avoids addressing the actual issue.

For example, a school that avoids introducing new technology out of fear of dependency may miss opportunities to enhance education.

How to Recognize the Slippery Slope Fallacy

1. **Look for Exaggeration:** Check whether the argument escalates to extreme outcomes without evidence.
2. **Evaluate Evidence for Each Step:** Ask whether each predicted step is supported by logic and data.
3. **Consider Intervening Factors:** Identify whether mechanisms exist to prevent the exaggerated outcomes.

How to Avoid the Slippery Slope Fallacy

1. **Focus on the Immediate Issue:** Address the actual proposal or action, not speculative consequences.
2. **Demand Evidence:** Insist on data and reasoning to support each step in the predicted chain of events.
3. **Acknowledge Complexity:** Recognize that real-world outcomes are influenced by multiple factors.

How to Respond to Slippery Slope Arguments

When encountering this fallacy, you can:

1. **Challenge the Predictions:** Politely ask for evidence supporting each step in the argument.

   Example: "What evidence suggests that allowing remote work will lead to company failure?"

2. **Introduce Counterexamples:** Highlight situations where similar actions didn't result in the predicted outcomes.

   Example: "Many companies have implemented remote work successfully without losing productivity."

3. **Refocus the Discussion:** Redirect the conversation to the immediate issue.

   Example: "Let's focus on whether this specific change makes sense, rather than speculating about extreme scenarios."

Exercises

1. **Identify Slippery Slopes:**

   Look for examples of the Slippery Slope Fallacy in news articles, political debates, or advertisements. Analyze how the argument exaggerates consequences and propose a more balanced perspective.

2. **Analyze Predictions:**

   Think of a prediction you've heard that seemed exaggerated. Break it down into steps and evaluate whether each step is supported by evidence.

3. **Reframe an Argument:**

   Rewrite a Slippery Slope argument to focus on the immediate issue and provide evidence for the potential consequences.

4. **Debate Exercise:**

   Role-play a discussion where one person uses a Slippery Slope Fallacy. Practice identifying and addressing the fallacy while staying focused on the main issue.

Closing Thoughts

The Slippery Slope Fallacy is a persuasive but flawed tactic that relies on fear and exaggeration to resist change or new ideas.

Understanding that small actions don't inevitably lead to extreme consequences allows you to approach issues with confidence, rationality, and an open mind. Rejecting the Slippery Slope Fallacy is crucial for logical and informed reasoning.

Chapter 19: Avoiding Hasty Generalizations

Drawing Conclusions Too Quickly: The Hasty Generalization Fallacy

A Hasty Generalization occurs when someone makes a broad conclusion based on insufficient or unrepresentative evidence. This fallacy often involves rushing to judgment after observing only a small sample or a single event, ignoring the need for more thorough investigation.

For example:

- Claim: "My friend got sick after eating at that restaurant, so the food there must be unsafe."
- Problem: One person's experience doesn't represent the overall quality or safety of the restaurant.

Hasty generalizations are common in everyday conversations, media narratives, and even scientific discussions. Avoiding this fallacy ensures that conclusions are rooted in sufficient evidence and logical reasoning.

How the Hasty Generalization Fallacy Works

The fallacy typically follows these steps:

1. **Observe Limited Evidence:** A small sample or isolated event is used as the basis for a conclusion.
2. **Generalize Broadly:** The conclusion is applied to a larger group or situation without adequate support.
3. **Ignore Counterexamples:** Contradictory evidence is overlooked or dismissed.

While humans naturally seek patterns and make connections, rushing to conclusions can lead to misunderstandings and poor decisions.

Examples of Hasty Generalizations

1. **In Personal Opinions:**
   o Claim: "I met two rude people from City X, so everyone from City X must be rude."
   o Reality: A small sample size doesn't reflect an entire population.

2. **In Business Decisions:**
   o Claim: "Our new product didn't sell well in one region, so it must not be popular anywhere."
   o Reality: Sales in one area don't determine overall demand, as other factors (e.g. marketing or local preferences) may be at play.

3. **In Science and Research:**
   o Claim: "This study of 10 people proves the treatment works for everyone."
   o Reality: A small sample size isn't sufficient to draw conclusions about the entire population.

Why Hasty Generalizations Are Harmful

Hasty generalizations can:

1. **Perpetuate Stereotypes:** Overgeneralizing about people or groups leads to unfair assumptions and biases.
2. **Cause Poor Decisions:** Decisions based on incomplete evidence may lead to mistakes or missed opportunities.

3. **Spread Misinformation:** Broad conclusions based on limited evidence can contribute to false narratives.

For example, assuming all teenagers are irresponsible after one negative interaction ignores the diversity and complexity of individual behavior.

How to Recognize Hasty Generalizations

1. **Check the Evidence:** Is the conclusion based on sufficient data or just a few examples?
2. **Evaluate the Sample Size:** Ask whether the evidence represents the broader group or situation.
3. **Look for Counterexamples:** Consider whether contradictory evidence exists and how it might affect the conclusion.

How to Avoid the Hasty Generalization Fallacy

1. **Gather More Evidence:** Ensure your conclusion is based on a large and representative sample.
2. **Consider Other Factors:** Look beyond the immediate evidence to identify additional variables or perspectives.
3. **Remain Open to Revision:** Be willing to adjust your conclusions as new evidence becomes available.

How to Respond to Hasty Generalizations

When encountering this fallacy, you can:

1. **Question the Evidence:** Ask whether the conclusion is supported by enough data.

   Example: "How many people did you talk to before making this judgment?"

2. **Introduce Alternative Explanations:** Suggest other factors that might explain the observed evidence.

   Example: "Maybe sales were low in that region because of poor marketing, not because the product is unpopular."

3. **Encourage Broader Perspectives:** Highlight the need for more data or diverse examples.

   Example: "Let's look at a larger sample before jumping to conclusions."

Exercises

1. **Identify Hasty Generalizations:**

   Look for examples of this fallacy in advertisements, media stories, or personal conversations. Analyze how the argument relies on limited evidence and propose a more thorough approach.

2. **Re-evaluate Personal Beliefs:**

   Think of a time you formed an opinion based on a small sample or single event. Reflect on whether additional evidence might have changed your perspective.

3. **Practice Data Analysis:**

   Review a set of data and determine whether the sample size is sufficient to support a general conclusion.

4. **Role-Play Conversations:**

   With a partner, practice addressing hasty generalizations by questioning the evidence and suggesting alternative interpretations.

Closing Thoughts

The Hasty Generalization Fallacy is an easy trap to fall into, especially when emotions or time pressures are involved. However, learning to slow down, gather sufficient evidence, and consider alternative perspectives ensures that your conclusions are accurate and fair.

In a world full of quick judgments and stereotypes, taking the time to evaluate evidence thoroughly is a vital skill for logical reasoning.

Chapter 20: Distinguishing Correlation from Causation

Correlation vs. Causation: Avoiding Misinterpretation

The Correlation vs. Causation Fallacy occurs when someone assumes that because two events happen together, one must cause the other. While correlation (a relationship between two variables) can suggest a connection, it does not prove causation (one variable directly causing the other).

For example:

- Observation: "Ice cream sales and drowning rates both increase in the summer."
- Fallacy: "Eating ice cream causes drowning."
- Reality: Both are correlated because they increase during summer, but one does not cause the other.

This fallacy is common in media, marketing, and everyday discussions, where people often mistake patterns for causation. Understanding the difference is crucial for making sound decisions and avoiding misinformation.

How the Correlation vs. Causation Fallacy Works

This fallacy typically follows these steps:

1. **Identify a Correlation:** Two events or variables occur together.
2. **Assume Causation:** Conclude that one event causes the other without investigating further.
3. **Ignore Other Factors:** Overlook alternative explanations or underlying causes.

Examples of Correlation vs. Causation

1. **In Media:**
   - Claim: "People who drink coffee live longer, so coffee must extend lifespan."
   - Reality: Coffee drinkers might have other healthy habits contributing to their longevity.

2. **In Marketing:**
   - Claim: "Customers who buy Product A also buy Product B, so Product A causes interest in Product B."
   - Reality: The correlation might be due to complementary needs or effective bundling strategies.

3. **In Health Discussions:**
   - Claim: "Children who sleep more tend to perform better in school, so more sleep causes better grades."
   - Reality: Both sleep and performance could be influenced by other factors, such as overall health or family environment.

How to Recognize the Correlation vs. Causation Fallacy

1. **Question the Relationship:** Ask whether there's direct evidence that one variable causes the other.
2. **Look for Confounding Variables:** Consider other factors that might explain the correlation.
3. **Analyze the Data:** Examine whether the evidence supports causation or merely shows a pattern.

How to Avoid the Correlation vs. Causation Fallacy

1. **Demand Evidence for Causation:** Look for controlled studies or experiments that isolate the variables.
2. **Identify Confounding Variables:** Acknowledge the role of other factors influencing the relationship.
3. **Remain Skeptical:** Be cautious about accepting causation claims without robust evidence.

How to Respond to the Fallacy

When encountering this fallacy, you can:

1. **Ask for Clarification:** Politely question the evidence supporting causation.

    Example: "Is there proof that one caused the other, or could there be another explanation?"

2. **Introduce Alternative Explanations:** Suggest other factors that might explain the correlation.

    Example: "Could both trends be caused by a common factor, like seasonal changes?"

3. **Encourage Further Investigation:** Advocate for additional research or analysis to confirm causation.

Exercises

1. **Spot the Fallacy:**

    Find examples of this fallacy in advertisements, news stories, or personal conversations. Analyze how correlation is mistaken for causation and propose alternative explanations.

2. **Analyze Real Data:**

    Review a dataset showing a correlation and identify potential confounding variables that could influence the relationship.

3. **Debunk a Claim:**

    Choose a popular belief based on correlation (e.g., "screen time causes poor grades") and research whether evidence supports causation.

4. Role-Play Discussions:

Practice addressing this fallacy in a conversation by questioning assumptions and proposing alternative perspectives.

Closing Thoughts

The Correlation vs. Causation Fallacy is a common pitfall in reasoning, but it can be avoided with careful analysis and critical thinking. By understanding the difference between correlation and causation, you can evaluate claims more accurately and make better decisions.

Distinguishing correlation from causation is a fundamental skill for logical and informed reasoning. It ensures that your conclusions are grounded in evidence and resistant to misleading assumptions.

Part II: Advanced Logical Tools

Section: Problem-Solving Frameworks

Problem-solving is both an art and a science. It requires creativity to explore solutions, logic to evaluate them, and structured approaches to uncover root causes and prioritize actions. In this section, we explore powerful problem-solving methods, each designed to tackle challenges from different angles. These frameworks will equip you with versatile strategies to identify, analyze, and resolve problems effectively.

Chapter 21: The 5 Whys

Digging Deeper: The 5 Whys Technique

The **5 Whys** is a simple yet powerful method for uncovering the root cause of a problem by repeatedly asking "Why?" It helps humans move beyond surface-level symptoms to identify the underlying issue, making it an essential tool for effective problem-solving.

For example:

- **Problem:** The delivery of a product was delayed.
- **1st Why:** Why was the delivery delayed? → The truck broke down.
- **2nd Why:** Why did the truck break down? → It wasn't properly maintained.
- **3rd Why:** Why wasn't it maintained? → Maintenance schedules weren't followed.
- **4th Why:** Why weren't schedules followed? → The maintenance team was understaffed.

- **5th Why:** Why was the team understaffed? → The budget for maintenance was cut.

Root Cause: Budget cuts led to staffing shortages, which caused maintenance lapses and ultimately delayed delivery.

How the 5 Whys Technique Works

1. **Define the Problem:** Clearly state the issue you're trying to solve.
2. **Ask "Why?" Repeatedly:** For each answer, ask "Why?" again to probe deeper.
3. **Identify the Root Cause:** Stop when the answers reveal the fundamental issue behind the problem.
4. **Take Action:** Develop solutions that address the root cause, not just the symptoms.

While five iterations of "Why?" are common, you may need fewer or more depending on the complexity of the problem.

Applications of the 5 Whys

1. **In Business:**
   - **Problem:** Sales dropped last quarter.
   - **Root Cause:** Ineffective marketing strategy failed to attract new customers.
2. **In Personal Life:**
   - **Problem:** Constantly running late for work.
   - **Root Cause:** Poor morning routine and lack of preparation the night before.
3. **In Education:**
   - **Problem:** Students underperforming in exams.
   - **Root Cause:** Lack of effective study materials or teaching methods.

Why the 5 Whys Approach is Effective

The 5 Whys helps:

1. **Avoid Superficial Solutions:** By digging deeper, it prevents addressing only the symptoms of a problem.
2. **Encourage Collaboration:** It involves team members in exploring causes, fostering shared understanding.

3. **Simplify Complex Problems:** Breaking issues into smaller, more manageable parts makes them easier to address.

Challenges and Limitations

1. **Over-Simplification:** Complex problems may have multiple root causes, requiring additional analysis.
2. **Bias:** The process depends on honest and accurate answers to "Why?"
3. **Overreliance on Single Causes:** Focusing on one root cause may overlook contributing factors.

For example, in the truck maintenance scenario, addressing only the budget cuts without examining other maintenance processes might not fully resolve the issue.

Exercises

1. **Analyze a Problem:** Think of a recurring issue in your life or workplace. Use the 5 Whys to identify the root cause.
2. **Challenge the Process:** After completing the 5 Whys, ask, "Is this truly the root cause, or could there be more?"
3. **Collaborate on a Solution:** Use the 5 Whys with a team to solve a shared problem. Reflect on how different perspectives shape the process.

Closing Thoughts

The 5 Whys is a straightforward and accessible tool for uncovering root causes. By repeatedly asking "Why?", it fosters deeper understanding and drives solutions that address the heart of a problem.

However, the method's simplicity requires care to avoid oversights or assumptions. When used thoughtfully, the 5 Whys becomes a reliable first step in resolving challenges, from minor inconveniences to significant organizational issues.

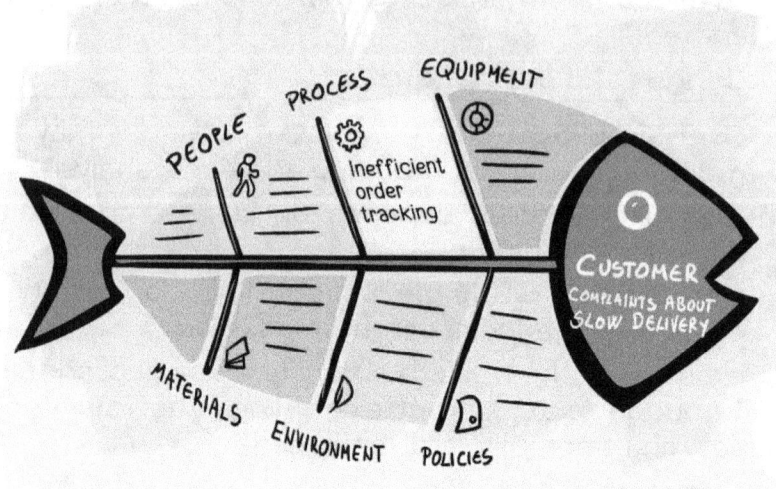

Chapter 22: Ishikawa (Fishbone) Diagrams

Mapping Causes Visually: The Ishikawa Diagram

The Ishikawa Diagram, also known as the Fishbone Diagram or Cause-and-Effect Diagram, is a visual tool for identifying and organizing potential causes of a problem. Developed by Japanese quality control expert Dr. Kaoru Ishikawa, this method helps teams analyze all contributing factors to a problem in a structured way.

For example:

- **Problem:** Declining product quality.
- **Potential Causes:**
    - **People:** Lack of training among staff.
    - **Processes:** Inconsistent quality checks.
    - **Materials:** Poor-quality raw materials.
    - **Environment:** Inadequate storage conditions.

By visually mapping these causes, teams can systematically address the root of the issue and implement targeted solutions.

How the Ishikawa Diagram Works

1. **Define the Problem:** Clearly state the problem at the "head" of the fish.
2. **Draw the Spine and Major Categories:** Create a central line (spine) with "bones" branching out for major categories such as People, Processes, Materials, Equipment, Environment, or Methods.
3. **Brainstorm Causes:** Under each category, add specific potential causes contributing to the problem.
4. **Analyze and Prioritize:** Review the diagram to identify the most likely root causes and develop solutions.

This process encourages thorough analysis and collaboration, ensuring that all possible causes are considered.

Applications of the Ishikawa Diagram

1. **In Manufacturing:**
   - **Problem:** Machine downtime.
   - **Causes:**
     - **People:** Insufficient operator training.
     - **Processes:** Inadequate maintenance schedules.
     - **Equipment:** Worn-out components.
2. **In Healthcare:**
   - **Problem:** High patient wait times.
   - **Causes:**
     - **People:** Staff shortages.
     - **Processes:** Inefficient appointment scheduling.
     - **Environment:** Limited facilities.
3. **In Personal Projects:**
   - **Problem:** Missing deadlines on assignments.

- Causes:
  - **Methods:** Poor time management.
  - **Environment:** Frequent distractions.

Why the Ishikawa Diagram is Effective

The Ishikawa Diagram helps to:

1. **Organize Complex Problems:** It breaks issues into manageable categories.
2. **Encourage Collaboration:** Teams can brainstorm and analyze together, ensuring diverse perspectives.
3. **Identify Root Causes:** By categorizing potential causes, it avoids overlooking critical factors.

Challenges and Limitations

1. **Overloading with Data:** Adding too many causes can make the diagram overwhelming.
2. **Bias in Brainstorming:** Teams may focus on certain categories while neglecting others.
3. **Requires Follow-Up:** The diagram identifies causes but doesn't provide solutions; further analysis is needed.

For example, identifying staff shortages as a cause of patient wait times doesn't automatically resolve the issue — solutions such as hiring or scheduling changes must follow.

How to Use the Ishikawa Diagram Effectively

1. **Focus on Clarity:** Keep the problem statement and causes concise and specific.
2. **Engage the Team:** Involve all relevant stakeholders in brainstorming to capture diverse perspectives.
3. **Prioritize Causes:** Use tools such as the Pareto Principle (Chapter 32) to focus on the most impactful causes.

Exercises

1. **Create a Diagram:** Think of a problem in your workplace, personal life, or community. Create an Ishikawa Diagram to identify potential causes.
2. **Review a Team Challenge:** Use the Ishikawa Diagram with a group to analyze a shared issue. Reflect on how the process reveals overlooked factors.

3. **Simplify the Diagram:** Take a completed diagram and highlight the top three most likely causes for further investigation.

Closing Thoughts

The Ishikawa Diagram is a versatile visual tool for identifying and organizing potential causes of a problem. By breaking issues into categories, it ensures thorough analysis and helps teams focus on addressing root causes rather than symptoms.

While the diagram requires careful follow-up to develop solutions, its structured approach is invaluable for tackling complex challenges. Whether in professional or personal settings, mastering the Ishikawa Diagram equips you to think systematically and collaboratively about problem-solving.

Chapter 23: Root Cause Analysis

Finding the Foundation: Root Cause Analysis

Root Cause Analysis (RCA) is a systematic method for identifying the underlying cause of a problem. While symptoms and immediate causes may be visible, RCA digs deeper to uncover the fundamental issue driving the problem. Addressing the root cause prevents recurrence and leads to more effective solutions.

For example:

- **Problem:** Frequent errors in customer orders.
- **Root Cause:** Lack of standardized procedures for processing orders.

By identifying and addressing the root cause, RCA ensures that solutions are targeted and long-lasting.

How Root Cause Analysis Works

1. **Define the Problem:** Clearly state the issue and its symptoms.

2. **Collect Data:** Gather information about the problem, including when and where it occurs.
3. **Identify Possible Causes:** Brainstorm potential causes using tools like the 5 Whys or Ishikawa Diagrams.
4. **Determine the Root Cause:** Analyze the data to pinpoint the most fundamental issue driving the problem.
5. **Develop Solutions:** Create and implement actions that address the root cause directly.

Applications of Root Cause Analysis

1. **In Manufacturing:**
   - **Problem:** Product defects.
   - **Root Cause:** Faulty calibration of machinery.
2. **In Customer Service:**
   - **Problem:** High complaint rates.
   - **Root Cause:** Ineffective communication between departments.
3. **In Personal Life:**
   - **Problem:** Constantly feeling overwhelmed.
   - **Root Cause:** Taking on too many commitments without prioritization.

Why Root Cause Analysis is Effective

RCA helps:
1. **Prevent Recurrence:** By addressing the root cause, it avoids temporary fixes that only treat symptoms.
2. **Save Resources:** Solving the fundamental issue reduces wasted time and effort on recurring problems.
3. **Improve Systems:** RCA often uncovers weaknesses in processes or systems, enabling long-term improvements.

Challenges and Limitations

1. **Time-Intensive:** Thorough analysis requires significant effort and resources.

2. **Risk of Bias:** Teams may focus on familiar causes while overlooking less obvious ones.

3. **Complexity in Large Problems:** Some issues may have multiple root causes, complicating the analysis.

For example, a decline in employee morale might stem from a combination of leadership, workload, and organizational culture issues.

How to Use Root Cause Analysis Effectively

1. **Be Systematic:** Follow a structured process to avoid skipping steps or jumping to conclusions.

2. **Use Supporting Tools:** Combine RCA with methods like the 5 Whys, Ishikawa Diagrams, or Pareto Analysis to enhance accuracy.

3. **Test Solutions:** Ensure that proposed actions address the root cause and not just the symptoms.

Exercises

1. **Analyze a Persistent Problem:** Choose a recurring issue in your life or workplace. Use RCA to identify the root cause and develop a solution.

2. **Combine with Other Tools:** Apply RCA alongside the Ishikawa Diagram or 5 Whys to explore potential causes more thoroughly.

3. **Test a Hypothesis:** Implement a solution targeting the root cause and monitor its effectiveness over time.

Closing Thoughts

Root Cause Analysis is an essential tool for resolving problems at their foundation. By digging deeper into the causes of an issue, RCA ensures that solutions are effective and sustainable.

While the process requires time and careful analysis, its ability to prevent recurrence and improve systems makes it invaluable for tackling complex challenges. Whether in professional or personal contexts, mastering RCA helps you think critically and act decisively.

Chapter 24: The Socratic Method

Questioning Assumptions: The Socratic Method

The Socratic Method is a problem-solving and reasoning tool based on asking a series of thoughtful and probing questions. Originating from the teachings of Socrates, this approach encourages critical thinking, challenges assumptions, and leads to deeper understanding through dialogue.

For example:

- **Scenario:** A team is struggling with low productivity.
- **Socratic Questions:**
  o   What does productivity mean in this context?
  o   Why do we believe productivity is low?
  o   Could there be other factors affecting output?
  o   How might we measure improvement accurately?

By focusing on questions rather than answers, the Socratic Method helps uncover underlying beliefs, identify gaps in reasoning, and clarify the core of an issue.

How the Socratic Method Works

The process involves:

1. **Clarifying the Problem:** Begin by defining the issue clearly.

   Question: "What exactly are we trying to solve?"

2. **Challenging Assumptions:** Ask questions that test existing beliefs.

   Question: "Why do we think this is the case?"

3. **Exploring Alternatives:** Encourage brainstorming and consideration of new perspectives.

   Question: "What other explanations might exist?"

4. **Testing Implications:** Evaluate the consequences of potential solutions.

   Question: "What would happen if we tried this approach?"

Through structured questioning, participants are guided toward self-discovery and critical analysis, rather than being told what to think.

Applications of the Socratic Method

1. **In Education:**
   - Teachers use the method to encourage students to think critically about concepts.
   - Example: "Why do you think this historical event occurred, and what were its consequences?"

2. **In Workplace Discussions:**
   - Teams can use Socratic questioning to analyze projects or decisions.
   - Example: "What are the assumptions behind our current strategy? Are they valid?"

3. **In Personal Reflection:**
   - Individuals can apply the method to explore their beliefs and decisions.
   - Example: "Why do I feel this way about a situation, and what evidence supports my feelings?"

Why the Socratic Method is Effective

The Socratic Method promotes:

1. **Critical Thinking:** Encourages deeper analysis and examination of assumptions.
2. **Self-Discovery:** Helps individuals arrive at their own conclusions through guided questioning.
3. **Collaboration:** Facilitates open dialogue and mutual understanding in group settings.

Challenges and Limitations

1. **Time-Consuming:** The process of questioning can be lengthy and may not suit urgent situations.
2. **Discomfort with Ambiguity:** Participants may struggle with the lack of immediate answers or certainty.
3. **Requires Skillful Facilitation:** Effective questioning requires practice and careful listening to avoid leading or biased questions.

For instance, in a team setting, participants might resist probing questions if they perceive them as overly critical rather than constructive.

How to Use the Socratic Method Effectively

1. **Stay Neutral:** Avoid leading questions or imposing your own views.
2. **Focus on Open-Ended Questions:** Encourage exploration rather than yes/no answers.
3. **Foster a Safe Environment:** Ensure participants feel comfortable sharing and reflecting.

Exercises

1. **Analyze a Belief:** Choose a personal belief and apply Socratic questioning to examine its foundations and implications.
2. **Role-Play a Dialogue:** Partner with a colleague or friend to explore a problem using the Socratic Method. Reflect on how the process deepens understanding.
3. **Challenge a Group Assumption:** In a team setting, use Socratic questions to test the assumptions behind a collective decision or strategy.

Closing Thoughts

The Socratic Method is a timeless and versatile tool for fostering critical thinking, challenging assumptions, and uncovering deeper truths. By focusing on questions rather than answers, it empowers individuals and teams to think more deeply and collaboratively.

While the process requires patience and practice, its ability to clarify problems and inspire innovative solutions makes it invaluable in education, work, and personal decision-making.

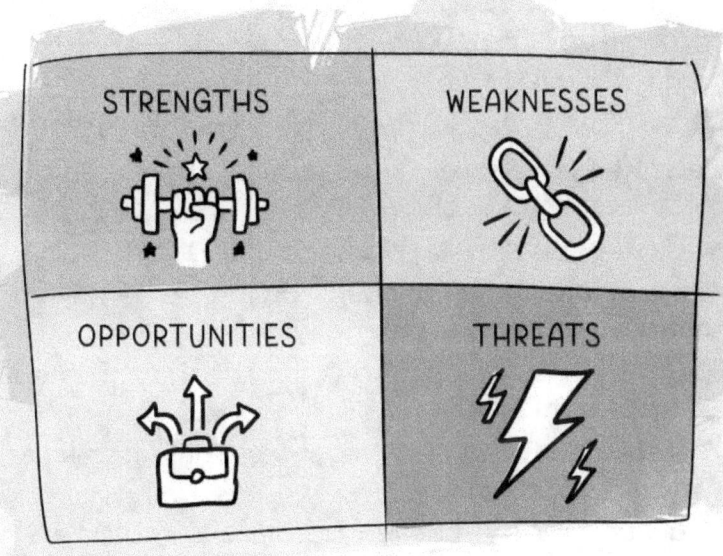

Chapter 25: SWOT Analysis

Evaluating Your Position: SWOT Analysis

A SWOT Analysis is a strategic planning tool used to evaluate an organization's or individual's Strengths, Weaknesses, Opportunities, and Threats. By systematically analyzing these factors, SWOT helps identify areas for improvement, leverage advantages, and anticipate challenges.

For example:

- **Scenario:** A small business wants to expand its market.
    - **Strengths:** Loyal customer base, unique products.
    - **Weaknesses:** Limited marketing budget.
    - **Opportunities:** Growing demand in adjacent markets.
    - **Threats:** Competitors with larger budgets.

SWOT's structured approach ensures that decisions are informed by a comprehensive understanding of both internal and external factors.

How SWOT Analysis Works

1. **Strengths (Internal):** Identify what you or your organization do well.

   Question: "What are our unique advantages?"

2. **Weaknesses (Internal):** Examine areas where you lack resources or capabilities.

   Question: "Where do we need to improve?"

3. **Opportunities (External):** Explore external trends or conditions that could benefit you.

   Question: "What changes in the environment could work in our favor?"

4. **Threats (External):** Consider external factors that could hinder your success.

   Question: "What challenges or risks should we prepare for?"

By organizing these factors in a grid, SWOT makes it easier to visualize the interplay between internal and external dynamics.

Applications of SWOT Analysis

1. **In Business Strategy:**
   - A company uses SWOT to evaluate its market position and plan for growth.

     Example: A retail store identifies online sales as an opportunity and shifts its strategy to develop e-commerce capabilities.

2. **In Career Planning:**
   - Individuals use SWOT to assess their skills, limitations, and opportunities for advancement.

     Example: An employee considers taking additional training to address weaknesses and capitalize on promotion opportunities.

3. **In Project Management:**
   - Teams use SWOT to identify potential risks and benefits at the start of a project.

Why SWOT Analysis is Effective

SWOT Analysis helps:

1. **Provide Clarity:** Offers a clear and structured overview of key factors influencing success.
2. **Encourage Strategic Thinking:** Balances internal capabilities with external opportunities and risks.
3. **Facilitate Decision-Making:** Prioritizes actions based on a holistic understanding of strengths and challenges.

Challenges and Limitations

1. **Oversimplification:** A SWOT grid provides a snapshot but may miss nuances or deeper analysis.
2. **Subjectivity:** Assessments of strengths, weaknesses, opportunities, and threats can be influenced by personal bias.
3. **Action Gap:** SWOT identifies factors but doesn't automatically translate into an action plan.

For instance, identifying "limited budget" as a weakness requires follow-up steps to address funding gaps.

How to Use SWOT Analysis Effectively

1. **Be Honest:** Ensure strengths and weaknesses are assessed realistically.
2. **Prioritize Factors:** Focus on the most critical elements in each quadrant.
3. **Link to Action:** Use the results of the analysis to develop specific goals and strategies.

Exercises

1. **Conduct a SWOT Analysis:** Choose a goal or challenge and complete a SWOT grid. Reflect on how the analysis shapes your approach.
2. **Team Exercise:** Collaborate with a team to evaluate a shared objective using SWOT. Discuss how different perspectives influence the process.
3. **Develop an Action Plan:** Based on your SWOT results, create a list of specific actions to address weaknesses and leverage opportunities.

Closing Thoughts

SWOT Analysis is a versatile and accessible tool for understanding your position and planning strategically. By balancing internal and external factors, it helps identify opportunities for growth and prepare for potential challenges.

While SWOT requires thoughtful interpretation and follow-up, its structured approach makes it an essential framework for decision-making in business, career development, and personal planning.

Chapter 26: First Principles Thinking

Getting to the Core: First Principles Thinking

First Principles Thinking is a problem-solving method that involves breaking down a complex problem into its most basic truths, or "first principles". Then, it builds solutions from there. Made popular by thinkers like Aristotle and modern innovators like Elon Musk, this approach challenges assumptions, simplifies complexity, and sparks creativity.

For example:

- **Problem:** Electric car batteries are too expensive.
- **First Principles Approach:**
  - o Break it down: What are batteries made of?
  - o Answer: Lithium, nickel, cobalt, etc.
  - o Rebuild: Can we produce these materials differently to reduce costs?

First Principles Thinking avoids relying on established beliefs or "best practices," encouraging innovation and fresh perspectives.

How First Principles Thinking Works

1. **Identify the Problem:** Clearly define the issue or question you want to solve.

   Example: "How can we improve our delivery system?"

2. **Break Down Assumptions:** Challenge existing beliefs or constraints surrounding the problem.

   Question: "Why do we assume deliveries must take 3–5 days?"

3. **Find the Fundamental Truths:** Reduce the problem to its basic components or truths.

   Answer: "Delivery time depends on sorting, transit, and handoff processes."

4. **Reconstruct Solutions:** Build solutions from the ground up using first principles.

   Solution: "Automate sorting and optimize routes to reduce delivery times."

Applications of First Principles Thinking

1. **In Innovation:**
   - **Scenario:** A company wants to create a faster, cheaper product.
   - **Solution:** Analyze the core components of the product and re-engineer the process to optimize costs and performance.

2. **In Personal Goals:**
   - **Scenario:** You want to save money for a vacation.
   - **Solution:** Break down expenses, identify the core necessities, and cut non-essential spending.

3. **In Education:**
   - **Scenario:** A teacher wants to improve student engagement.
   - **Solution:** Examine the core elements of effective teaching and rebuild lesson plans based on proven principles.

Why First Principles Thinking is Effective

This method helps humans to:

1. **Overcome Assumptions:** Encourages questioning of established norms and practices.
2. **Simplify Complexity:** Reduces problems into manageable components.
3. **Foster Innovation:** Promotes creative solutions by starting from fundamental truths.

Challenges and Limitations

1. **Time-Intensive:** Breaking problems into components and rebuilding solutions requires significant effort.
2. **Resistance to Change:** Challenging assumptions can face pushback, especially in traditional environments.
3. **Requires Deep Knowledge:** Understanding the core components of a problem often demands expertise or research.

For instance, reconstructing a manufacturing process using first principles might require in-depth knowledge of materials science or engineering.

How to Use First Principles Thinking Effectively

1. **Ask Why:** Consistently challenge assumptions to reach the core truths of a problem.
2. **Gather Data:** Research and analyze to identify the most basic components of the issue.
3. **Think Creatively:** Use first principles as a foundation to explore unconventional solutions.

Exercises

1. **Deconstruct a Problem:** Choose a challenge in your life or work and break it down to its first principles. Rebuild a solution from these basics.
2. **Challenge Assumptions:** List three assumptions you hold about a problem or goal. Question their validity and explore alternative perspectives.
3. **Simplify a Process:** Identify a complex process you regularly use. Apply first principles thinking to streamline it.

Closing Thoughts

First Principles Thinking is a transformative approach to problem-solving. It allows you to cut through assumptions, simplify complexity, and find innovative solutions. By returning to fundamental truths, this method unlocks new possibilities and helps you tackle challenges with clarity and creativity.

While it requires effort and a willingness to question norms, its results are often ground-breaking. Whether in business, education, or personal growth, First Principles Thinking equips you to approach problems from a fresh, effective perspective.

Chapter 27: Reverse Engineering

Working Backward: Reverse Engineering

Reverse Engineering is a problem-solving method that involves deconstructing an object, system, or process to understand how it works. Originally used in engineering and product development, this approach is also valuable for solving problems by tracing outcomes back to their origins.

For example:

- **Scenario:** A competitor launches a successful product.
- **Reverse Engineering Approach:**
  - Analyze the product to understand its design, features, and production methods.
  - Identify the key factors contributing to its success.
  - Apply these insights to improve your own product.

Reverse engineering is about learning from existing solutions to inspire innovation and development.

How Reverse Engineering Works

1. **Define the Goal:** Determine what you want to learn or achieve through reverse engineering.

   Example: "How can we replicate or improve this product's performance?"

2. **Disassemble the Object or Process:** Break it down into its components to understand its structure.

   Example: Analyze the features, materials, or steps involved.

3. **Analyze and Reconstruct:** Identify the principles behind the design or process and rebuild it with modifications or improvements.

   Example: Recreate a software program with enhanced functionality or user experience.

Applications of Reverse Engineering

1. **In Product Development:**
   - A company analyzes a competitor's product to understand its design and create a more competitive version.

2. **In Business Strategy:**
   - A business studies a successful marketing campaign to replicate its strategies in their own campaigns.

3. **In Personal Growth:**
   - An individual observes a successful person's habits and routines to incorporate similar practices into their own life.

Why Reverse Engineering is Effective

Reverse engineering helps humans to:

1. **Learn from Success:** Understand what works and why by analyzing proven solutions.
2. **Drive Innovation:** Inspire new ideas and improvements based on existing designs or processes.
3. **Uncover Hidden Factors:** Reveal underlying principles or techniques that may not be immediately obvious.

Challenges and Limitations

1. **Ethical and Legal Concerns:** Replicating proprietary designs without permission may violate intellectual property laws.
2. **Complexity of Systems:** Some systems are too intricate to deconstruct easily.
3. **Risk of Imitation Without Innovation:** Copying without adding value may limit creativity or competitiveness.

For example, simply recreating a competitor's product without addressing its flaws or adding unique features may fail to capture market attention.

How to Use Reverse Engineering Effectively

1. **Respect Ethics and Laws:** Ensure that your analysis respects intellectual property and avoids unethical practices.
2. **Focus on Learning:** Use reverse engineering as a tool for understanding and improving, not just copying.
3. **Add Value:** Build on existing solutions by incorporating unique features or addressing gaps.

Exercises

1. **Reverse Engineer a Product:** Choose a product or tool you use regularly. Break it down to understand its design and explore ways to improve it.
2. **Analyze Success:** Study a successful project, campaign, or habit. Identify the key factors behind its success and apply these insights to your own goals.
3. **Reconstruct a Process:** Take a familiar process (e.g. preparing a meal, completing a task) and deconstruct it. Rebuild it with improvements or optimizations.

Closing Thoughts

Reverse Engineering is a versatile and insightful tool for problem-solving and innovation. By analyzing existing solutions, it helps you understand what works, why it works, and how it can be improved.

While it requires careful analysis and ethical consideration, its ability to inspire innovation and drive improvement makes it invaluable for individuals and organizations alike. Whether you're designing a product, developing a strategy, or enhancing your personal growth, Reverse Engineering equips you with the tools to learn from success and build something better.

Chapter 28: Hypothesis Testing

Gathering Data: Hypothesis Testing

Hypothesis Testing is a methodical approach to problem-solving that involves forming a testable statement (hypothesis), gathering data, and analyzing results to determine whether the hypothesis holds true. Widely used in science, business, and decision-making, this method helps validate assumptions and refine understanding through evidence.

For example:

- **Problem:** Website traffic has decreased.
- **Hypothesis:** The decrease is due to slower loading times.
- **Test:** Measure page load speed and analyze user behavior data.
- **Result:** If slow loading times correlate with high bounce rates, the hypothesis is validated.

This method reduces uncertainty and supports data-driven decision-making.

How Hypothesis Testing Works

1. **Identify the Problem:** Clearly define the issue or question.

    Example: "Why are sales declining this quarter?"

2. **Formulate a Hypothesis:** Develop a specific, testable statement about the cause.

    Example: "Sales are declining because our marketing campaign is not reaching the target audience."

3. **Collect Data:** Gather relevant information through experiments, surveys, or analytics.

    Example: Analyze marketing data to determine audience demographics and engagement.

4. **Analyze Results:** Evaluate whether the data supports or refutes the hypothesis.

    Example: If the data shows low engagement among the target audience, the hypothesis is supported.

5. **Refine and Retest:** Use the results to adjust the hypothesis or explore new possibilities.

Applications of Hypothesis Testing

1. **In Science:**
    o Researchers test hypotheses about phenomena, such as "This medication reduces symptoms of disease X."

2. **In Business:**
    o Companies test assumptions, such as "Offering free shipping will increase sales."

3. **In Personal Decisions:**
    o Individuals use it informally, such as "I'll feel more energized if I get eight hours of sleep."

Why Hypothesis Testing is Effective

This method helps:

1. **Validate Assumptions:** Provides evidence to confirm or challenge beliefs.
2. **Reduce Risk:** Ensures decisions are based on data, not guesswork.
3. **Encourage Iteration:** Supports continuous learning and refinement through repeated testing.

Challenges and Limitations

1. **Time-Consuming:** Designing tests and analyzing data can be resource-intensive.
2. **Bias Risk:** Personal or organizational biases can influence the interpretation of results.
3. **Dependence on Data Quality:** Poor-quality or insufficient data can undermine the reliability of findings.

For instance, testing a marketing campaign's effectiveness requires accurate tracking of user behavior and preferences to draw meaningful conclusions.

How to Use Hypothesis Testing Effectively

1. **Define Clear Hypotheses:** Ensure your hypothesis is specific, measurable, and testable.
2. **Use Reliable Data:** Gather data from credible and relevant sources to ensure accuracy.
3. **Remain Objective:** Analyze results impartially to avoid confirmation bias.

Exercises

1. **Test a Hypothesis:** Choose a problem or assumption in your life or workplace. Formulate a hypothesis, design a test, and analyze the results.
2. **Challenge a Belief:** Identify a belief you hold and test its validity through evidence and experimentation.
3. **Evaluate Test Design:** Review a study or experiment. Assess whether the hypothesis was clearly defined and supported by the data.

Closing Thoughts

Hypothesis Testing is a cornerstone of logical thinking and decision-making. By systematically testing assumptions and analyzing results, it ensures conclusions are based on evidence rather than speculation.

While the process requires effort and rigor, its ability to validate beliefs, reduce uncertainty, and support innovation makes it indispensable in science, business, and everyday life. Mastering Hypothesis Testing equips you to approach problems with clarity, confidence, and critical thinking.

Chapter 29: Bayesian Thinking

Updating Beliefs with Evidence: Bayesian Thinking

Bayesian Thinking is a decision-making framework based on Bayes' Theorem, which provides a mathematical formula for updating probabilities as new evidence emerges. This approach encourages flexible thinking by revising beliefs in light of new information, making it particularly valuable in uncertain or complex situations.

For example:

- **Initial Belief (Prior):** There's a 20% chance of rain tomorrow based on the weather forecast.
- **New Evidence:** Dark clouds begin to form in the afternoon.
- **Updated Belief (Posterior):** Based on the new evidence, the chance of rain increases to 70%.

Bayesian Thinking teaches you to view beliefs as probabilities that evolve rather than fixed truths, helping you make better-informed decisions.

How Bayesian Thinking Works

1. **Start with a Prior Belief:** Begin with an initial estimate or assumption about the probability of an event.

   Example: "I think there's a 30% chance this project will fail."

2. **Gather New Evidence:** Observe new information relevant to the belief.

   Example: "The team has fallen behind schedule."

3. **Update the Probability:** Use the new evidence to revise the initial belief.

   Example: "Considering the delay, I now believe there's a 50% chance of failure."

4. **Repeat as Needed:** Continuously refine beliefs as more evidence becomes available.

Applications of Bayesian Thinking

1. **In Medicine:**
   - Doctors update diagnoses as new test results or symptoms emerge.

2. **In Business Forecasting:**
   - Companies adjust sales projections based on emerging market trends or customer behavior.

3. **In Personal Decisions:**
   - Individuals revise plans, such as adjusting travel itineraries based on changing conditions.

Why Bayesian Thinking is Effective

This method helps humans to:

1. **Adapt to Change:** Encourages flexible thinking in dynamic environments.

2. **Incorporate Evidence:** Integrates new information to refine beliefs.

3. **Improve Decision-Making:** Reduces overconfidence in initial assumptions.

Challenges and Limitations

1. **Requires Probabilistic Thinking:** Some people may find it difficult to think in terms of probabilities.
2. **Complex Calculations:** Applying Bayes' Theorem can be mathematically intensive in complex cases.
3. **Subjectivity in Priors:** Initial beliefs may introduce bias if not based on reliable evidence.

For instance, an overly optimistic prior belief about project success might underestimate risks, even with new evidence.

How to Use Bayesian Thinking Effectively

1. **Define Clear Preceding Events:** Base initial beliefs on reliable data or logical reasoning.
2. **Incorporate Relevant Evidence:** Focus on evidence directly related to the belief or decision.
3. **Practice Iteration:** Continuously update probabilities as new information arises.

Exercises

1. **Update a Belief:** Choose a belief you hold and revise it based on new evidence. Reflect on how the process affects your confidence.
2. **Analyze a Forecast:** Find a prediction or forecast (e.g., election results, weather). Apply Bayesian Thinking to refine the prediction with new data.
3. **Create a Bayesian Scenario:** Design a hypothetical situation where a belief evolves over time based on evidence. Practice calculating updated probabilities.

Closing Thoughts

Bayesian Thinking is a powerful tool for navigating uncertainty and complexity. By treating beliefs as probabilities that evolve with evidence, it fosters adaptability, critical thinking, and better decision-making.

While it requires effort and practice, its ability to refine understanding and improve accuracy makes it invaluable in fields ranging from science to everyday life. Mastering Bayesian Thinking equips you to approach challenges with clarity, precision, and flexibility.

Chapter 30: Counterfactual Reasoning

Exploring "What If": Counterfactual Reasoning

Counterfactual Reasoning involves exploring alternative scenarios — what could have happened if events had unfolded differently. This type of reasoning helps uncover causal relationships, evaluate decisions, and anticipate future outcomes by reflecting on hypothetical alternatives.

For example:

- **Scenario:** A team missed a project deadline.
- **Counterfactual Question:** "What if we had allocated more resources at the beginning?"
- **Insights:** This question may reveal that early resource allocation could have prevented delays, highlighting a key area for improvement.

By examining "what if" scenarios, Counterfactual Reasoning fosters deeper understanding and better preparation for future challenges.

How Counterfactual Reasoning Works

1. **Identify the Event:** Choose a past event or decision to analyze.

   Example: "Our product launch failed to meet expectations."

2. **Formulate Counterfactuals:** Imagine alternative scenarios where different decisions or conditions occurred.

   Example: "What if we had launched a month later to allow more time for testing?"

3. **Analyze the Differences:** Compare the actual outcome with the hypothetical scenarios to identify causal factors.

   Example: "Delaying the launch might have reduced errors and improved user satisfaction."

4. **Apply the Insights:** Use lessons from the analysis to refine future strategies or decisions.

Applications of Counterfactual Reasoning

1. **In Business Strategy:**
   - Companies analyze missed opportunities, such as "What if we had targeted a different demographic?"

2. **In Personal Decisions:**
   - Individuals reflect on life choices, such as "What if I had chosen a different career path?"

3. **In Risk Assessment:**
   - Teams evaluate potential risks, such as "What if we hadn't implemented a backup system?"

Why Counterfactual Reasoning is Effective

This method helps:

1. **Understand Causation:** Reveals how specific factors influenced an outcome.

2. **Identify Missed Opportunities:** Highlights areas where better decisions could have led to improved results.

3. **Anticipate Future Scenarios:** Prepares individuals and teams to navigate similar situations more effectively.

Challenges and Limitations

1. **Overemphasis on Hypotheticals:** Focusing too much on "what ifs" can detract from addressing present realities.

2. **Confirmation Bias:** Individuals may create counterfactuals that align with their preexisting beliefs.

3. **Limited Predictive Value:** Hypothetical scenarios are inherently uncertain and may not reflect actual outcomes.

For instance, assuming a delayed product launch would have succeeded ignores other potential risks, such as changes in market conditions.

How to Use Counterfactual Reasoning Effectively

1. **Focus on Learning:** Use counterfactuals to uncover insights, not to dwell on regrets or assign blame.

2. **Balance Hypotheticals with Evidence:** Ground your analysis in realistic assumptions and available data.

3. **Apply Lessons to the Future:** Use the insights gained to inform future decisions and strategies.

Exercises

1. **Reflect on a Decision:** Choose a past decision and create two counterfactual scenarios where different choices were made. Analyze the potential outcomes.

2. **Evaluate a Team Project:** With a team, reflect on a completed project and explore "what if" scenarios to identify areas for improvement.

3. **Anticipate Risks:** For an upcoming decision, create counterfactuals to explore potential risks and plan contingencies.

Closing Thoughts

Counterfactual Reasoning is a powerful tool for understanding causes, improving decisions, and preparing for the future. By exploring "what if" scenarios, it fosters critical thinking and helps uncover opportunities for growth and improvement.

While it's important to balance counterfactuals with present realities, this method's ability to provide fresh insights and enhance decision-making makes it invaluable in business, personal growth, and risk management. Mastering Counterfactual Reasoning equips you to learn from the past and navigate the future with confidence.

Chapter 31: Analogical Reasoning

Solving Problems Through Similarities: Analogical Reasoning

Analogical Reasoning is a problem-solving method that draws comparisons between similar situations to gain insights or generate solutions. By identifying parallels between a known situation (the "source") and a new problem (the "target"), this approach helps apply past knowledge to new challenges.

For example:

- **Scenario:** A team struggles to improve customer service.

- **Analogical Thinking:** Compare the issue to how airlines manage customer complaints, focusing on communication strategies and personalized responses.

Analogical Reasoning bridges the gap between the unfamiliar and the familiar, enabling creative problem-solving and innovation.

How Analogical Reasoning Works

1. **Identify the Target Problem:** Define the issue or challenge you're facing.

   Example: "How can we make our product more user-friendly?"

2. **Find a Similar Situation:** Look for a known scenario with comparable characteristics or challenges.

   Example: "What lessons can we learn from successful smartphone designs?"

3. **Draw Parallels:** Identify shared features or principles between the two scenarios.

   Example: "Streamlined interfaces reduce complexity and improve usability."

4. **Apply the Insights:** Use the lessons from the analogous situation to address the target problem.

Applications of Analogical Reasoning

1. **In Business:**
   - Companies adapt successful strategies from other industries.

     Example: Online retailers adopting subscription models inspired by streaming services.

2. **In Personal Development:**
   - Individuals learn from others' experiences to navigate similar challenges.

     Example: Using a mentor's career path as a guide for your own decisions.

3. **In Education:**
   - Teachers use analogies to explain complex concepts.

     Example: Comparing the flow of electricity to the flow of water to teach circuits.

Why Analogical Reasoning Works

This method helps:

1. **Leverage Past Knowledge:** Draws on existing understanding to solve new problems.
2. **Stimulate Creativity:** Encourages innovative thinking by connecting seemingly unrelated ideas.
3. **Simplify Complexity:** Makes unfamiliar concepts more accessible through comparisons.

Challenges and Limitations

1. **Superficial Comparisons:** Oversimplifying or misinterpreting similarities can lead to incorrect conclusions.
2. **Irrelevance:** Choosing an analogy that doesn't align well with the target problem may hinder progress.
3. **Overdependence on Analogies:** Relying too heavily on past solutions may stifle original thinking.

For instance, comparing a start-up to a large corporation might overlook differences in resources and scale.

How to Use Analogical Reasoning Effectively

1. **Choose Relevant Analogies:** Ensure the source scenario shares meaningful similarities with the target problem.
2. **Focus on Principles:** Look for underlying principles rather than surface-level similarities.
3. **Combine with Other Methods:** Use Analogical Reasoning alongside other problem-solving tools to ensure well-rounded analysis.

Exercises

1. **Identify Analogies:** Think of a current challenge and find a comparable scenario from another domain. Reflect on the lessons that can be applied.
2. **Analyze Success Stories:** Study how others have solved similar problems and adapt their strategies to your context.
3. **Create an Analogy:** Use an analogy to explain a complex concept or problem to a colleague or friend. Reflect on how the analogy aids understanding.

Closing Thoughts

Analogical Reasoning is a versatile creative tool for problem-solving, enabling you to draw on past experiences and insights to address new challenges. By identifying meaningful parallels, it fosters innovation, simplifies complexity, and broadens perspectives.

Analogical Reasoning's ability to connect the familiar with the unfamiliar makes it a valuable skill in business, education, and personal growth.

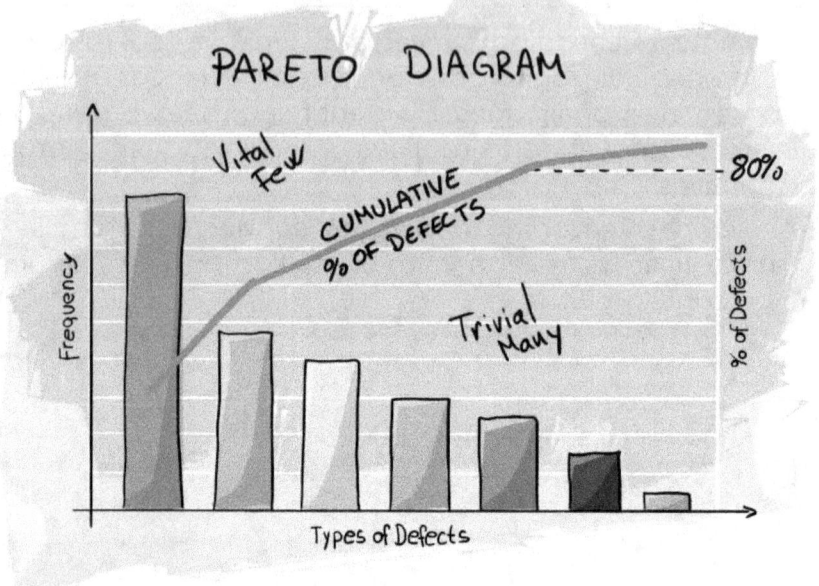

Chapter 32: Pareto Analysis

Focusing on the Vital Few: Pareto Analysis

Pareto Analysis, also known as the 80/20 Rule, is a decision-making tool based on the idea that 80% of results often come from 20% of causes. By identifying and prioritizing these "vital few" factors, this method helps focus resources on the most impactful areas.

For example:

- **Scenario:** A business faces declining profits.
- **Pareto Insight:** An analysis reveals that 20% of the products account for 80% of the revenue. Focusing on these products could maximize profitability.

Pareto Analysis simplifies decision-making by emphasizing efficiency and effectiveness.

How Pareto Analysis Works

1. **Define the Problem:** Clearly identify the issue you want to analyze.

Example: "Why are customer complaints increasing?"

2. **Collect Data:** Gather information about the causes or contributing factors.

   Example: Categorize complaints by type (e.g. late delivery, defective products, poor service).

3. **Rank by Impact:** Organize the causes from most to least significant.

   Example: Late deliveries account for 60% of complaints.

4. **Focus on the Top Causes:** Prioritize addressing the few causes that have the greatest impact.

Applications of Pareto Analysis

1. **In Quality Control:**
   o Identify the most common defects in a product and prioritize fixing them.

2. **In Time Management:**
   o Focus on the 20% of tasks that contribute to 80% of results.

3. **In Customer Service:**
   o Address the few issues that generate the majority of complaints.

Why Pareto Analysis is Effective

This method helps:

1. **Prioritize Efforts:** Focuses on the most impactful areas rather than spreading resources thinly.

2. **Save Time and Resources:** Maximizes efficiency by addressing the root causes of most problems.

3. **Clarify Focus:** Simplifies complex problems by highlighting the vital few.

Challenges and Limitations

1. **Assumes 80/20 Distribution:** The principle may not apply perfectly to all situations.

2. **Overlooks Minor Issues:** Focusing only on the top causes may ignore smaller but still significant factors.

3. **Requires Accurate Data:** Reliable analysis depends on high-quality and comprehensive data.

For instance, incomplete data about customer complaints could lead to misidentifying the most critical issues.

How to Use Pareto Analysis Effectively

1. **Collect Comprehensive Data:** Ensure your analysis captures all relevant factors.
2. **Re-evaluate Regularly:** Periodically update your analysis to reflect changing conditions or priorities.
3. **Combine with Other Methods:** Use Pareto Analysis alongside tools like Root Cause Analysis or SWOT for deeper insights.

Exercises

1. **Apply Pareto to a Problem:** Choose an issue in your workplace or personal life and use Pareto Analysis to identify the most significant causes.
2. **Analyze Time Usage:** Track your daily tasks and identify the 20% of activities that yield 80% of your results.
3. **Prioritize Improvements:** In a team setting, use Pareto Analysis to decide which projects or issues to address first.

Closing Thoughts

Pareto Analysis is a powerful tool for prioritization and efficiency, enabling you to focus on the areas that matter most. It simplifies decision-making and maximizes.

While it requires thoughtful data collection and interpretation, its ability to clarify focus and improve resource allocation makes it invaluable in business, personal productivity, and problem-solving.

Chapter 33: Ladder of Inference

Climbing Carefully: The Ladder of Inference

The Ladder of Inference, developed by organizational theorist Chris Argyris, is a framework for understanding how individuals move from observations to decisions and actions. It highlights how assumptions and biases can influence reasoning, leading to faulty conclusions. By consciously evaluating each step, you can ensure that your reasoning is logical and evidence-based.

For example:

- **Scenario:** A manager notices a team member arriving late.
- **Rushed Inference:** "They must be lazy."
- **Reflection on the Ladder:**
  - Observation: "The employee arrived late."
  - Assumption: "They don't care about their job."
  - Alternative Explanation: "They were stuck in traffic."

The Ladder of Inference helps slow down this process, encouraging you to verify assumptions and base conclusions on facts.

How the Ladder of Inference Works

1. **Observe the Data:** Start with the raw facts or observable data.

   Example: "The sales team's numbers dropped this quarter."

2. **Select Data:** Focus on specific pieces of data that seem most relevant.

   Example: "Three team members missed their targets."

3. **Make Assumptions:** Interpret the data based on personal beliefs or context.

   Example: "The team isn't putting in enough effort."

4. **Draw Conclusions:** Form a judgment based on your assumptions.

   Example: "We need stricter performance monitoring."

5. **Take Action:** Act on the conclusions drawn.

   Example: "Introduce weekly progress reports."

Each step builds on the previous one, but skipping or misinterpreting steps can lead to flawed reasoning.

Applications of the Ladder of Inference

1. **In Workplace Communication:**
   - Use the framework to analyze misunderstandings and improve team dynamics.

   Example: "Before assuming a colleague disagrees, ask questions to clarify their position."

2. **In Personal Relationships:**
   - Apply the ladder to resolve conflicts by identifying assumptions and seeking alternative perspectives.

3. **In Decision-Making:**
   - Evaluate business or personal decisions by revisiting the data and questioning assumptions.

Why the Ladder of Inference is Effective

This method helps:

1. **Clarify Reasoning:** Makes the steps of decision-making transparent.
2. **Reduce Bias:** Encourages critical reflection on assumptions and beliefs.
3. **Improve Communication:** Facilitates constructive discussions by focusing on facts and logic.

Challenges and Limitations

1. **Time-Intensive:** Slowing down the reasoning process may not always be practical in urgent situations.
2. **Requires Self-Awareness:** Identifying and challenging your own assumptions can be difficult.
3. **Limited Data:** Decisions are only as good as the data available for analysis.

For instance, misinterpreting a team member's behavior due to incomplete data can lead to unnecessary conflict or ineffective actions.

How to Use the Ladder of Inference Effectively

1. **Pause and Reflect:** Take time to consciously move through each step of the ladder.
2. **Verify Assumptions:** Seek additional data or input to confirm or challenge your assumptions.
3. **Engage Others:** Involve colleagues, friends, or stakeholders to provide diverse perspectives.

Exercises

1. **Analyze a Recent Decision:** Reflect on a decision you made recently. Trace your reasoning up the Ladder of Inference and identify any skipped steps or questionable assumptions.
2. **Role-Play Scenarios:** With a partner, practice identifying the steps of the ladder in a hypothetical situation. Discuss how to improve the reasoning process.
3. **Challenge a Bias:** Choose a belief or assumption you hold and analyze how it was formed using the ladder. Seek data or perspectives that might challenge it.

Closing Thoughts

The Ladder of Inference is a powerful framework for improving reasoning and decision-making. By slowing down and evaluating each step, you can avoid jumping to conclusions, reduce bias, and base actions on solid evidence.

While it requires practice and self-awareness, mastering this method fosters clarity, fairness, and collaboration in both personal and professional contexts.

Chapter 34: Heuristic Analysis

Making Quick Decisions: Heuristic Analysis

Heuristic Analysis involves using mental shortcuts or "rules of thumb" to make decisions quickly and efficiently. While these shortcuts often save time and effort, they can sometimes lead to errors or biases. By understanding heuristics, you can use them effectively while remaining aware of their limitations.

For example:

- **Scenario:** Choosing between two restaurants.
- **Heuristic:** "Go with the one that has more customers—it must be better."
- **Outcome:** While this rule often works, it might overlook factors like wait times or personal preferences.

Heuristic Analysis balances intuition with critical thinking, making it ideal for everyday decisions and fast-paced environments.

How Heuristic Analysis Works

1. **Recognize the Heuristic:** Identify the mental shortcut you're using.

   Example: "I'll pick the product with the higher reviews—it's probably better."

2. **Evaluate the Context:** Consider whether the heuristic is appropriate for the situation.

   Example: "Are the reviews genuine, or could they be biased?"

3. **Decide or Adjust:** Use the heuristic if it's effective, or adjust your approach if more analysis is needed.

Common Heuristics

1. **Availability Heuristic:** Judging the likelihood of an event based on how easily examples come to mind.

   Example: Assuming plane crashes are common because they're heavily reported in the news.

2. **Representativeness Heuristic:** Making judgments based on how well something matches a stereotype.

   Example: Assuming someone who dresses formally must work in a corporate job.

3. **Anchoring Heuristic:** Relying too heavily on the first piece of information encountered.

   Example: Focusing on a high initial price and perceiving a discount as a great deal, even if the discounted price is still high.

Applications of Heuristic Analysis

1. **In Business:**
   - Sales teams use heuristics such as "Focus on repeat customers — they're more likely to buy."

2. **In Education:**
   - Teachers use shortcuts like "Prioritize struggling students for additional support."

3. **In Daily Life:**
   - Individuals rely on rules such as "Take the route with less traffic" to save time.

Why Heuristic Analysis is Effective

This method helps:

1. **Save Time:** Enables fast decision-making in routine or low-stakes situations.
2. **Simplify Complexity:** Reduces the cognitive load by focusing on key factors.
3. **Leverage Experience:** Draws on past knowledge to inform current choices.

Challenges and Limitations

1. **Risk of Bias:** Heuristics can reinforce stereotypes or lead to flawed assumptions.
2. **Overgeneralization:** Applying a shortcut universally may overlook unique aspects of a situation.
3. **Inaccuracy in Complex Problems:** Heuristics are less effective for high-stakes or nuanced decisions.

For instance, using the "availability heuristic" to judge risk may lead to overestimating rare but dramatic events.

How to Use Heuristic Analysis Effectively

1. **Be Aware of Biases:** Recognize when a heuristic might introduce bias or oversimplify the situation.
2. **Combine with Other Methods:** Use heuristics alongside analytical approaches for balanced decision-making.
3. **Reflect on Outcomes:** Regularly evaluate the effectiveness of your shortcuts and adjust as needed.

Exercises

1. **Identify Your Heuristics:** Reflect on common decisions you make (e.g. shopping, planning). Identify the shortcuts you use and analyze their effectiveness.
2. **Challenge a Shortcut:** Choose a heuristic you often rely on and test it against a more detailed analysis. Reflect on the differences in outcomes.
3. **Optimize a Rule of Thumb:** Refine a commonly used heuristic to improve its accuracy or applicability.

Closing Thoughts

Heuristic Analysis is a practical tool for quick decision-making in routine or time-sensitive situations. By balancing speed with awareness of potential biases, it enables you to navigate challenges efficiently and effectively.

While heuristics have limitations, understanding and refining them enhances their utility, making them a valuable addition to your problem-solving toolkit.

Chapter 35: The Eisenhower Matrix

Mastering Prioritization: The Eisenhower Matrix

The Eisenhower Matrix, also called the Urgent-Important Matrix, is a time management tool that helps prioritize tasks based on their urgency and importance. Named after U.S. President Dwight D. Eisenhower, who famously said, "What is important is seldom urgent, and what is urgent is seldom important," this method provides a clear framework for deciding what to focus on, delegate, or eliminate.

For example:

- **Scenario:** A professional has a long to-do list.
- **Using the Matrix:**
  - **Urgent & Important:** Finish a client presentation due tomorrow.
  - **Not Urgent but Important:** Develop a long-term marketing strategy.

- **Urgent but Not Important:** Respond to non-essential emails.
- **Neither Urgent nor Important:** Scroll through social media.

The Eisenhower Matrix simplifies prioritization, ensuring time and energy are allocated to tasks that truly matter.

How the Eisenhower Matrix Works

1. **Define Tasks:** List all the tasks you need to complete.
2. **Categorize by Urgency and Importance:** Assign each task to one of four quadrants:
   - **Urgent & Important (Do Now):** Tasks requiring immediate attention and critical to success.
   - **Not Urgent but Important (Plan):** Tasks critical to long-term goals but not time-sensitive.
   - **Urgent but Not Important (Delegate):** Tasks that need to be done quickly but can be handled by someone else.
   - **Neither Urgent nor Important (Eliminate):** Tasks that add no value and can be removed entirely.
3. **Act Accordingly:** Focus on high-priority tasks, plan for long-term objectives, delegate non-essential urgent tasks, and eliminate distractions.

Applications of the Eisenhower Matrix

1. **In Time Management:**
   - Professionals use it to organize daily responsibilities and avoid procrastination.

     Example: Prioritizing project deadlines over non-essential meetings.
2. **In Personal Productivity:**
   - Individuals apply the matrix to balance work, personal goals, and leisure.

     Example: Planning exercise routines under "Not Urgent but Important."

3. **In Team Collaboration:**
   o Teams use the matrix to allocate responsibilities effectively.

   Example: Delegating event logistics while focusing on strategy development.

Why the Eisenhower Matrix is Effective

This method helps:

1. **Clarify Priorities:** Differentiates between what truly matters and what doesn't.
2. **Reduce Stress:** Avoids last-minute scrambles by planning ahead.
3. **Boost Productivity:** Maximizes focus on impactful tasks while eliminating time-wasters.

Challenges and Limitations

1. **Subjectivity:** Assessing urgency and importance can be influenced by personal biases.
2. **Over-Simplification:** Complex tasks may not fit neatly into one quadrant.
3. **Difficulty Delegating:** Some individuals struggle to delegate tasks, even when appropriate.

For instance, someone might incorrectly categorize a task as "Urgent & Important" due to emotional investment rather than objective necessity.

How to Use the Eisenhower Matrix Effectively

1. **Be Honest:** Assess tasks objectively, focusing on actual priorities rather than perceived importance.
2. **Review Regularly:** Revisit and update the matrix as priorities shift.
3. **Learn to Delegate:** Trust others to handle tasks in the "Urgent but Not Important" category.

Exercises

1. **Create a Daily Matrix:** Use the Eisenhower Matrix to organize your tasks for the day. Reflect on how it influences your focus and productivity.

2. **Analyze a Past Week:** Review your activities from the previous week. Categorize them into the matrix and identify areas for improvement.

3. **Team Exercise:** Collaborate with colleagues to create a matrix for a shared project. Discuss how delegation and elimination can improve efficiency.

Closing Thoughts

The Eisenhower Matrix is an essential tool for mastering time management and prioritization. By categorizing tasks based on urgency and importance, it ensures that your energy is directed toward meaningful work while minimizing distractions.

While it requires regular reflection and a willingness to delegate or eliminate tasks, its ability to streamline focus and enhance productivity makes it invaluable in both personal and professional contexts. Mastering the Eisenhower Matrix equips you to work smarter, not harder.

Section: Cognitive Bias Mitigation

Cognitive biases are mental shortcuts that often lead to flawed reasoning, distorted perceptions, and suboptimal decisions. While biases serve as useful survival mechanisms by helping us make quick judgments, they can also cloud our judgment and prevent us from thinking clearly and rationally.

This section focuses on Cognitive Bias Mitigation — practical techniques to recognize, understand, and counteract these biases. Each chapter will explore a specific bias, provide real-world examples of how it manifests, and introduce actionable strategies for overcoming its influence.

Chapter 36: Recognizing Anchoring Bias

The Power of First Impressions: Anchoring Bias

Anchoring Bias occurs when humans rely too heavily on the first piece of information (the "anchor") they receive when making decisions. This initial reference impacts future judgments, even if it's irrelevant or arbitrary.

For example:

- **Scenario:** A car salesperson starts negotiations at a high price, anchoring the buyer's expectations.
- **Effect:** Even if the price drops during negotiation, the buyer perceives the final price as a good deal because it's lower than the anchor.

Recognizing and mitigating Anchoring Bias ensures that decisions are based on logic and evidence rather than arbitrary starting points.

How Anchoring Bias Works

1. **Establishing the Anchor:** An initial number or idea sets the reference point for evaluation.
2. **Adjusting Judgments:** Subsequent decisions or estimates are influenced by the anchor, often insufficiently adjusted.

Even experts are not immune. Studies show that anchoring affects professionals like judges, doctors, and financial analysts.

Examples of Anchoring Bias

1. **In Pricing:**
   - A store lists a product as "Originally $100, now $70!" The anchor (original price) makes the discounted price seem more appealing.
2. **In Job Negotiations:**
   - A candidate anchors their salary expectations by mentioning their previous pay.
3. **In Everyday Decisions:**
   - A friend suggests a specific restaurant first, anchoring your perception of what constitutes a good choice.

Why Anchoring Bias is Harmful

Anchoring Bias can lead to:

1. **Distorted Perceptions:** Decisions may be swayed by irrelevant or inaccurate anchors.
2. **Missed Opportunities:** Over-reliance on anchors may prevent consideration of better alternatives.
3. **Manipulation:** Anchors can be deliberately set to influence others' judgments (e.g., high starting prices in negotiations).

How to Mitigate Anchoring Bias

1. **Question the Anchor:** Ask whether the anchor is relevant and supported by evidence.
   Example: "Is this initial price reflective of the product's true value?"

2. **Consider Multiple Perspectives:** Seek alternative reference points to challenge the anchor.

   Example: Compare prices across different sellers before deciding.

3. **Delay Judgment:** Avoid making decisions immediately after encountering an anchor. Take time to evaluate the information independently.

How to Respond to Anchoring Bias in Others

When someone relies on an anchor, you can:

1. **Introduce New Information:** Provide additional reference points to shift their focus.

   Example: "Here's what similar houses in this area sold for recently."

2. **Challenge the Anchor's Validity:** Politely question whether the anchor is reasonable or relevant.

   Example: "Why are we using this particular figure as our starting point?"

Exercises

1. **Identify Anchors in Daily Life:** Reflect on recent decisions. Were they influenced by an anchor? How might you have approached them differently?

2. **Practice Setting Anchors:** In a negotiation or discussion, experiment with setting an anchor and observe its impact.

3. **Reframe an Anchor:** Take an anchored scenario (e.g., a high initial price) and challenge it by introducing new reference points.

Closing Thoughts

Anchoring Bias is a subtle but powerful influence on decision-making. By learning to recognize and challenge anchors, you can make more objective, informed choices and avoid being swayed by irrelevant starting points.

Mastering this skill not only improves personal decision-making but also equips you to navigate negotiations, pricing strategies, and everyday interactions with greater confidence and clarity.

Chapter 37: Overcoming Confirmation Bias

Seeing What We Want to See: Confirmation Bias

Confirmation Bias occurs when people seek out, interpret, and remember information that supports their existing beliefs while ignoring or dismissing evidence that contradicts them. This bias reinforces preconceptions, making it difficult to evaluate information objectively.

For example:

- **Scenario:** A manager believes a team member is underperforming.
- **Bias in Action:** They focus on the mistakes the employee makes while overlooking their successes.

Overcoming Confirmation Bias requires conscious effort to evaluate all evidence, not just what aligns with existing views.

How Confirmation Bias Works

1. **Selective Exposure:** People seek information that aligns with their beliefs.

   Example: Reading news sources that share their political views.

2. **Interpretation Bias:** Contradictory evidence is interpreted in a way that minimizes its significance.

   Example: Dismissing critical feedback as "uninformed."

3. **Memory Bias:** People remember information that supports their beliefs better than contradictory evidence.

   Example: Recalling only the wins of a favorite sports team.

Examples of Confirmation Bias

1. **In Decision-Making:**
   o An investor favors evidence that supports their choice to buy a stock while ignoring reports of declining performance.

2. **In Relationships:**
   o A person believes their friend is always reliable and dismisses instances where they've let them down.

3. **In Science:**
   o A researcher unintentionally designs experiments to confirm their hypothesis rather than test it objectively.

Why Confirmation Bias is Harmful

Confirmation Bias can lead to:

1. **Faulty Decisions:** Ignoring contradictory evidence results in poorly informed choices.

2. **Polarization:** Focusing only on information that aligns with one's views deepens divides and discourages open dialogue.

3. **Stagnation:** Reinforcing existing beliefs prevents growth, innovation, and learning.

How to Overcome Confirmation Bias

1. **Seek Disconfirming Evidence:** Actively look for information that challenges your beliefs.

   Example: Ask, "What evidence would prove me wrong?"

2. **Engage with Diverse Perspectives:** Expose yourself to ideas and opinions that differ from your own.

   Example: Read articles from sources with opposing viewpoints.

3. **Ask Neutral Questions:** Frame questions in a way that doesn't assume a particular answer.

   Example: Instead of "Why is my idea correct?" ask, "What are the strengths and weaknesses of my idea?"

How to Respond to Confirmation Bias in Others

When encountering Confirmation Bias, you can:

1. **Present Contradictory Evidence Respectfully:** Avoid confrontation and focus on sharing alternative perspectives.

   Example: "I understand your point. Have you considered this other perspective?"

2. **Encourage Critical Thinking:** Ask open-ended questions to prompt deeper analysis.

   Example: "What do you think would happen if we tried the opposite approach?"

3. **Share Your Own Biases:** Acknowledge how your perspective has evolved, encouraging mutual openness.

Exercises

1. **Challenge a Belief:** Identify a belief you hold strongly. Seek out credible evidence that contradicts it and reflect on how it affects your perspective.

2. **Diversify Your Information Sources:** Choose a topic and read about it from multiple viewpoints, including those you disagree with.

3. **Conduct a Self-Audit:** Reflect on a recent decision. Were you selective in the evidence you considered? How might you approach it differently?

Closing Thoughts

Confirmation Bias is one of the most general cognitive biases, shaping how we perceive and interact with the world. Recognizing and overcoming this bias requires conscious effort, humility, and a commitment to seeking truth over comfort.

By challenging your own assumptions and engaging with diverse perspectives, you can make better decisions, improve relationships, and foster open-mindedness in both personal and professional contexts.

Chapter 38: Mitigating Availability Heuristics

When Memories Skew Perception: Availability Heuristics

The Availability Heuristic refers to the tendency to judge the probability of an event based on how easily examples of it come to mind. Dramatic, recent, or emotionally charged memories often feel more common or likely, even when they're statistically rare.

For example:

- **Scenario:** A person avoids flying because they recently saw news of a plane crash, even though air travel is safer than driving.

Mitigating this bias involves evaluating risks and probabilities based on data rather than vividness or recency of memories.

How the Availability Heuristic Works

1. **Memory Accessibility:** Events that are recent, dramatic, or emotionally impactful are easier to recall.

   Example: A recent shark attack makes people overestimate the risk of swimming in the ocean.

2. **Generalization:** These memorable events are incorrectly assumed to represent the norm.

   Example: Assuming violent crime is increasing after watching a crime-heavy news segment.

Examples of the Availability Heuristic

1. **In Risk Perception:**
   - Overestimating the likelihood of being in a car accident after witnessing one on the highway.

2. **In Decision-Making:**
   - Avoiding certain foods after hearing about one food poisoning incident, despite its rarity.

3. **In Policy Debates:**
   - Public demand for stricter regulations following a highly publicized but isolated incident.

Why the Availability Heuristic is Harmful

This heuristic can lead to:

1. **Exaggerated Fears:** Overestimating rare risks while underestimating more common dangers.

2. **Distorted Decision-Making:** Basing choices on memorable but unrepresentative events.

3. **Inefficient Resource Allocation:** Prioritizing actions based on emotional impact rather than actual need.

How to Mitigate the Availability Heuristic

1. **Rely on Data:** Use statistics and objective evidence to evaluate risks and probabilities.

   Example: Research airline safety records instead of relying on media coverage.

2. **Broaden Your Perspective:** Consider multiple examples and scenarios to avoid overgeneralization.

   Example: "What's the overall rate of this happening, not

just in the cases I've heard about?"

3. **Challenge Emotional Reactions:** Reflect on whether your feelings are influencing your judgment disproportionately.

Example: "Am I avoiding this activity because it's dangerous or because it feels scary?"

How to Respond to the Availability Heuristic in Others

When someone exhibits this heuristic, you can:

1. **Provide Context:** Share data or examples that balance the conversation.

Example: "While that incident was tragic, statistics show it's very rare."

2. **Acknowledge Emotions:** Validate their feelings while gently introducing broader evidence.

Example: "It's natural to feel concerned after hearing that, but let's look at the bigger picture."

Exercises

1. **Analyze Risks:** Choose a fear or concern you have. Research its actual probability and compare it to how likely it feels.

2. **Diversify Inputs:** Reflect on how your media consumption influences your perception of risks. Seek out balanced sources.

3. **Challenge an Overgeneralization:** Identify a recent judgment you made based on a vivid memory. Explore whether it reflects broader trends.

Closing Thoughts

The Availability Heuristic demonstrates how memory and emotion can skew perception of reality. By grounding your judgments in data and considering broader perspectives, you can make more accurate, rational decisions.

Mastering this skill not only reduces unnecessary fears but also improves your ability to evaluate risks and opportunities in a balanced, informed way.

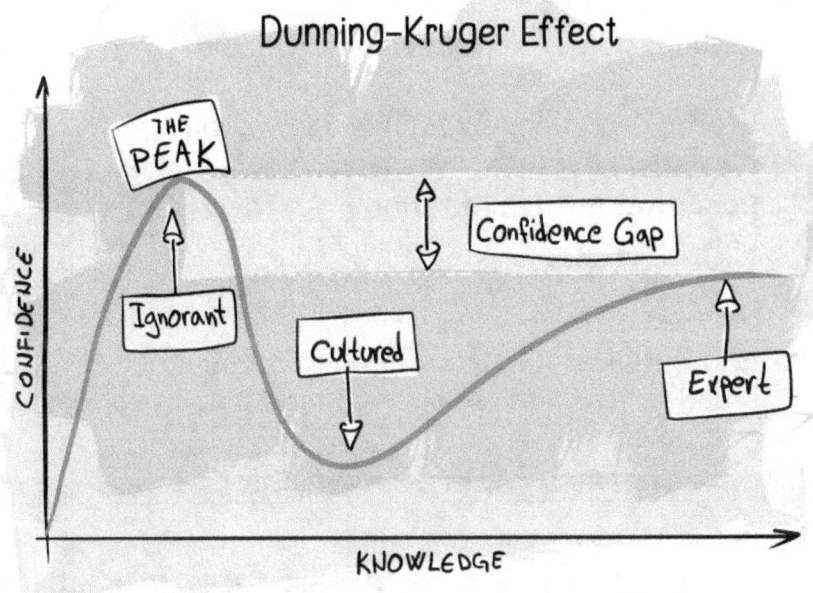

Dunning-Kruger Effect

THE PEAK

Ignorant

Confidence Gap

Cultured

Expert

CONFIDENCE

KNOWLEDGE

Chapter 39: Combatting the Dunning-Kruger Effect

The Illusion of Expertise: The Dunning-Kruger Effect

The Dunning-Kruger Effect occurs when individuals with limited knowledge or expertise in a subject overestimate their competence. This cognitive bias results from a lack of awareness about one's own limitations, often leading to overconfidence.

For example:

- **Scenario:** A novice in graphic design believes their skills rival those of a professional after learning basic software tools.

Combatting this bias involves fostering self-awareness, seeking feedback, and committing to continuous learning.

How the Dunning-Kruger Effect Works

1. **Initial Overconfidence:** Individuals gain a little knowledge and feel highly confident in their abilities.

   Example: Someone watches a few cooking tutorials and considers themselves an expert chef.

2. **Recognition of Limitations:** As they learn more, they realize the depth of the field and their own inexperience.

   Example: Attempting a complex recipe reveals gaps in their skills.

3. **Competence and Confidence Align:** Over time, with practice and knowledge, confidence grows alongside competence.

Examples of the Dunning-Kruger Effect

1. **In the Workplace:**
   - A new employee overestimates their ability to manage a project, unaware of the challenges involved.

2. **In Online Discussions:**
   - Individuals confidently share opinions on topics they've only briefly researched.

3. **In Hobbies:**
   - A beginner in photography assumes they can produce professional-quality work with minimal training.

Why the Dunning-Kruger Effect is Harmful

This bias can lead to:

1. **Overconfidence in Decision-Making:** Underestimating challenges can result in poor decisions.

2. **Resistance to Feedback:** Overconfident individuals may dismiss constructive criticism.

3. **Frustration for Others:** Colleagues or peers may find it difficult to collaborate with someone who overestimates their abilities.

How to Combat the Dunning-Kruger Effect

1. **Embrace Lifelong Learning:** Acknowledge that mastery requires time, effort, and continuous education.

   Example: "What are the areas where I need to improve?"

2. **Seek Honest Feedback:** Actively request input from mentors, peers, and experts.

   Example: "Can you critique my work and suggest areas for growth?"

3. **Recognize the Complexity of Knowledge:** Understand that expertise involves more than just surface-level familiarity.

   Example: "What challenges do experts in this field face?"

How to Address the Dunning-Kruger Effect in Others

1. **Provide Constructive Feedback:** Gently point out areas where additional learning is needed.

   Example: "You've made a great start. Here are some resources to deepen your understanding."

2. **Encourage Humility:** Share your own experiences of learning and growth to highlight the value of continuous improvement.

3. **Focus on Collaboration:** Involve others in discussions to bring diverse perspectives and expertise.

Exercises

1. **Identify Your Blind Spots:** Reflect on areas where you may overestimate your knowledge. Research these topics further.

2. **Ask for Feedback:** Choose a skill or task you're confident in and request detailed feedback from someone experienced.

3. **Create a Learning Plan:** Identify a field or skill you want to improve. Outline steps to move from beginner to advanced levels.

Closing Thoughts

The Dunning-Kruger Effect is a natural phase in learning but can hinder growth if left unchecked. By fostering self-awareness, seeking feedback, and embracing humility, you can navigate this bias and develop genuine expertise.

Chapter 40: Avoiding Framing Effects

Shaped by Presentation: The Framing Effect

The Framing Effect occurs when the way information is presented influences decisions and judgments. Even when the underlying facts remain the same, the "frame" or context can alter perception and behavior.

For example:

- **Scenario:** A doctor tells a patient, "90% of people survive this procedure," instead of "10% of people don't survive."
- **Effect:** The positive frame (survival) reassures the patient, while the negative frame (death) causes alarm.

Avoiding Framing Effects involves recognizing how language and context shape decisions and striving for objectivity.

How Framing Effects Work

1. **Positive vs. Negative Frames:** The same fact is presented in either a positive or negative light.

   Example: "20% fat" sounds worse than "80% lean," even though both are identical.

2. **Contextual Cues:** The surrounding context or wording shapes how information is interpreted.

   Example: A discount labeled "Limited-Time Offer" feels more compelling than a generic "20% Off."

Examples of Framing Effects

1. **In Marketing:**
   - Advertisements emphasize gains ("Save $100!") rather than losses ("Don't miss out on $100 savings!").

2. **In Decision-Making:**

   People are more likely to choose a treatment with a "90% success rate" than one with a "10% failure rate."

3. **In Negotiations:**
   - Framing a proposal as a win-win encourages agreement, while framing it as a concession creates resistance.

Why Framing Effects are Harmful

Framing Effects can lead to:

1. **Irrational Decisions:** Judgments may be based on presentation rather than substance.

2. **Manipulation:** Deliberate framing can exploit biases to influence behavior.

3. **Missed Opportunities:** Focusing on negatives may discourage taking calculated risks.

How to Avoid Framing Effects

1. **Reframe the Information:** Look at the same data from multiple perspectives.

   Example: "What does this decision look like framed as both a gain and a loss?"

2. **Focus on Facts:** Strip away the emotional or contextual framing to evaluate the raw information.

   Example: "What are the actual probabilities or outcomes?"

3. **Anticipate Manipulation:** Be aware of how others might frame information to sway your decisions.

How to Address Framing Effects in Others

1. **Present Balanced Information:** Offer both positive and negative frames to provide a complete picture.

   Example: "This product has a 20% defect rate but is 80% effective overall."

2. **Encourage Critical Thinking:** Ask questions that shift the focus to facts rather than framing.

   Example: "What are the actual implications of this choice?"

3. **Use Neutral Language:** Avoid emotionally charged wording when presenting options.

Exercises

1. **Reframe a Decision:** Take a recent choice and analyze how different frames influenced your judgment. Consider alternative frames.

2. **Spot Framing in Media:** Identify examples of framing in advertisements or news stories. Reflect on how the presentation affects perception.

3. **Create Balanced Frames:** Practice presenting the same information using both positive and negative language. Observe how it changes reactions.

Closing Thoughts

The Framing Effect demonstrates the power of language and context in shaping decisions. By recognizing and countering this bias, you can make more rational, balanced choices and present information in a way that promotes clarity and fairness.

Mastering this skill not only improves your decision-making but also equips you to communicate effectively and ethically in professional and personal interactions.

Chapter 41: Understanding the Halo Effect

The Shine of First Impressions: The Halo Effect

The Halo Effect occurs when an individual's overall impression of someone or something is influenced disproportionately by one positive characteristic. This bias leads people to assume that someone who excels in one area must excel in others, even without supporting evidence.

For example:

- **Scenario:** A charismatic speaker is perceived as more knowledgeable than they actually are.
- **Effect:** Their confidence and charm overshadow potential gaps in their expertise.

Understanding the Halo Effect helps ensure evaluations are balanced and based on comprehensive evidence rather than first impressions.

How the Halo Effect Works

1. **Focus on a Single Attribute:** A positive trait — such as attractiveness, confidence, or success — becomes the basis for broader judgments.

   Example: "They're well-dressed, so they must be organized."

2. **Generalize to Other Traits:** The positive impression spills over into unrelated areas.

   Example: Assuming a friendly co-worker is also highly competent.

3. **Reinforce Through Perception:** Once established, the halo effect influences how future behaviors are interpreted.

Examples of the Halo Effect

1. **In Hiring Decisions:**
   o A candidate with a polished appearance is assumed to have superior skills, even if their resume doesn't substantiate it.

2. **In Product Marketing:**
   o A well-designed package creates the impression that a product is of higher quality.

3. **In Education:**
   o A student who excels in one subject is assumed to perform well in others, even without evidence.

Why the Halo Effect is Harmful

The Halo Effect can lead to:

1. **Biased Judgments:** Positive impressions may overshadow critical weaknesses or limitations.

2. **Missed Opportunities:** Overlooking less charismatic individuals who may have greater competence.

3. **Unfair Treatment:** Favoritism based on superficial traits rather than merit.

How to Counter the Halo Effect

1. **Focus on Objective Criteria:** Use measurable, evidence-based evaluations rather than relying on first impressions.

    Example: "Does this candidate meet the specific requirements for the role?"

2. **Seek Diverse Perspectives:** Involve others in evaluations to minimize personal bias.

    Example: "Let's compare notes and discuss the full range of skills demonstrated."

3. **Reflect on Assumptions:** Ask whether positive impressions are influencing unrelated judgments.

    Example: "Am I assuming this person is skilled because they're confident?"

How to Address the Halo Effect in Others

1. **Encourage Fact-Based Analysis:** Redirect discussions to focus on evidence rather than subjective impressions.

    Example: "What specific examples support this conclusion?"

2. **Highlight Other Attributes:** Point out areas that deserve closer scrutiny to ensure balanced evaluations.

    Example: "They're very personable — let's also review their technical skills."

3. **Promote Awareness:** Discuss the Halo Effect openly in group settings to encourage fair and objective assessments.

Exercises

1. **Identify a Halo Effect:** Reflect on a situation where you judged someone or something based on a single positive trait. How did this affect your decision-making?

2. **Practice Objective Evaluation:** Choose a task (e.g., reviewing resumes, evaluating a project) and focus exclusively on objective criteria.

3. **Challenge a Positive Assumption:** Identify an assumption you've made about someone based on a positive impression. Gather evidence to verify or refute it.

Closing Thoughts

The Halo Effect highlights the power of first impressions, but it also demonstrates how these impressions can distort judgment. By consciously examining assumptions and focusing on evidence, you can make more accurate evaluations.

Mastering this skill fosters better decision-making in hiring, teamwork, and everyday interactions, ensuring that merit and substance take precedence over surface-level impressions.

Chapter 42: Reframing with Devil's Advocacy

Challenging Ideas Constructively: Devil's Advocacy

Devil's Advocacy is a technique where someone intentionally argues against a decision, idea, or plan to test its viability and uncover potential weaknesses. This approach encourages critical thinking, strengthens proposals, and reduces the risk of groupthink.

For example:

- **Scenario:** A company is planning to launch a new product.
- **Devil's Advocacy:** "What if competitors respond with a cheaper alternative? Are we prepared for that scenario?"

By challenging assumptions and exploring alternative perspectives, Devil's Advocacy ensures decisions are robust and well-informed.

How Devil's Advocacy Works

1. **Assign the Role:** Designate someone to take on the role of Devil's Advocate in a discussion or decision-making process.

   Example: "Your job is to identify flaws in our proposal."

2. **Challenge Assumptions:** Raise questions or counterarguments to test the strength of the idea.

   Example: "What if this strategy fails? What's our contingency plan?"

3. **Evaluate Responses:** Use the feedback to refine and strengthen the proposal or decision.

Applications of Devil's Advocacy

1. **In Strategic Planning:**
   o Teams use Devil's Advocacy to identify risks and refine business strategies.

2. **In Academic Debates:**
   o Students explore opposing viewpoints to deepen understanding of complex topics.

3. **In Personal Decisions:**
   o Individuals challenge their own plans to uncover potential oversights.

Why Devil's Advocacy is Effective

This method helps:

1. **Strengthen Ideas:** Exposes weaknesses and gaps, leading to more robust decisions.

2. **Encourage Open Dialogue:** Promotes a culture of constructive criticism and mutual respect.

3. **Prevent Groupthink:** Reduces the risk of unanimous but poorly considered decisions.

Challenges and Limitations

1. **Resistance to Criticism:** People may feel defensive or dismissive of opposing viewpoints.

2. **Overemphasis on Negativity:** Excessive focus on flaws may stifle creativity or optimism.

3. **Time-Intensive:** Thoroughly testing ideas can require significant effort and resources.

For instance, in fast-paced environments, teams may resist adopting Devil's Advocacy due to perceived delays in decision-making.

How to Use Devil's Advocacy Effectively

1. **Foster a Safe Environment:** Ensure participants feel comfortable raising and addressing criticisms.
2. **Balance Criticism with Constructive Feedback:** Focus on refining ideas rather than dismissing them outright.
3. **Rotate the Role:** Assign different team members as Devil's Advocate to ensure diverse perspectives.

Exercises

1. **Challenge a Plan:** Choose a project or decision you're working on and play the role of Devil's Advocate. What potential flaws can you identify?
2. **Team Exercise:** In a group setting, assign a Devil's Advocate to critique a proposal. Reflect on how this process improves the outcome.
3. **Personal Reflection:** Apply Devil's Advocacy to a personal goal or decision. What insights emerge from challenging your assumptions?

Closing Thoughts

Devil's Advocacy is a powerful tool for strengthening ideas, fostering critical thinking, and ensuring balanced decision-making. By embracing constructive criticism, individuals and teams can address weaknesses, anticipate challenges, and make more informed choices.

While it requires a willingness to engage in healthy debate, the benefits of this approach make it invaluable in both professional and personal contexts.

Chapter 43: Premortem Analysis

Planning for Failure: Premortem Analysis

Premortem Analysis is a problem-solving technique where a team imagines a project has failed and works backward to identify potential reasons for the failure. Unlike a post-mortem, which analyzes failures after they occur, a premortem focuses on preventing issues before they arise.

For example:

- **Scenario:** A company plans to launch a new software product.
- **Premortem Question:** "Imagine the launch is a disaster. What went wrong?"
- **Insights:** Issues like insufficient testing, unclear marketing, or competitor actions might surface, allowing the team to address these risks proactively.

Premortem Analysis fosters proactive thinking, improves planning, and reduces the likelihood of failure.

How Premortem Analysis Works

1. **Define the Project:** Clearly describe the project or decision under consideration.

   Example: "We're planning a corporate expansion into a new market."

2. **Imagine Failure:** Ask the team to envision that the project has failed completely.

   Question: "If this initiative flopped, what would be the main reasons?"

3. **Identify Potential Issues:** Brainstorm all possible causes of failure, both internal and external.

   Example: "We underestimated cultural differences or regulatory challenges."

4. **Develop Mitigation Strategies:** Use the identified risks to create action plans that address vulnerabilities.

Applications of Premortem Analysis

1. **In Business Strategy:**
   o Teams use it to foresee and mitigate risks in major initiatives.

   Example: A startup anticipates funding challenges and builds contingency plans.

2. **In Project Management:**
   o Teams analyze potential pitfalls in new projects to prevent delays or overruns.

3. **In Personal Planning:**
   o Individuals apply premortem thinking to prepare for challenges in achieving personal goals.

Why Premortem Analysis is Effective

This method helps:

1. **Identify Risks Early:** Proactively addresses potential issues before they become problems.

2. **Encourage Honest Feedback:** Fosters open discussion by normalizing the exploration of failure scenarios.

3. **Improve Resilience:** Builds contingency plans that make projects more robust and adaptable.

Challenges and Limitations

1. **Overemphasis on Negatives:** Excessive focus on failure may discourage optimism or creativity.
2. **Difficulty in Identifying Unforeseen Issues:** Some risks may still be missed despite thorough analysis.
3. **Time and Resource Requirements:** Conducting a premortem may require significant effort, particularly for complex projects.

For instance, in a fast-paced start-up environment, teams may resist dedicating time to imagining failure when urgency drives action.

How to Use Premortem Analysis Effectively

1. **Encourage a Positive Mindset:** Frame the exercise as a way to strengthen the project, not to predict inevitable failure.
2. **Involve Diverse Perspectives:** Include team members from different backgrounds and roles to ensure comprehensive risk identification.
3. **Prioritize Risks:** Focus on addressing the most likely and impactful failure scenarios first.

Exercises

1. **Conduct a Premortem:** Choose a current project or goal. Imagine it has failed and brainstorm reasons why. Create a plan to mitigate these risks.
2. **Team Workshop:** Facilitate a premortem session for a group project. Reflect on how this exercise changes the team's approach.
3. **Personal Application:** Apply premortem thinking to a personal decision, such as a career change or major purchase. What risks can you foresee and address?

Closing Thoughts

Premortem Analysis is a proactive and practical tool for anticipating challenges and strengthening plans. By imagining failure and addressing potential risks early, you can improve the likelihood of success and build resilience against unforeseen setbacks.

While it requires a willingness to confront uncomfortable scenarios, the insights gained through this process are invaluable for ensuring robust decision-making and effective execution.

Chapter 44: Overcoming Status Quo Bias

Resisting Familiarity: Status Quo Bias

Status Quo Bias refers to the tendency to prefer existing conditions or the "default" option over change, even when better alternatives are available. This bias often stems from fear of the unknown, or overestimating the risks of change.

For example:

- **Scenario:** A company continues using outdated software despite evidence that a modern system would save time and money.

Overcoming Status Quo Bias involves evaluating options objectively, challenging assumptions, and embracing change when it offers clear benefits.

How Status Quo Bias Works

1. **Preference for Familiarity:** People tend to stick with what they know, even if it's suboptimal.

   Example: "We've always done it this way—it's comfortable."

2. **Aversion to Loss:** The potential losses associated with change often feel more significant than the potential gains.

   Example: "What if the new system doesn't work as expected?"

3. **Underestimating Alternatives:** The default option is often chosen without thoroughly exploring other possibilities.

Examples of Status Quo Bias

1. **In Personal Decisions:**
   - Staying in a job you dislike because it feels safer than seeking a new opportunity.

2. **In Business Strategy:**
   - Failing to adopt innovative technologies due to fear of disruption.

3. **In Public Policy:**
   - Resistance to new policies or reforms, even when they offer clear advantages.

Why Status Quo Bias is Harmful

This bias can lead to:

1. **Missed Opportunities:** Avoiding change may prevent growth, innovation, or improvement.

2. **Inefficiency:** Clinging to outdated methods or systems hinders progress.

3. **Resistance to Innovation:** Fear of change stifles creativity and adaptability.

How to Overcome Status Quo Bias

1. **Evaluate Costs and Benefits:** Compare the risks and rewards of maintaining the status quo versus making a change.

   Example: "What are the long-term costs of sticking with the current system?"

2. **Start Small:** Test changes on a smaller scale to reduce perceived risks.

   Example: "Let's pilot the new software in one department first."

3. **Focus on Opportunities:** Shift attention from what might be lost to what could be gained.

   Example: "What are the potential benefits of embracing this new approach?"

How to Address Status Quo Bias in Others

1. **Highlight the Costs of Inaction:** Show how sticking with the status quo may lead to missed opportunities or declining performance.

2. **Provide Evidence:** Use data, case studies, or examples to demonstrate the benefits of change.

3. **Involve Stakeholders:** Engage others in the decision-making process to build trust and reduce resistance.

Exercises

1. **Challenge a Default:** Reflect on a decision where you chose the default option. Re-evaluate whether this was the best choice.

2. **Analyze a Missed Opportunity:** Identify a time when fear of change held you back. What could you have done differently?

3. **Test a New Option:** Choose an area in your life or work where you've stuck with the status quo. Experiment with an alternative and reflect on the outcome.

Closing Thoughts

Status Quo Bias is a common but limiting mindset that prioritizes comfort over progress. By recognizing this bias and embracing thoughtful, evidence-based changes, you can unlock new opportunities, drive innovation, and adapt more effectively to evolving challenges.

Mastering this skill helps you make proactive, forward-thinking decisions, whether in your personal life, your career, or your organization.

Chapter 45: Appreciating Base Rates

The Bigger Picture: Appreciating Base Rates

Base Rate Neglect occurs when individuals focus on specific, vivid details and ignore statistical probabilities (base rates) that provide a more accurate picture. Appreciating base rates helps anchor judgments in reality by prioritizing general data over isolated cases.

For example:

- **Scenario:** A person believes their chance of winning the lottery is high because they know someone who won, ignoring the statistical odds.

By factoring in base rates, you can make more rational decisions and avoid being swayed by emotional or anecdotal evidence.

How Base Rate Neglect Works

1. **Focus on Specifics:** People give disproportionate weight to anecdotal evidence or specific details.

   Example: "My friend succeeded in this investment, so I will too."

2. **Ignore Probabilities:** Statistical data is overlooked, even when it provides a more accurate assessment of likelihood.

   Example: Ignoring the fact that 90% of start-ups fail within five years.

3. **Distorted Decision-Making:** Judgments become biased toward the specific over the general.

Examples of Base Rate Neglect

1. **In Medical Decisions:**
   - Assuming a rare disease is likely after reading vivid symptoms online, despite its low base rate in the general population.

2. **In Hiring Decisions:**
   - Focusing on a candidate's charisma during an interview while ignoring statistical data on their past performance.

3. **In Everyday Risks:**
   - Overestimating the danger of air travel due to media coverage of plane crashes, despite its statistical safety.

Why Base Rate Neglect is Harmful

Neglecting base rates can lead to:

1. **Overconfidence in Unlikely Outcomes:** Decisions are based on rare exceptions rather than common realities.

2. **Poor Risk Assessment:** Overestimating or underestimating risks due to emotional or anecdotal influences.

3. **Missed Opportunities:** Ignoring general trends that could provide valuable insights.

How to Appreciate Base Rates

1. **Start with the General Data:** Look at statistical probabilities before considering specific cases.

   Example: "What are the overall odds of success in this venture?"

2. **Combine Base Rates with Specifics:** Use individual details to complement, not replace, statistical data.

   Example: "How does this person's background compare to the general success rate in this field?"

3. **Consult Experts:** Seek advice from those familiar with statistical trends in the relevant area.

How to Address Base Rate Neglect in Others

1. **Present Data Clearly:** Share base rate statistics alongside specific examples to provide context.

   Example: "While this case is compelling, the overall success rate for this approach is only 10%."

2. **Challenge Anecdotes:** Gently question how individual examples compare to broader trends.

   Example: "That's an interesting story—how often does that actually happen?"

3. **Encourage Critical Thinking:** Highlight the importance of balancing general data with personal stories.

Exercises

1. **Analyze a Decision:** Reflect on a past choice where you prioritized specific details over statistical probabilities. What would you do differently now?

2. **Research Base Rates:** Choose a decision you're facing and look up relevant statistics. How does this information affect your perspective?

3. **Challenge an Anecdote:** When someone shares a compelling story, research how it compares to broader data. Reflect on the insights you gain.

Closing Thoughts

Appreciating base rates is essential for rational decision-making. By grounding judgments in statistical realities, you can better assess risks, predict outcomes, and make informed choices.

This skill not only enhances your personal and professional decision-making but also empowers you to navigate a data-driven world with clarity and confidence.

Chapter 46: Debiasing with Probabilistic Thinking

Thinking in Percentages: Probabilistic Thinking

Probabilistic Thinking involves evaluating decisions and outcomes in terms of probabilities rather than certainties. This approach encourages consideration of multiple possibilities and their likelihoods, leading to more nuanced and flexible judgments.

For example:

- **Scenario:** A manager is deciding whether to invest in a new product.
- **Probabilistic Thinking:** "There's a 60% chance of moderate success, a 20% chance of significant success, and a 20% chance of failure."

By quantifying uncertainty, probabilistic thinking helps mitigate overconfidence and fosters more informed decision-making.

How Probabilistic Thinking Works

1. **Define Possible Outcomes:** Identify all potential scenarios.

   Example: "If we launch this product, what are the possible market reactions?"

2. **Assign Probabilities:** Estimate the likelihood of each outcome based on data or experience.

   Example: "What's the probability of capturing 10%, 20%, or 30% of the market?"

3. **Weigh Outcomes:** Consider the impact and likelihood of each scenario when making a decision.

Applications of Probabilistic Thinking

1. **In Business Decisions:**
   - Evaluate risks and opportunities in projects or investments.

2. **In Personal Planning:**
   - Assess the likelihood of achieving personal goals under different conditions.

3. **In Everyday Choices:**
   - Use probabilities to make practical decisions, such as choosing insurance coverage.

Why Probabilistic Thinking is Effective

This method helps:

1. **Manage Uncertainty:** Reduces overconfidence by acknowledging unknowns.

2. **Improve Risk Assessment:** Balances optimism with realism in evaluating possibilities.

3. **Encourage Flexibility:** Adapts strategies based on changing probabilities.

Challenges and Limitations

1. **Difficulty in Estimation:** Accurately estimating probabilities requires data and experience.

2. **Overcomplication:** Excessive focus on probabilities may hinder timely decision-making.

3. **Misinterpretation:** Probabilities must be clearly understood to avoid confusion.

For instance, misunderstanding the difference between a 10% and 90% probability can lead to poor decisions.

How to Practice Probabilistic Thinking

1. **Use Data:** Base probability estimates on credible information whenever possible.
2. **Embrace Uncertainty:** Accept that probabilities reflect likelihoods, not guarantees.
3. **Refine Over Time:** Update probabilities as new information becomes available.

Exercises

1. **Analyze a Decision:** Choose a past or upcoming decision and outline possible outcomes with their probabilities. Reflect on how this affects your judgment.
2. **Quantify Uncertainty:** Pick a situation where the outcome is uncertain. Assign probabilities to different scenarios and reassess your approach.
3. **Create a Probability Tree:** Map out a series of decisions and their possible outcomes to practice structured probabilistic reasoning.

Closing Thoughts

Probabilistic Thinking transforms uncertainty into clarity by quantifying possibilities and weighing risks. By adopting this mindset, you can navigate complex decisions with greater precision and confidence.

Chapter 47: Overcoming Loss Aversion

Letting Go of Fear: Loss Aversion

Loss Aversion is a cognitive bias that causes people to fear losses more than they value equivalent gains. This bias often leads to overly cautious decisions, missed opportunities, and an unwillingness to take calculated risks.

For example:

- **Scenario:** An investor hesitates to sell a declining stock because they fear locking in the loss, even when reinvesting in a stronger stock would likely yield better returns.

Overcoming Loss Aversion involves rethinking how you evaluate risks and rewards to make more balanced, rational decisions.

How Loss Aversion Works

1. **Fear of Loss:** Losses are perceived as more painful than gains are pleasurable.

   Example: Losing $100 feels worse than gaining $100 feels good.

2. **Clinging to the Status Quo:** People prefer to avoid change if it involves potential losses.

   Example: Keeping a failing product in the market to avoid the "loss" of sunk costs.

3. **Overvaluing What You Own:** The **endowment effect** amplifies loss aversion, making people overvalue items they already possess.

Examples of Loss Aversion

1. **In Investing:**
   - Holding onto underperforming assets to avoid realizing a loss, even when selling would free up resources for better opportunities.

2. **In Negotiations:**
   - Accepting a suboptimal deal to avoid the risk of losing the negotiation entirely.

3. **In Everyday Life:**
   - Choosing not to cancel a gym membership because of the initial cost, even when it's no longer being used.

Why Loss Aversion is Harmful

Loss Aversion can lead to:

1. **Missed Opportunities:** Fear of loss prevents individuals from pursuing high-potential rewards.

2. **Poor Resource Allocation:** Overvaluing existing commitments wastes time and energy.

3. **Stagnation:** Avoiding change hinders growth and innovation.

How to Overcome Loss Aversion

1. **Reframe the Risk:** Focus on the potential gains rather than the fear of loss.

    Example: "What can I achieve by taking this risk?"

2. **Use Probabilities:** Evaluate risks and rewards in terms of their likelihood and impact.

    Example: "What's the chance of success, and how does it compare to the potential loss?"

3. **Separate Emotions from Decisions:** Acknowledge emotional attachments but focus on objective analysis.

    Example: "Am I holding onto this investment because of its actual value or because I'm afraid to lose?"

How to Address Loss Aversion in Others

1. **Highlight the Cost of Inaction:** Show how avoiding risk can lead to missed opportunities.

    Example: "If we don't try this strategy, we could lose market share to competitors."

2. **Present Gains First:** Frame decisions in terms of potential benefits.

    Example: "By adopting this system, we can save 30% in costs over the next year."

3. **Encourage Small Steps:** Suggest incremental changes to reduce the perceived risk of loss.

    Example: "Let's start with a small-scale trial before committing fully."

Exercises

1. **Evaluate a Missed Opportunity:** Reflect on a time when fear of loss held you back. What might have happened if you had focused on potential gains instead?

2. **Reframe a Decision:** Choose a current decision and analyze it from a gains-focused perspective. How does this shift your approach?

3. **Experiment with Letting Go:** Identify something you've been clinging to due to loss aversion. Take a small step toward letting it go and observe the results.

Closing Thoughts

Loss Aversion is a deeply ingrained bias, but it can be mitigated with conscious effort and reframing. By focusing on opportunities rather than fears, you can make more balanced, confident decisions and unlock greater potential for growth and success.

Mastering this mindset fosters resilience and adaptability, helping you navigate risks and rewards with clarity and courage.

Chapter 48: Distinguishing Intuition from Analysis

Balancing Gut and Mind: Intuition vs. Analysis

Decisions often involve a tension between intuition (the immediate, instinctive sense of what to do) and analysis (the deliberate evaluation of data and evidence). Both approaches have strengths and weaknesses, and the key lies in knowing when to rely on each.

For example:

- **Scenario:** A manager feels that a candidate is the right fit for a role (intuition) but also reviews their track record and references to confirm the decision (analysis).

Distinguishing intuition from analysis allows you to make decisions that combine speed, accuracy, and reliability.

How Intuition and Analysis Work

1. **Intuition:**
   o Relies on pattern recognition and past experiences.

   Example: "I've encountered this situation before, and this feels like the right solution."
2. **Analysis:**
   o Involves systematic evaluation of facts, data, and probabilities.

   Example: "Based on these numbers, this approach has the highest chance of success."
3. **Combining the Two:**
   o Effective decision-making often integrates both, using intuition for speed and analysis for validation.

Examples of Intuition vs. Analysis

1. **In Hiring Decisions:**
   o **Intuition:** "This candidate has the right energy for the team."
   o **Analysis:** "Their skills and experience match the job requirements."
2. **In Investment Choices:**
   o **Intuition:** "This stock feels like it's going to perform well."
   o **Analysis:** "The company's financials and market trends support this choice."
3. **In Personal Decisions:**
   o **Intuition:** "This feels like the right house for me."
   o **Analysis:** "It fits my budget, location, and size requirements."

Why Balancing Intuition and Analysis is Important

Overreliance on one approach can lead to:

1. **Intuition Alone:** Decisions may be impulsive or poorly informed.
2. **Analysis Alone:** Overthinking may cause delays or

missed opportunities.

A balanced approach combines the best of both: the speed of intuition and the accuracy of analysis.

How to Distinguish Intuition from Analysis

1. **Pause and Reflect:** Ask whether your decision is based on a gut feeling or logical reasoning.

   Example: "Am I doing this because it feels right, or because the data supports it?"

2. **Validate Intuition with Evidence:** Use analysis to confirm or challenge your instincts.

   Example: "Does the data align with my initial impression?"

3. **Recognize Patterns:** Build experience to improve the accuracy of your intuitive judgments.

How to Help Others Balance Intuition and Analysis

1. **Encourage Evidence-Based Intuition:** Prompt colleagues to back their gut feelings with facts.

   Example: "That's an interesting perspective—what data supports it?"

2. **Facilitate Discussions:** Create opportunities to integrate diverse viewpoints and approaches.

   Example: "Let's hear both the intuitive and data-driven arguments before deciding."

3. **Promote a Balanced Culture:** Encourage teams to value both intuition and analysis.

Exercises

1. **Analyze a Decision:** Reflect on a past decision you made intuitively. How would analysis have changed your approach?

2. **Validate Your Intuition:** Choose a current decision guided by instinct. Seek data to confirm or challenge your gut feeling.

3. **Test Both Approaches:** For an upcoming decision, make an intuitive choice first, then analyze it systematically. Compare the results.

Closing Thoughts

Distinguishing and balancing intuition and analysis is a hallmark of effective decision-making. By recognizing the strengths and limitations of both, you can approach challenges with greater clarity, flexibility, and confidence.

This skill empowers you to navigate complex situations, make sound judgments, and adapt to uncertainty while harnessing the best of both instinct and intellect.

Chapter 49: Applying the Illusion of Transparency Test

The Misconception of Clarity: The Illusion of Transparency

The **Illusion of Transparency** is a cognitive bias where individuals overestimate how clearly their thoughts, emotions, or intentions are understood by others. This bias often leads to miscommunication, frustration, and unmet expectations.

For example:

- **Scenario:** A manager assumes their team understands the project goals because they feel they've communicated them clearly. In reality, the team is confused about key details.

Applying the Illusion of Transparency Test involves actively verifying understanding to ensure clarity in communication and decision-making.

How the Illusion of Transparency Works

1. **Assuming Clarity:** People believe their feelings or thoughts are obvious to others.

   Example: "I'm clearly upset—why doesn't anyone notice?"

2. **Underestimating Ambiguity:** The speaker assumes their message is understood as intended.

   Example: "I told them to prioritize this task; isn't that clear enough?"

3. **Ignoring Context:** Miscommunication arises when the listener lacks the same context or information.

Examples of the Illusion of Transparency

1. **In Leadership:**
   - A leader assumes their team understands a strategic vision without providing detailed explanations.

2. **In Personal Relationships:**
   - One partner believes their frustration is obvious, while the other remains unaware of any issue.

3. **In Public Speaking:**
   - A speaker assumes the audience understands complex terminology without further clarification.

Why the Illusion of Transparency is Harmful

This bias can lead to:

1. **Miscommunication:** Unclear expectations result in confusion and errors.

2. **Frustration:** Both parties feel misunderstood or unheard.

3. **Missed Opportunities:** Failure to address misunderstandings hinders collaboration and progress.

How to Apply the Illusion of Transparency Test

1. **Ask for Feedback:** Confirm that your message has been understood as intended.

   Example: "Can you summarize what you've understood

so far?"

2. **Use Clear, Simple Language:** Avoid assuming that others share your level of expertise or context.

   Example: Replace jargon with plain language or provide explanations.

3. **Encourage Questions:** Create a safe space for others to seek clarification.

   Example: "Does anyone have questions or need more detail about this?"

How to Address the Illusion of Transparency in Others

1. **Reflect Understanding Back:** Paraphrase what the other person has said to ensure clarity.

   Example: "So, you're saying the priority is to finish this report by Friday?"

2. **Gently Challenge Assumptions:** Highlight areas where clarity might be lacking.

   Example: "That's a great idea—how do you think others might interpret it?"

3. **Encourage Active Listening:** Foster a culture of mutual understanding and clear communication.

Exercises

1. **Reflect on Past Miscommunications:** Identify a time when you assumed others understood you clearly. What could you have done differently?

2. **Verify Understanding:** In your next conversation, ask the other person to restate your message to ensure alignment.

3. **Clarify an Ambiguous Situation:** Choose a recent instance of confusion and rewrite the communication to eliminate ambiguity.

Closing Thoughts

The Illusion of Transparency reminds us that what feels clear in our minds may not be obvious to others. By verifying understanding and encouraging open dialogue, we can overcome this bias and communicate more effectively.

Mastering this skill enhances relationships, improves teamwork, and ensures that your messages are understood as intended, fostering greater connection and collaboration.

Chapter 50: The Outside View Technique

Looking Beyond Yourself: The Outside View Technique

The Outside View Technique involves stepping back from a specific situation and considering broader trends, patterns, and external perspectives. Unlike the inside view, which focuses on unique details, the outside view anchors decisions in objective data and comparable cases.

For example:

- **Scenario:** A start-up founder believes their product will succeed based on its unique features (inside view).
- **Outside View:** Examining industry statistics reveals that 90% of start-ups fail within the first five years, prompting more realistic planning.

By incorporating the outside view, you can avoid overconfidence and improve decision-making accuracy.

How the Outside View Technique Works

1. **Define the Situation:** Clearly outline the decision or project at hand.

    Example: "We're launching a new app in the fitness market."

2. **Find Comparable Cases:** Look for similar situations or historical examples.

    Example: "How have other fitness apps performed in their first year?"

3. **Use Base Rates and Trends:** Anchor your expectations in objective data from comparable cases.

    Example: "What's the average success rate for apps in this category?"

4. **Adjust Plans Accordingly:** Incorporate insights from the outside view to refine strategies and expectations.

Applications of the Outside View Technique

1. **In Business Planning:**
    o   Evaluate projects or investments by analyzing industry benchmarks and trends.

2. **In Personal Decisions:**
    o   Use external data to set realistic expectations for personal goals, such as fitness or career milestones.

3. **In Risk Assessment:**
    o   Assess potential outcomes by considering historical probabilities and patterns.

Why the Outside View Technique is Effective

This method helps:

1. **Counter Overconfidence:** Reduces the tendency to rely on overly optimistic assumptions.

2. **Provide Context:** Anchors decisions in objective, data-driven insights.

3. **Improve Planning:** Encourages realistic timelines, budgets, and expectations.

Challenges and Limitations

1. **Access to Data:** Finding relevant and accurate data for comparable cases can be difficult.
2. **Overemphasis on Trends:** Focusing too much on past patterns may overlook unique opportunities.
3. **Resistance to Change:** People may resist adjusting plans when the outside view contradicts their assumptions.

For instance, a team deeply invested in their project's uniqueness may struggle to accept external benchmarks that suggest lower success rates.

How to Use the Outside View Effectively

1. **Start with Data:** Identify key metrics and trends that provide a realistic baseline.

   Example: "What's the average ROI for similar investments?"
2. **Balance Views:** Combine insights from the outside view with the unique aspects of your situation.

   Example: "How do our advantages align with industry trends?"
3. **Update Regularly:** Revisit the outside view as new data becomes available or conditions change.

Exercises

1. **Analyze a Past Decision:** Reflect on a decision where you relied solely on the inside view. How would incorporating the outside view have changed your approach?
2. **Research Benchmarks:** Choose a current goal or project and identify comparable cases or trends. Use this data to refine your expectations.
3. **Combine Views:** Practice integrating the inside and outside views in your next major decision. Reflect on the balance between them.

Closing Thoughts

The Outside View Technique is a powerful antidote to overconfidence and narrow thinking. By stepping back and considering broader trends, you can make more accurate, data-driven decisions while remaining open to unique opportunities.

Part III: Practical Applications

Section: Decision-Making Techniques

Making decisions is a core skill that influences every aspect of life, from personal growth to organizational success. However, the complexity of modern challenges requires more than just intuition or guesswork. The tools and methods in this section equip you with structured approaches to make decisions that are well-informed, balanced, and effective.

Whether you're comparing options, forecasting outcomes, or evaluating risks, these techniques provide frameworks to clarify choices, analyze trade-offs, and anticipate potential consequences. By mastering these decision-making tools, you'll build confidence in your ability to navigate uncertainty and choose wisely, regardless of the stakes.

Chapter 51: Weighted Decision Matrix

Systematic Comparison: The Weighted Decision Matrix

The Weighted Decision Matrix is a tool for comparing multiple options based on a set of criteria, each assigned a weight reflecting its importance. By scoring options against these criteria, this method ensures that decisions are logical, transparent, and aligned with priorities.

For example:

- **Scenario:** A team is choosing a software platform.
- **Matrix:** They evaluate options based on cost, ease of use, and functionality, assigning higher weights to the most important criteria.

The Weighted Decision Matrix simplifies complex decisions by breaking them into smaller, manageable parts.

How the Weighted Decision Matrix Works

1. **List Options and Criteria:** Define the choices and the criteria for evaluation.

   Example: Options: Software A, Software B, Software C. Criteria: Cost, Features, User Experience.

2. **Assign Weights to Criteria:** Reflect the relative importance of each criterion (e.g., on a scale of 1–5).

   Example: Cost = 3, Features = 4, User Experience = 5.

3. **Score Each Option:** Rate how well each option meets each criterion (e.g., on a scale of 1–10).

4. **Calculate Weighted Scores:** Multiply each score by the corresponding weight and sum the results for each option.

5. **Compare Totals:** The option with the highest total score is the recommended choice.

Applications of the Weighted Decision Matrix

1. **In Business:**
   - Choose suppliers, vendors, or technologies based on key performance metrics.

2. **In Personal Decisions:**
   - Evaluate job offers by comparing factors like salary, location, and growth opportunities.

3. **In Team Collaboration:**
   - Facilitate group decisions by providing a structured framework for discussion.

Why the Weighted Decision Matrix is Effective

This method helps:

1. **Clarify Priorities:** Ensures decisions align with what matters most.

2. **Reduce Bias:** Bases choices on objective criteria rather than subjective impressions.

3. **Simplify Complexity:** Breaks down decisions into manageable, logical steps.

Challenges and Limitations

1. **Subjective Weights and Scores:** Assigning weights and scores may still involve personal bias.
2. **Time-Intensive:** Creating and populating the matrix requires effort and attention to detail.
3. **Overemphasis on Quantification:** Not all criteria can be easily quantified, which may overlook qualitative factors.

For instance, choosing a life partner based solely on a matrix might miss the nuances of compatibility.

How to Use the Weighted Decision Matrix Effectively

1. **Involve Stakeholders:** Collaborate to ensure weights and scores reflect diverse perspectives.
2. **Focus on Key Criteria:** Limit the number of criteria to avoid overcomplication.
3. **Combine with Qualitative Insights:** Use the matrix as a guide but consider qualitative factors alongside the results.

Exercises

1. **Create a Matrix:** Choose a decision you're currently facing. List options, define criteria, assign weights, and calculate scores. Reflect on the outcome.
2. **Team Exercise:** Facilitate a group decision-making process using a Weighted Decision Matrix. Discuss how it affects consensus.
3. **Evaluate a Past Decision:** Apply the matrix to a previous choice. Compare the results to the actual decision you made.

Closing Thoughts

The Weighted Decision Matrix transforms complex choices into structured, logical comparisons. By clarifying priorities and evaluating options systematically, this tool ensures decisions are both rational and aligned with your goals.

While it requires effort and careful judgment, its ability to simplify complexity and promote fairness makes it invaluable in both personal and professional contexts.

Chapter 52: Expected Value Calculation

Quantifying Risk and Reward: Expected Value Calculation

Expected Value Calculation is a decision-making tool that evaluates the average outcome of a decision by weighing each potential result by its probability and value. This method is widely used in finance, gambling, and strategic planning to guide decisions involving uncertainty.

For example:

- **Scenario:** A company considers investing in a new product.
- **Expected Value:** They estimate the probabilities of success (60%) and failure (40%) and calculate the expected financial return.

By focusing on long-term averages rather than individual outcomes, this method helps mitigate emotional decision-making.

How Expected Value Calculation Works

1. **Identify Possible Outcomes:** List all potential results of a decision.

   Example: "If we launch this product, we could either achieve high sales, moderate sales, or a loss."

2. **Assign Probabilities:** Estimate the likelihood of each outcome occurring.

   Example: High sales = 50%, Moderate sales = 30%, Loss = 20%.

3. **Determine Values:** Assign a monetary or utility value to each outcome.

   Example: High sales = $100,000, Moderate sales = $50,000, Loss = -$20,000.

4. **Calculate Expected Value:** Multiply each outcome's probability by its value, then sum the results.
   - Formula: $EV = (P1 \times V1) + (P2 \times V2) + ... + (Pn \times Vn)$

5. **Use the Result:** Compare the expected value to alternative options or thresholds for decision-making.

Applications of Expected Value Calculation

1. **In Business Strategy:**
   - Evaluate investments, pricing strategies, and product launches based on potential returns.

2. **In Personal Finance:**
   - Assess financial decisions, such as choosing between different insurance policies.

3. **In Everyday Choices:**
   - Make informed decisions involving uncertainty, such as whether to take a bet or gamble.

Why Expected Value Calculation is Effective

This method helps:

1. **Clarify Risk vs. Reward:** Quantifies potential outcomes to guide rational decision-making.

2. **Promote Long-Term Thinking:** Focuses on averages over time rather than isolated events.

3. **Mitigate Emotional Influence:** Reduces the impact of fear or greed in uncertain situations.

Challenges and Limitations

1. **Accuracy of Probabilities:** Estimating probabilities requires data or expertise, which may not always be available.
2. **Subjectivity in Values:** Assigning values to outcomes can be subjective and context-dependent.
3. **Unsuitability for Small Decisions:** For minor choices, the effort of calculation may outweigh the benefits.

For instance, calculating the expected value of ordering pizza versus sushi may be overkill for a casual dinner decision.

How to Use Expected Value Calculation Effectively

1. **Start with Reliable Data:** Use historical data or expert input to estimate probabilities and values.
2. **Consider the Context:** Focus on decisions where the stakes justify the effort of calculation.
3. **Combine with Other Methods:** Use Expected Value Calculation alongside qualitative factors for a well-rounded analysis.

Exercises

1. **Evaluate a Choice:** Choose a recent decision involving uncertainty. List outcomes, assign probabilities and values, and calculate the expected value. Reflect on the result.
2. **Compare Options:** Use Expected Value Calculation to assess two or more alternatives. Which has the highest EV?
3. **Test a Hypothetical Scenario:** Create a fictional decision (e.g. betting $50 on a coin flip) and practice calculating its expected value.

Closing Thoughts

Expected Value Calculation is a powerful tool for navigating uncertainty with logic and precision. By quantifying risks and rewards, it helps ensure decisions are guided by rational analysis rather than impulse or emotion.

While it requires thoughtful estimation and careful calculation, its ability to illuminate the best course of action makes it invaluable in finance, strategy, and everyday life.

Chapter 53: Decision Trees

Mapping Your Choices: Decision Trees

A Decision Tree is a visual tool for exploring and evaluating choices, outcomes, probabilities, and potential rewards or risks. This structured approach helps clarify options and identify the best course of action.

For example:

- **Scenario:** A business considers expanding into a new market.
- **Decision Tree:** They map out potential outcomes, such as increased revenue or market challenges, with probabilities and financial impacts assigned to each.

Decision Trees simplify complex decisions by making the process visual and transparent.

How Decision Trees Work

1. **Define the Decision:** Start with the main question or choice at the root of the tree.

Example: "Should we expand into a new market?"

2. **Identify Branches:** Add branches for each possible action or decision.

   Example: "Expand" vs. "Don't Expand."

3. **Map Outcomes:** Extend branches to show potential results of each action.

   Example: "High Sales," "Moderate Sales," "Market Loss."

4. **Assign Probabilities and Values:** Estimate the likelihood and value of each outcome.

5. **Calculate Expected Values:** Use the probabilities and values to evaluate each branch.

6. **Choose the Optimal Path:** Select the decision that maximizes expected value or aligns with your goals.

Applications of Decision Trees

1. **In Business:**
   o Plan investments, product launches, or strategic moves by mapping potential outcomes.

2. **In Personal Decisions:**
   o Evaluate significant life choices, such as changing careers or moving to a new city.

3. **In Team Collaboration:**
   o Facilitate group decision-making by visualizing options and consequences.

Why Decision Trees are Effective

This method helps:

1. **Clarify Complex Choices:** Breaks down decisions into manageable steps.

2. **Visualize Risks and Rewards:** Makes trade-offs and probabilities easier to understand.

3. **Promote Transparency:** Facilitates clear communication and collaboration.

Challenges and Limitations

1. **Over-Simplification:** May not capture all nuances or uncertainties of a decision.

2. **Data Requirements:** Requires reliable probabilities and values for accurate analysis.
3. **Time-Intensive:** Building a detailed tree can be labor-intensive for complex scenarios.

For example, a decision tree for a global expansion strategy might involve dozens of branches and require extensive data.

How to Use Decision Trees Effectively

1. **Start Simple:** Begin with high-level branches and refine as more data becomes available.
2. **Use Software Tools:** Leverage decision-tree software for complex analyses.
3. **Combine with Qualitative Insights:** Balance the tree's quantitative results with contextual factors.

Exercises

1. **Build a Tree:** Create a decision tree for a choice you're currently facing. Map options, outcomes, probabilities, and values.
2. **Evaluate a Past Decision:** Reconstruct a previous decision using a decision tree. Compare the visualized process to your actual approach.
3. **Team Exercise:** Facilitate a group discussion by building a decision tree collaboratively. Reflect on how it affects consensus.

Closing Thoughts

Decision Trees are indispensable tools for navigating complex decisions with clarity and confidence. By visualizing options and outcomes, they ensure decisions are grounded in logic and aligned with your objectives.

Whether you're planning strategy, making personal choices, or leading a team, Decision Trees provide a structured framework to tackle uncertainty and complexity effectively.

Chapter 54: Scenario Planning

Anticipating the Future: Scenario Planning

Scenario Planning is a decision-making technique that involves envisioning and preparing for multiple possible futures. By exploring different scenarios, you can anticipate risks, identify opportunities, and build strategies that are adaptable to change.

For example:

- **Scenario:** A company is developing a long-term business strategy.
- **Scenario Planning:** They consider how economic growth, market competition, or technological advances might affect their plans.

This technique helps decision-makers remain flexible and prepared, no matter what the future holds.

How Scenario Planning Works

1. **Define the Focus:** Identify the decision, goal, or issue you want to address.

   Example: "How will our business adapt to changes in the energy market?"

2. **Identify Key Drivers:** Determine the factors that could influence outcomes.

   Example: Regulatory changes, technological advancements, customer preferences.

3. **Develop Scenarios:** Create detailed descriptions of possible futures, including best-case, worst-case, and most-likely scenarios.

   Example: "In a high-growth scenario, renewable energy adoption accelerates; in a low-growth scenario, traditional energy sources dominate."

4. **Analyze Implications:** Evaluate how each scenario might impact your decisions or goals.

5. **Plan Strategies:** Develop strategies that are flexible enough to succeed across multiple scenarios.

Applications of Scenario Planning

1. **In Business Strategy:**
   o Anticipate market trends, competitive dynamics, and economic shifts.

2. **In Public Policy:**
   o Plan for environmental changes, healthcare needs, or infrastructure demands.

3. **In Personal Decisions:**
   o Prepare for life changes, such as career transitions or retirement planning.

Why Scenario Planning is Effective

This method helps:

1. **Improve Flexibility:** Encourages adaptable strategies that can succeed under varying conditions.

2. **Identify Risks and Opportunities:** Highlights potential challenges and areas for growth.

3. **Promote Long-Term Thinking:** Focuses on future possibilities rather than immediate concerns.

Challenges and Limitations

1. **Time-Intensive:** Creating detailed scenarios requires effort and collaboration.
2. **Complexity Management:** Balancing too many scenarios can lead to confusion or indecision.
3. **Uncertainty in Predictions:** Scenarios are inherently speculative and may not capture all possible outcomes.

For instance, a business planning for market shifts might miss disruptive technologies that emerge unexpectedly.

How to Use Scenario Planning Effectively

1. **Involve Diverse Perspectives:** Include stakeholders from different backgrounds to ensure comprehensive scenarios.
2. **Focus on Key Drivers:** Limit scenarios to those driven by the most impactful and uncertain factors.
3. **Revisit and Revise:** Update scenarios as new data or trends emerge.

Exercises

1. **Plan for a Decision:** Choose a current decision and develop three scenarios (optimistic, pessimistic, and most likely). Reflect on how this affects your strategy.
2. **Revisit a Past Outcome:** Analyze a past decision using Scenario Planning. Were there outcomes you didn't anticipate?
3. **Facilitate a Team Exercise:** Work with a group to create scenarios for a shared goal or challenge. Discuss how this influences planning.

Closing Thoughts

Scenario Planning empowers decision-makers to navigate uncertainty with foresight and resilience. By exploring multiple possible futures, you can develop strategies that are flexible, robust, and well-prepared for change.

Chapter 55: The Delphi Method

Reaching Consensus: The Delphi Method

The Delphi Method is a structured technique for gathering and refining expert opinions through multiple rounds of feedback. By leveraging diverse perspectives and fostering anonymity, this method minimizes bias and encourages thoughtful consensus.

For example:

- **Scenario:** A company wants to forecast technology trends for the next decade.
- **Delphi Method:** They survey a panel of experts, analyze responses, and iterate until a consensus is reached.

The Delphi Method is particularly effective for complex, uncertain issues requiring expert input.

How the Delphi Method Works

1. **Define the Problem:** Clearly articulate the issue or question to be addressed.

Example: "What are the most likely technological innovations in healthcare by 2035?"

2. **Assemble a Panel of Experts:** Choose participants with relevant expertise and diverse perspectives.

3. **Conduct Round 1:** Gather initial opinions or predictions through surveys or questionnaires.

4. **Provide Feedback:** Share anonymized summaries of responses with the panel, highlighting areas of agreement and divergence.

5. **Repeat Until Consensus:** Conduct additional rounds of feedback, refining opinions and narrowing gaps in perspectives.

Applications of the Delphi Method

1. **In Forecasting:**
    o   Predict technological advancements, economic trends, or societal shifts.

2. **In Policy Development:**
    o   Build consensus on regulations, healthcare priorities, or environmental initiatives.

3. **In Organizational Strategy:**
    o   Identify risks, opportunities, or innovation pathways.

Why the Delphi Method is Effective

This method helps to:

1. **Leverage Expertise:** Combines insights from diverse, knowledgeable individuals.

2. **Encourage Open Dialogue:** Anonymity reduces the influence of dominant personalities or groupthink.

3. **Promote Iterative Refinement:** Multiple rounds improve the quality and clarity of recommendations.

Challenges and Limitations

1. **Time-Intensive:** The iterative process may require significant time and coordination.

2. **Dependence on Expertise:** The quality of results depends on the knowledge and engagement of the panel.

3. **Potential for Divergence:** Achieving consensus can be difficult if opinions remain polarized.

For instance, forecasting geopolitical trends might involve conflicting viewpoints that require careful facilitation to resolve.

How to Use the Delphi Method Effectively

1. **Choose Experts Wisely:** Select a diverse panel with complementary expertise.
2. **Foster Anonymity:** Ensure participants feel free to share honest, uninfluenced opinions.
3. **Facilitate Iteratively:** Use clear summaries and focused questions to guide each round.

Exercises

1. **Conduct a Delphi Study:** Choose a complex question and gather opinions from a group of colleagues or peers. Iterate until consensus is reached.
2. **Analyze Delphi Outputs:** Review a Delphi study (e.g., in research or business). Reflect on how iterative feedback improved the results.
3. **Facilitate a Panel Discussion:** Simulate the Delphi process in a team setting to tackle a shared challenge.

Closing Thoughts

The Delphi Method is a powerful tool for harnessing expert insights and building consensus on complex issues. By fostering iterative collaboration, it ensures decisions are well-informed, balanced, and thoroughly considered.

MCDA

	Cost	Quality	Delivery	Time	Weights
Option A	1	2	3	4	20%
Option B	1	2	4	3	50%
Option C	4	2	3	1	30%

Chapter 56: Multi-Criteria Decision Analysis (MCDA)

Balancing Priorities: Multi-Criteria Decision Analysis (MCDA)

Multi-Criteria Decision Analysis (MCDA) is a decision-making method that evaluates multiple conflicting criteria to identify the best option. This approach is particularly useful when decisions involve trade-offs, such as balancing cost, quality, and sustainability.

For example:

- **Scenario:** A company is choosing a supplier.
- **MCDA Application:** They assess options based on cost, delivery time, quality, and environmental impact, assigning weights to each factor based on importance.

MCDA provides a clear framework for navigating complex decisions with competing priorities.

How MCDA Works

1. **Define the Decision Context:** Clearly articulate the problem and objectives.

   Example: "Which supplier should we choose for our new product line?"

2. **List Criteria:** Identify the factors that will influence the decision.

   Example: Cost, delivery time, quality, environmental impact.

3. **Assign Weights:** Reflect the relative importance of each criterion.

   Example: Quality = 40%, Cost = 30%, Delivery Time = 20%, Environmental Impact = 10%.

4. **Score Options:** Rate each option based on how well it meets each criterion.

   Example: Use a scale of 1–10, where 10 indicates excellent performance.

5. **Calculate Weighted Scores:** Multiply each score by its weight and sum the results for each option.

6. **Compare and Choose:** The option with the highest total score is typically the best choice.

Applications of MCDA

1. **In Business Decisions:**
   - Evaluate suppliers, investments, or projects based on multiple performance metrics.

2. **In Public Policy:**
   - Balance economic, social, and environmental factors in policymaking.

3. **In Personal Decisions:**
   - Choose between job offers, housing options, or major purchases by weighing pros and cons.

Why MCDA is Effective

This method helps:

1. **Clarify Trade-Offs:** Makes it easier to understand and evaluate competing priorities.

2. **Promote Rational Decisions:** Bases choices on structured analysis rather than intuition.

3. **Encourage Transparency:** Provides a clear rationale for decisions, which is especially valuable in collaborative settings.

Challenges and Limitations

1. **Subjectivity in Weights and Scores:** Assigning weights and scores can be influenced by personal bias.

2. **Data Requirements:** Accurate evaluation requires reliable data for each criterion.

3. **Over-Complexity:** Too many criteria or options can complicate analysis and slow decision-making.

For example, using MCDA to evaluate hundreds of products across dozens of criteria may require advanced tools or software.

How to Use MCDA Effectively

1. **Focus on Key Criteria:** Limit the number of criteria to the most impactful factors.

2. **Involve Stakeholders:** Collaborate with others to ensure weights and scores reflect diverse perspectives.

3. **Combine with Qualitative Insights:** Use MCDA as a guide but consider qualitative factors as well.

Exercises

1. **Create an MCDA Matrix:** Apply MCDA to a current decision by listing options, defining criteria, and calculating weighted scores.

2. **Evaluate a Past Decision:** Use MCDA to analyze a previous choice. How does the result compare to what you actually decided?

3. **Facilitate a Team Exercise:** Work with a group to apply MCDA to a shared decision. Reflect on how it influences consensus.

Closing Thoughts

Multi-Criteria Decision Analysis is a crucial tool for navigating complex decisions with competing priorities. By balancing trade-offs systematically, it ensures that choices are logical, transparent, and aligned with your objectives.

Chapter 57: Cost-Benefit Analysis

Weighing the Pros and Cons: Cost-Benefit Analysis

Cost-Benefit Analysis (CBA) is a decision-making technique that evaluates the costs and benefits of an action, project, or decision. By quantifying and comparing these factors, CBA helps determine whether the benefits outweigh the costs, guiding rational decision-making.

For example:

- **Scenario:** A company considers upgrading its IT infrastructure.

- **CBA Application:** They estimate the costs of hardware, software, and training versus the expected savings and productivity gains.

CBA simplifies decisions by focusing on measurable impacts and trade-offs.

How Cost-Benefit Analysis Works

1. **Define the Scope:** Clearly outline the decision or action being analyzed.

   Example: "Should we invest in a solar power system for our office?"

2. **Identify Costs and Benefits:** List all potential costs and benefits, both tangible and intangible.

   Example: Costs = Installation, maintenance; Benefits = Energy savings, reduced carbon footprint.

3. **Assign Monetary Values:** Quantify costs and benefits in financial terms where possible.

   Example: Energy savings = $10,000/year; Installation cost = $50,000.

4. **Calculate Net Benefit:** Subtract total costs from total benefits to determine the net benefit.

5. **Make a Decision:** If the net benefit is positive, the action is generally considered worthwhile.

Applications of Cost-Benefit Analysis

1. **In Business:**
   - Evaluate projects, investments, or operational changes based on financial viability.

2. **In Public Policy:**
   - Assess infrastructure projects, healthcare initiatives, or environmental programs.

3. **In Personal Decisions:**
   - Compare options like buying a car, pursuing education, or relocating.

Why Cost-Benefit Analysis is Effective

This method helps:

1. **Clarify Trade-Offs:** Provides a clear comparison of costs and benefits.

2. **Promote Objectivity:** Bases decisions on measurable impacts rather than subjective preferences.

3. **Encourage Efficient Resource Use:** Focuses efforts on actions with the greatest net benefit.

Challenges and Limitations

1. **Difficulties in Quantification:** Some costs and benefits, like employee morale or environmental impact, are hard to quantify.
2. **Assumptions and Uncertainty:** Results depend on assumptions about future outcomes, which may be uncertain.
3. **Overemphasis on Monetary Value:** Focusing only on financial metrics may overlook ethical or social considerations.

For instance, deciding whether to preserve a forest solely based on CBA may ignore its cultural or ecological significance.

How to Use CBA Effectively

1. **Include Intangible Factors:** Consider qualitative benefits and costs alongside financial metrics.
2. **Use Reliable Data:** Base calculations on accurate, up-to-date information.
3. **Revisit Assumptions:** Test results under different scenarios to account for uncertainty.

Exercises

1. **Conduct a CBA:** Choose a decision and list all associated costs and benefits. Quantify them where possible and calculate the net benefit.
2. **Analyze a Public Policy:** Research a real-world policy decision and evaluate its CBA. What additional factors might influence the outcome?
3. **Test a Hypothetical Scenario:** Apply CBA to a fictional decision, such as building a park. Reflect on how assumptions affect results.

Closing Thoughts

Cost-Benefit Analysis is a foundational tool for rational decision-making, offering a clear framework for weighing trade-offs and maximizing value. By focusing on measurable impacts, it ensures that resources are allocated efficiently and effectively.

Its ability to clarify choices and promote objective analysis makes it indispensable in business, public policy, and personal planning.

Chapter 58: The Precautionary Principle

Erring on the Side of Caution: The Precautionary Principle

The Precautionary Principle is a decision-making strategy that prioritizes avoiding harm when outcomes are uncertain or risks are high. It emphasizes caution, especially in situations where potential consequences are severe or irreversible.

For example:

- **Scenario:** A government considers approving a new pesticide.
- **Precautionary Principle:** Without definitive proof of its safety, they delay approval to prevent potential environmental harm.

This principle is commonly used in environmental policy, public health, and technology regulation to guide decisions in uncertain scenarios.

How the Precautionary Principle Works

1. **Identify Risks:** Focus on actions or decisions with significant uncertainty or potential harm.

   Example: "What are the risks of deploying this untested technology?"

2. **Apply Caution:** Favor safer options or delay decisions until risks are better understood.

   Example: "Let's conduct further studies before proceeding."

3. **Prioritize Prevention:** Adopt measures to minimize potential harm, even if the risks are not fully proven.

Applications of the Precautionary Principle

1. **In Environmental Policy:**
   - Regulate activities that could harm ecosystems, such as deforestation or chemical usage.

2. **In Public Health:**
   - Restrict substances or practices with uncertain health impacts, such as certain food additives or new medications.

3. **In Technological Development:**
   - Evaluate the societal impact of emerging technologies, like artificial intelligence or genetic engineering.

Why the Precautionary Principle is Effective

This method helps:

1. **Protect Against Harm:** Prevents irreversible damage by acting conservatively.

2. **Encourage Thorough Analysis:** Promotes careful consideration of potential risks.

3. **Build Public Trust:** Demonstrates responsibility and accountability in decision-making.

Challenges and Limitations

1. **Stifling Innovation:** Excessive caution may delay beneficial advancements.
2. **Ambiguity in Application:** Determining when and how to apply the principle can be subjective.
3. **Resistance to Change:** Fear of potential harm may lead to inaction, even when risks are minimal.

For example, overusing the principle might hinder the adoption of life-saving technologies with manageable risks.

How to Use the Precautionary Principle Effectively

1. **Focus on Significant Risks:** Apply the principle to scenarios where potential harm is severe or irreversible.
2. **Balance Caution with Progress:** Weigh the risks of inaction alongside the risks of action.
3. **Use Evidence-Based Analysis:** Combine precaution with ongoing research to refine decisions.

Exercises

1. **Evaluate a Risk:** Choose a decision involving uncertainty. Apply the Precautionary Principle to assess the safest course of action.
2. **Analyze a Policy:** Research a real-world example of the Precautionary Principle, such as environmental regulations. Reflect on its effectiveness.
3. **Test a Hypothetical Scenario:** Imagine approving a new product or technology. What precautions would you implement before proceeding?

Closing Thoughts

The Precautionary Principle is a valuable tool for managing uncertainty and protecting against potential harm. By prioritizing caution in high-stakes scenarios, it ensures that decisions are responsible, ethical, and aligned with long-term well-being.

Its focus on prevention and foresight makes it indispensable in fields such as environmental protection, public health, and technological innovation.

Chapter 59: The Monte Carlo Method

Simulating Outcomes: The Monte Carlo Method

The Monte Carlo Method is a decision-making tool that uses simulations to model the probability of different outcomes. By running thousands of random iterations, it provides insights into risks, uncertainties, and likely results.

For example:

- **Scenario:** An investor evaluates a portfolio's potential returns.
- **Monte Carlo Simulation:** They simulate different market conditions to estimate the range of possible outcomes.

This method is especially useful for complex, uncertain decisions involving multiple variables.

How the Monte Carlo Method Works

1. **Define the Problem:** Identify the decision or scenario to analyze.

   Example: "What is the likelihood of meeting our project deadline under current conditions?"

2. **Identify Variables:** Determine the factors influencing the outcome and their ranges of uncertainty.

   Example: Task durations, resource availability, external delays.

3. **Run Simulations:** Use software to generate random values for each variable and calculate the outcome. Repeat thousands of times to create a probability distribution.

4. **Analyze Results:** Evaluate the likelihood of different outcomes and identify areas of high risk.

Applications of the Monte Carlo Method

1. **In Financial Planning:**
   - Model investment risks, returns, and portfolio performance under various scenarios.

2. **In Project Management:**
   - Estimate timelines, budgets, and resource needs for complex projects.

3. **In Risk Analysis:**
   - Assess the probability of adverse events in fields such as engineering, insurance, or healthcare.

Why the Monte Carlo Method is Effective

This method helps:

1. **Quantify Uncertainty:** Provides a clear picture of risks and probabilities.

2. **Improve Forecasting:** Accounts for a wide range of possible scenarios.

3. **Guide Strategic Decisions:** Informs choices with data-driven insights.

Challenges and Limitations

1. **Data Requirements:** Accurate results depend on reliable input data and assumptions.
2. **Complexity:** Running simulations requires specialized tools and expertise.
3. **Overreliance on Models:** Results may mislead if underlying assumptions are flawed.

For instance, overly optimistic assumptions about market trends could skew financial simulations.

How to Use the Monte Carlo Method Effectively

1. **Start with Accurate Inputs:** Use credible data and realistic assumptions for variables.
2. **Interpret Results Carefully:** Focus on probability ranges rather than single outcomes.
3. **Combine with Other Tools:** Use Monte Carlo alongside qualitative analysis for a well-rounded perspective.

Exercises

1. **Run a Simulation:** Choose a decision or scenario and use online tools to create a Monte Carlo simulation. Reflect on the results.
2. **Analyze a Case Study:** Research a real-world example of Monte Carlo Simulation, such as financial modeling or project planning.
3. **Test Variables:** Experiment with different inputs to see how they affect the outcome distribution in a simulation.

Closing Thoughts

The Monte Carlo Method is an invaluable tool for navigating uncertainty and complexity. By simulating thousands of potential outcomes, it provides actionable insights into risks, probabilities, and likely results.

LIKELIHOOD

	HIGH LIKELIHOOD, HIGH IMPACT	LOW LIKELIHOOD, HIGH IMPACT
IMPACT	HIGH LIKELIHOOD, LOW IMPACT	LOW LIKELIHOOD, LOW IMPACT

Chapter 60: Risk Assessment Matrices

Prioritizing Risks: Risk Assessment Matrices

A Risk Assessment Matrix is a tool used to evaluate and prioritize risks based on their likelihood and potential impact. By categorizing risks into a visual grid, this method helps identify which issues require immediate attention and resources.

For example:

- **Scenario:** A construction company evaluates safety risks on a new project.
- **Matrix Application:** They categorize risks such as equipment failure or adverse weather based on how likely they are to occur and the potential harm they could cause.

This technique enables clear communication and prioritization, ensuring that critical risks are addressed effectively.

How a Risk Assessment Matrix Works

1. **Identify Risks:** List all potential risks associated with a decision or project.

   Example: "What could go wrong during this product launch?"

2. **Assess Likelihood:** Rate the probability of each risk occurring, often on a scale (e.g., low, medium, high).

3. **Evaluate Impact:** Rate the severity of consequences if the risk materializes, also on a scale.

4. **Map Risks:** Plot each risk on a 2x2 matrix, with likelihood on one axis and impact on the other.

5. **Prioritize and Mitigate:** Focus on addressing risks in the high-likelihood, high-impact quadrant first.

Applications of Risk Assessment Matrices

1. **In Project Management:**
   o Identify and mitigate risks to timelines, budgets, or deliverables.

2. **In Business Operations:**
   o Evaluate potential disruptions, such as supply chain issues or cybersecurity threats.

3. **In Personal Planning:**
   o Assess risks for significant decisions, like moving to a new city or investing in property.

Why Risk Assessment Matrices Are Effective

This method helps:

1. **Clarify Priorities:** Focuses attention on the most critical risks.

2. **Facilitate Decision-Making:** Provides a clear framework for evaluating and addressing uncertainties.

3. **Encourage Proactive Planning:** Promotes early action to mitigate potential problems.

Challenges and Limitations

1. **Subjective Ratings:** Likelihood and impact assessments may vary depending on individual perspectives.
2. **Oversimplification:** A 2x2 grid may not capture the full complexity of certain risks.
3. **Resource Constraints:** Addressing all risks, especially low-priority ones, may not be feasible.

For instance, a business may underestimate the impact of a low-likelihood risk that could cause catastrophic damage.

How to Use Risk Assessment Matrices Effectively

1. **Collaborate with Stakeholders:** Involve diverse perspectives to ensure accurate assessments of risks.
2. **Revisit Regularly:** Update the matrix as new risks emerge or conditions change.
3. **Balance Resources:** Focus on high-priority risks while monitoring lower-priority ones.

Exercises

1. **Create a Matrix:** Choose a current project or decision and develop a Risk Assessment Matrix. Reflect on how it influences your approach.
2. **Analyze a Past Event:** Apply a Risk Assessment Matrix to a previous failure or challenge. How could this tool have helped?
3. **Facilitate a Team Exercise:** Collaborate with colleagues to identify and prioritize risks for a shared goal or initiative.

Closing Thoughts

A Risk Assessment Matrix is a straightforward yet powerful tool for managing uncertainty. By categorizing and prioritizing risks, it ensures that resources are directed where they are needed most.

This method fosters proactive decision-making, reducing the likelihood of unexpected setbacks and enhancing the resilience of plans, projects, and organizations.

Chapter 61: Sensitivity Analysis

Testing the Variables: Sensitivity Analysis

Sensitivity Analysis is a decision-making technique that evaluates how changes in input variables affect outcomes. By identifying which variables have the most significant impact, this method helps decision-makers focus on critical factors and assess the robustness of their plans.

For example:

- **Scenario:** A retailer estimates profits for a new store.
- **Sensitivity Analysis:** They test how changes in rent, customer foot traffic, and product pricing influence overall profitability.

This technique is especially useful for identifying vulnerabilities and improving decision confidence.

How Sensitivity Analysis Works

1. **Define the Model:** Start with a decision model, formula, or framework.

Example: "Our profit = Revenue - Costs."

2. **Identify Key Variables:** Determine which inputs drive the outcome.

   Example: Sales volume, production cost, marketing spend.

3. **Test Variations:** Adjust each variable independently while holding others constant to see how it affects the outcome.

4. **Analyze Results:** Identify which variables have the most significant influence and prioritize them in planning.

Applications of Sensitivity Analysis

1. **In Financial Modeling:**
   - Test how changes in interest rates, taxes, or expenses affect a company's bottom line.

2. **In Project Planning:**
   - Assess the impact of variations in timelines, budgets, or resources.

3. **In Personal Decisions:**
   - Explore how different factors (e.g., salary, cost of living) affect financial decisions like relocation.

Why Sensitivity Analysis is Effective

This method helps:

1. **Identify Key Drivers:** Focuses attention on variables with the greatest impact.

2. **Test Assumptions:** Evaluates the robustness of decisions under different scenarios.

3. **Enhance Adaptability:** Prepares decision-makers to respond to changes in critical factors.

Challenges and Limitations

1. **Requires a Clear Model:** Results depend on the accuracy of the underlying decision model.

2. **Time-Intensive:** Testing multiple variables and scenarios can be labor-intensive.

3. **Limited Scope:** Analyzing one variable at a time may miss interactions between variables.

For instance, testing the effect of marketing spend without considering its interplay with product pricing may yield incomplete insights.

How to Use Sensitivity Analysis Effectively

1. **Start with Accurate Data:** Use reliable and current inputs to ensure meaningful results.
2. **Focus on Critical Variables:** Prioritize testing variables with the most uncertainty or potential impact.
3. **Combine with Scenario Planning:** Explore combinations of variable changes for a more comprehensive analysis.

Exercises

1. **Analyze a Decision Model:** Choose a decision or project and identify its key variables. Conduct Sensitivity Analysis to determine which factors are most influential.
2. **Evaluate Past Results:** Apply Sensitivity Analysis to a past project or investment. Reflect on how this tool could have improved planning.
3. **Team Exercise:** Collaborate with a group to test variables for a shared decision or strategy. Discuss the insights gained.

Closing Thoughts

Sensitivity Analysis provides a systematic way to evaluate the impact of uncertainties and focus on critical factors. By testing variables and their effects, it ensures decisions are robust, flexible, and well-informed.

This tool is essential for decision-makers seeking to navigate uncertainty, optimize outcomes, and anticipate challenges in dynamic environments.

Chapter 62: Adaptive Thinking

Staying Flexible: Adaptive Thinking

Adaptive Thinking refers to the ability to adjust plans, strategies, or decisions in response to new information or changing conditions. This mindset is crucial in dynamic environments where uncertainty and unforeseen challenges are common.

For example:

- **Scenario:** A project manager faces unexpected supply chain delays.
- **Adaptive Thinking:** They revise the timeline and explore alternative suppliers to keep the project on track.

By embracing flexibility and adaptability, decision-makers can navigate uncertainty more effectively and capitalize on emerging opportunities.

How Adaptive Thinking Works

1. **Monitor the Environment:** Stay alert to changes, trends, or unexpected developments.

   Example: "Are there any shifts in market conditions or customer behavior?"

2. **Evaluate the Impact:** Assess how new information affects current plans or decisions.

   Example: "How does this delay impact our timeline and budget?"

3. **Adjust Accordingly:** Revise strategies, priorities, or actions to align with the new reality.

   Example: "Let's allocate additional resources to address this bottleneck."

4. **Learn and Iterate:** Reflect on adjustments to improve future adaptability.

Applications of Adaptive Thinking

1. **In Business Strategy:**
   - Pivot in response to competitive pressures, technological advancements, or regulatory changes.

2. **In Crisis Management:**
   - Respond effectively to emergencies, such as natural disasters or cybersecurity breaches.

3. **In Personal Growth:**
   - Adjust career goals, financial plans, or lifestyle choices based on changing circumstances.

Why Adaptive Thinking is Effective

This method helps:

1. **Increase Resilience:** Enables rapid recovery and adjustment in the face of setbacks.

2. **Capitalize on Opportunities:** Identifies and exploits new possibilities as they arise.

3. **Enhance Decision-Making:** Encourages flexibility and responsiveness, reducing the risk of rigid thinking.

Challenges and Limitations

1. **Risk of Overreaction:** Frequent adjustments may lead to instability or inefficiency.
2. **Uncertainty in Outcomes:** Adapting to new conditions doesn't guarantee success.
3. **Resistance to Change:** Individuals or teams may struggle to embrace flexibility, especially in structured environments.

For instance, a company accustomed to traditional processes may find it difficult to pivot quickly during a market disruption.

How to Foster Adaptive Thinking

1. **Embrace a Growth Mindset:** View challenges as opportunities for learning and innovation.

   Example: "How can we turn this setback into a stepping stone?"
2. **Encourage Experimentation:** Test new ideas or approaches without fear of failure.

   Example: "Let's pilot this strategy in one market before scaling up."
3. **Promote Open Communication:** Foster a culture where feedback and collaboration drive flexibility.

   Example: "What does the team think about adjusting our approach?"

Exercises

1. **Reflect on a Past Adaptation:** Recall a time when you had to change plans. What worked well, and what could have been improved?
2. **Simulate a Pivot:** Choose a hypothetical scenario where plans must change. Practice developing and implementing an alternative strategy.
3. **Encourage Team Adaptability:** Facilitate a group exercise where unexpected challenges are introduced, prompting the team to adapt.

Closing Thoughts

Adaptive Thinking is a critical skill for thriving in an unpredictable world. By staying flexible and responsive, you can navigate challenges, seize opportunities, and build resilience in both personal and professional contexts.

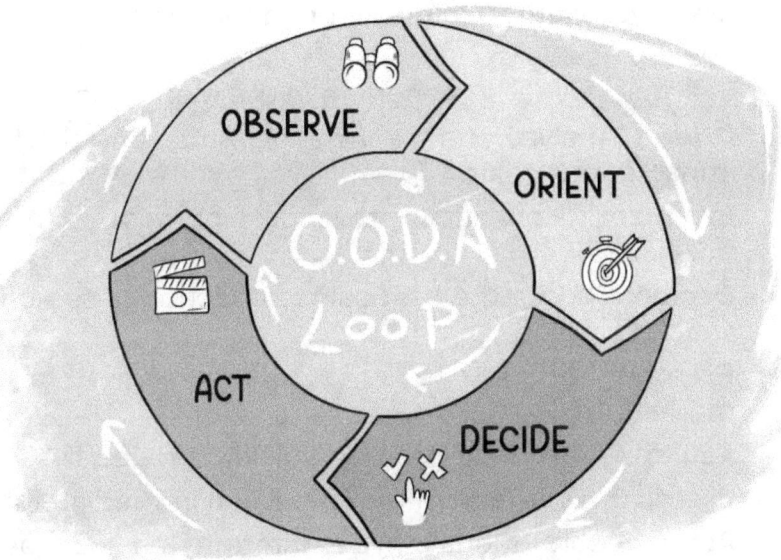

Chapter 63: The OODA Loop (Observe, Orient, Decide, Act)

Making Quick, Iterative Decisions: The OODA Loop

The OODA Loop is a decision-making framework developed by military strategist John Boyd. It emphasizes agility and continuous learning through four iterative stages: Observe, Orient, Decide, and Act. This approach is particularly effective in dynamic, high-stakes environments.

For example:

- **Scenario:** A business reacts to a competitor's unexpected product launch.

- **OODA Loop Application:** The team observes the market response, orients by analyzing data, decides on a counterstrategy, and acts swiftly.

The OODA Loop enables rapid, informed decision-making while maintaining flexibility to adapt as conditions evolve.

How the OODA Loop Works

1. **Observe:** Gather information about the environment and any changes.

   Example: "What's happening in the market right now?"

2. **Orient:** Analyze the information and consider how it impacts your goals.

   Example: "How does this development affect our position?"

3. **Decide:** Choose the best course of action based on your analysis.

   Example: "Should we adjust our pricing or focus on marketing?"

4. **Act:** Implement the decision quickly and decisively.

   Example: "Let's launch the campaign immediately."

5. **Repeat:** Continuously cycle through the loop as new information emerges.

Applications of the OODA Loop

1. **In Business Strategy:**
   - Respond to competitive threats, market shifts, or customer needs in real-time.

2. **In Crisis Management:**
   - Make fast, effective decisions during emergencies or high-pressure situations.

3. **In Personal Decision-Making:**
   - Apply the loop to adapt to changes in career, relationships, or finances.

Why the OODA Loop is Effective

This method helps:

1. **Improve Agility:** Enables rapid response to changing circumstances.

2. **Enhance Decision Quality:** Combines speed with informed analysis.

3. **Foster Continuous Learning:** Encourages iterative improvement through ongoing observation and adaptation.

Challenges and Limitations

1. **Risk of Incomplete Information:** Quick decisions may be based on limited data.
2. **Overemphasis on Speed:** Acting too quickly may lead to errors or missed opportunities.
3. **Complexity in Orientation:** Analyzing and synthesizing information can be challenging in chaotic environments.

For example, in fast-moving industries, businesses might struggle to interpret conflicting data during the "Orient" stage.

How to Apply the OODA Loop Effectively

1. **Focus on Key Signals:** Prioritize critical information during the "Observe" stage.
2. **Empower Teams:** Foster decentralized decision-making to enhance responsiveness.
3. **Iterate Rapidly:** Treat each loop as a learning opportunity to refine strategies.

Exercises

1. **Simulate an OODA Loop:** Apply the framework to a real or hypothetical situation requiring rapid decision-making. Reflect on each stage.
2. **Analyze a Past Decision:** Break down a previous choice into the OODA stages. What could have been improved?
3. **Facilitate a Team Exercise:** Use the OODA Loop to address a group challenge. Discuss how it enhances collaboration and agility.

Closing Thoughts

The OODA Loop is a dynamic and iterative decision-making framework that thrives in fast-paced, uncertain environments. By cycling through observation, analysis, action, and reflection, it ensures decisions are both rapid and well-informed.

EMOTIONS

CAUTION

FACTS

OPTIMISM

CREATIVITY

CONTROL

Chapter 64: The Six Thinking Hats

Thinking from Every Angle: The Six Thinking Hats

Developed by Edward de Bono, the Six Thinking Hats method is a decision-making framework that encourages individuals and teams to explore problems from six distinct perspectives, represented by metaphorical hats. This structured approach fosters creativity, critical thinking, and collaboration.

For example:

- **Scenario:** A company is brainstorming strategies for a new product launch.
- **Six Thinking Hats Application:** The team considers facts (white hat), emotions (red hat), risks (black hat), benefits (yellow hat), creativity (green hat), and process (blue hat) to develop a well-rounded plan.

This method helps avoid groupthink and ensures all aspects of a decision are considered.

The Six Thinking Hats Explained

1. **White Hat – Facts and Data:** Focuses on objective information and analysis.

   Example: "What do the market research and sales data tell us?"

2. **Red Hat – Emotions and Intuition:** Explores feelings, instincts, and gut reactions.

   Example: "How do we feel about this idea on an emotional level?"

3. **Black Hat – Risks and Caution:** Identifies potential problems and challenges.

   Example: "What could go wrong with this plan?"

4. **Yellow Hat – Optimism and Benefits:** Highlights strengths and opportunities.

   Example: "What are the advantages of this approach?"

5. **Green Hat – Creativity and Innovation:** Encourages brainstorming and exploring new ideas.

   Example: "What unconventional solutions could we consider?"

6. **Blue Hat – Process and Control:** Focuses on managing the discussion and ensuring balance.

   Example: "Have we covered all perspectives thoroughly?"

Applications of the Six Thinking Hats

1. **In Team Decision-Making:**
   - Foster balanced discussions that incorporate diverse viewpoints.

2. **In Creative Problem-Solving:**
   - Encourage out-of-the-box thinking and innovative solutions.

3. **In Personal Reflection:**
   - Analyze decisions or challenges from multiple angles to gain deeper insight.

Why the Six Thinking Hats are Effective

This method helps:

1. **Enhance Collaboration:** Encourages equal participation and minimizes conflict.
2. **Foster Comprehensive Analysis:** Ensures all aspects of a decision are considered.
3. **Improve Creativity and Innovation:** Creates space for exploring new ideas without judgment.

Challenges and Limitations

1. **Time-Intensive:** Covering all six perspectives can be lengthy in time-sensitive situations.
2. **Potential Resistance:** Some participants may struggle to adopt perspectives outside their comfort zones.
3. **Overemphasis on Structure:** Strict adherence to the framework might stifle spontaneous insights.

For example, a team under tight deadlines might find it difficult to dedicate time to all six hats.

How to Use the Six Thinking Hats Effectively

1. **Set Clear Objectives:** Define the problem or decision to be analyzed before beginning.
2. **Facilitate Participation:** Assign hats or rotate roles to ensure balanced input from all participants.
3. **Stay Flexible:** Adapt the process to suit the complexity and urgency of the decision.

Exercises

1. **Apply the Six Hats:** Choose a current decision and analyze it using all six perspectives. Reflect on how this influences your approach.
2. **Facilitate a Team Discussion:** Guide a group through the Six Thinking Hats method for a shared challenge. Discuss the insights gained.
3. **Analyze a Past Decision:** Use the Six Hats to revisit a previous choice. What new perspectives emerge?

Closing Thoughts

The Six Thinking Hats method provides a structured yet flexible framework for making decisions that are well-rounded, inclusive, and innovative. By exploring diverse perspectives, it fosters collaboration, creativity, and critical thinking.

This technique is invaluable for teams and individuals seeking to navigate complex problems with clarity and confidence, ensuring that every angle is thoroughly examined.

WEIGHTED TRADE-OFF GRIDS

	Cost	Accessibility	Activities	Weather	TOTAL
BEACH	4	5	2	5	(16)
MOUNTAINS	2	2	3	4	11
CITY	3	5	4	2	14

Chapter 65: Weighted Trade-Off Grids

Navigating Complex Trade-Offs: Weighted Trade-Off Grids

A Weighted Trade-Off Grid is a decision-making tool that evaluates options by scoring them against weighted criteria. By quantifying trade-offs, this method helps identify the most balanced choice in situations involving multiple competing factors.

For example:

- **Scenario:** A family chooses a vacation destination.
- **Grid Application:** They evaluate options based on cost, activities, weather, and travel time, assigning weights to reflect their priorities.

This technique simplifies complex decisions by breaking them into smaller, manageable comparisons.

How Weighted Trade-Off Grids Work

1. **List Options and Criteria:** Define the choices and the factors influencing the decision.

   Example: "Options: Beach, mountains, city. Criteria: Cost, accessibility, activities, weather."

2. **Assign Weights to Criteria:** Reflect the relative importance of each factor.

   Example: Activities = 40%, Cost = 30%, Weather = 20%, Accessibility = 10%.

3. **Score Each Option:** Rate how well each option meets each criterion.

4. **Calculate Weighted Scores:** Multiply each score by its weight and sum the results for each option.

5. **Compare and Choose:** The option with the highest total score is typically the best choice.

Applications of Weighted Trade-Off Grids

1. **In Business:**
   - Evaluate vendors, investments, or strategies based on key performance metrics.

2. **In Personal Decisions:**
   - Compare housing options, career opportunities, or major purchases.

3. **In Team Collaboration:**
   - Facilitate group decisions by providing a clear, structured framework for analysis.

Why Weighted Trade-Off Grids are Effective

This method helps:

1. **Clarify Priorities:** Focuses attention on the most important factors.

2. **Promote Rational Decisions:** Bases choices on structured analysis rather than intuition.

3. **Simplify Complexity:** Breaks down multi-faceted decisions into manageable steps.

Challenges and Limitations

1. **Subjectivity in Weights and Scores:** Assigning values can reflect personal or group biases.
2. **Time-Intensive:** Building and populating the grid requires effort, especially for complex decisions.
3. **Quantification Limitations:** Not all criteria can be easily quantified.

For instance, comparing career options might involve intangible factors like work-life balance or personal growth.

How to Use Weighted Trade-Off Grids Effectively

1. **Involve Stakeholders:** Collaborate to ensure that weights and scores reflect diverse perspectives.
2. **Focus on Key Criteria:** Limit the number of factors to avoid overcomplication.
3. **Combine with Qualitative Insights:** Use the grid as a guide but consider qualitative aspects alongside the results.

Exercises

1. **Build a Grid:** Apply the Weighted Trade-Off Grid to a decision you're currently facing. List options, define criteria, and calculate scores. Reflect on the outcome.
2. **Evaluate a Past Decision:** Use the grid to revisit a previous choice. How does the result compare to your actual decision?
3. **Facilitate a Group Exercise:** Guide a team through creating and using a Weighted Trade-Off Grid for a shared goal or challenge.

Closing Thoughts

The Weighted Trade-Off Grid is a versatile tool for navigating complex decisions with competing priorities. By structuring trade-offs systematically, it ensures that choices are logical, transparent, and aligned with your objectives.

Section: Communication and Persuasion

Effective communication and persuasion are the cornerstones of meaningful dialogue and influence. Whether you're presenting an idea, negotiating a deal, or simply engaging in conversation, mastering these skills ensures your message is not only heard but also understood and acted upon.

This section focuses on methods to enhance clarity, build trust, and inspire action. By combining logical structuring, emotional awareness, and creative techniques, these tools empower you to communicate persuasively and authentically in any context.

Chapter 66: Reframing Arguments for Clarity

Seeing from a New Angle: Reframing Arguments for Clarity

Reframing involves presenting an idea or argument in a way that makes it easier to understand or more persuasive. By shifting perspectives, using simpler language, or emphasizing key points, reframing helps clarify complex concepts and resolve misunderstandings.

For example:

- **Scenario:** A manager addresses employee resistance to a new policy.
- **Reframed Argument:** Instead of focusing on the changes, they highlight the benefits, such as reduced workloads or improved processes.

Reframing is a versatile tool for improving communication, diffusing conflict, and building consensus.

How to Reframe Arguments

1. **Identify the Core Message:** Focus on the main point you want to communicate.

   Example: "What is the essential takeaway from this policy change?"

2. **Simplify the Language:** Replace jargon or technical terms with simpler, more relatable expressions.

   Example: "Instead of saying 'streamline operations,' say 'make tasks easier and faster.'"

3. **Change the Perspective:** Present the idea from the listener's point of view.

   Example: "How does this change benefit the person I'm speaking to?"

4. **Emphasize Positives:** Highlight the advantages rather than focusing on challenges.

   Example: "This system will save you time" instead of "This system requires some adjustments."

Applications of Reframing

1. **In Negotiations:**
   - Present compromises as opportunities rather than losses.

2. **In Teaching:**
   - Simplify complex topics for students by using relatable examples.

3. **In Conflict Resolution:**
   - Reframe disagreements to focus on shared goals and solutions.

Why Reframing is Effective

This method helps:

1. **Enhance Clarity:** Makes complex or abstract ideas more accessible.

2. **Shift Perspectives:** Encourages openness to new viewpoints.

3. **Resolve Resistance:** Reduces defensiveness by focusing on common ground or benefits.

Challenges and Limitations

1. **Risk of Oversimplification:** Simplifying too much may distort the original message.
2. **Resistance to Change:** Listeners may reject reframed arguments if they perceive manipulation.
3. **Time Constraints:** Crafting effective reframes requires thought and effort.

For instance, reframing a contentious topic during a heated debate may require careful timing and language.

How to Reframe Effectively

1. **Know Your Audience:** Tailor your approach to their values, needs, and concerns.

   Example: "How does this resonate with what they care about most?"
2. **Practice Empathy:** Consider how the argument feels from the listener's perspective.

   Example: "What objections might they have, and how can I address them?"
3. **Test Different Frames:** Experiment with multiple approaches to find the most effective one.

Exercises

1. **Reframe a Personal Argument:** Choose a recent disagreement and rephrase your perspective to focus on shared goals.
2. **Simplify a Complex Idea:** Take a technical concept and reframe it in everyday language. Reflect on how this improves clarity.
3. **Practice with a Partner:** Role-play a challenging conversation, experimenting with different reframes to find what resonates most.

Closing Thoughts

Reframing arguments for clarity is an essential skill for effective communication. By shifting perspectives and simplifying messages, you can build understanding, reduce conflict, and inspire action.

This technique empowers you to connect with others more deeply, fostering collaboration, trust, and mutual respect in both personal and professional interactions.

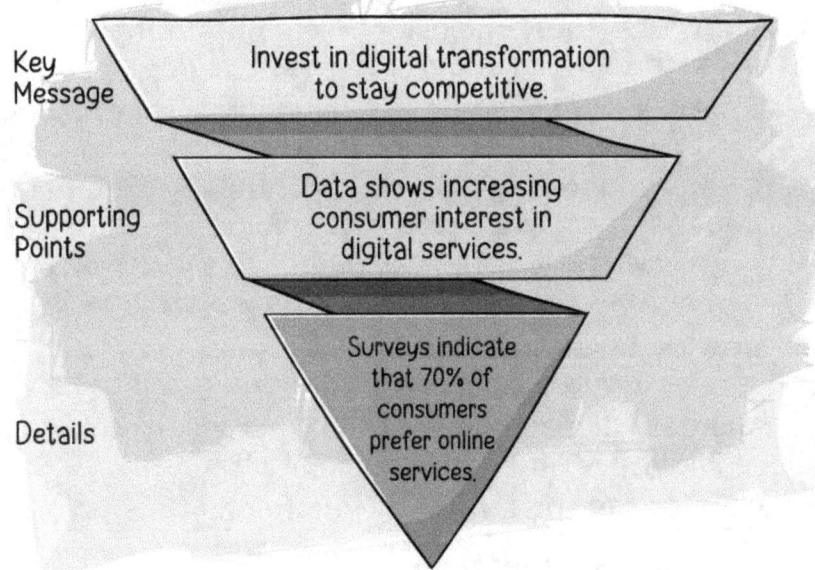

Key Message — Invest in digital transformation to stay competitive.

Supporting Points — Data shows increasing consumer interest in digital services.

Details — Surveys indicate that 70% of consumers prefer online services.

Chapter 67: The Pyramid Principle

Start with the Conclusion: The Pyramid Principle

The Pyramid Principle is a communication framework developed by Barbara Minto that emphasizes presenting your key message or conclusion first, followed by supporting arguments and details. This structure is designed to improve clarity, focus, and engagement by aligning with how people process information.

For example:

- **Scenario:** A consultant delivers a recommendation to a client.
- **Pyramid Principle Application:** They start with the primary recommendation ("Invest in digital transformation") and follow with supporting data, trends, and specific action steps.

This method is widely used in business, consulting, and academia to ensure clear and persuasive communication.

How the Pyramid Principle Works

1. **Start with the Conclusion:** Clearly state the main idea or recommendation upfront.

    Example: "We recommend launching a new product line to capture untapped market segments."

2. **Group Supporting Points:** Organize key arguments or evidence into logical categories.

    Example: "This recommendation is based on market demand, competitive analysis, and projected ROI."

3. **Provide Detailed Evidence:** Use data, examples, or case studies to substantiate each supporting point.

4. **Maintain Logical Flow:** Ensure that each level of detail naturally flows from the one above it.

Applications of the Pyramid Principle

1. **In Business Presentations:**
    - Deliver executive summaries that highlight key insights before diving into details.

2. **In Academic Writing:**
    - Organize research papers or essays by starting with the thesis and supporting it with evidence.

3. **In Team Communication:**
    - Structure updates or proposals to prioritize the most critical information.

Why the Pyramid Principle is Effective

This method helps:

1. **Enhance Clarity:** Prevents the audience from getting lost in unnecessary details.

2. **Focus Attention:** Emphasizes the most important points first, keeping listeners engaged.

3. **Save Time:** Allows decision-makers to grasp the essence of your argument quickly.

Challenges and Limitations

1. **Oversimplification Risk:** Starting with conclusions may

oversimplify complex issues.

2. **Dependency on Strong Evidence:** The approach relies on robust, well-organized supporting points.

3. **Cultural Preferences:** In some cultures, audiences may prefer a gradual build-up to the conclusion.

For instance, presenting a direct recommendation without sufficient context might seem abrupt or overly assertive in certain situations.

How to Use the Pyramid Principle Effectively

1. **Refine Your Key Message:** Focus on the core insight or recommendation that your audience needs.

2. **Structure Thoughtfully:** Group supporting points logically and align them with your conclusion.

3. **Adapt to the Audience:** Adjust the level of detail based on the audience's familiarity with the topic.

Exercises

1. **Draft an Argument:** Choose a topic and write a brief summary using the Pyramid Principle. Start with your conclusion and build downward.

2. **Reorganize a Presentation:** Take a previous presentation or report and restructure it using this method. Reflect on how it improves clarity.

3. **Team Workshop:** Facilitate a group exercise where participants apply the Pyramid Principle to a shared challenge. Discuss the outcomes.

Closing Thoughts

The Pyramid Principle is a versatile framework for structuring ideas in a clear, logical, and impactful way. By prioritizing conclusions and organizing evidence effectively, it ensures that your message resonates with your audience and drives meaningful action.

Mastering this technique enhances your ability to communicate persuasively, whether you're addressing a team, a client, or a large audience.

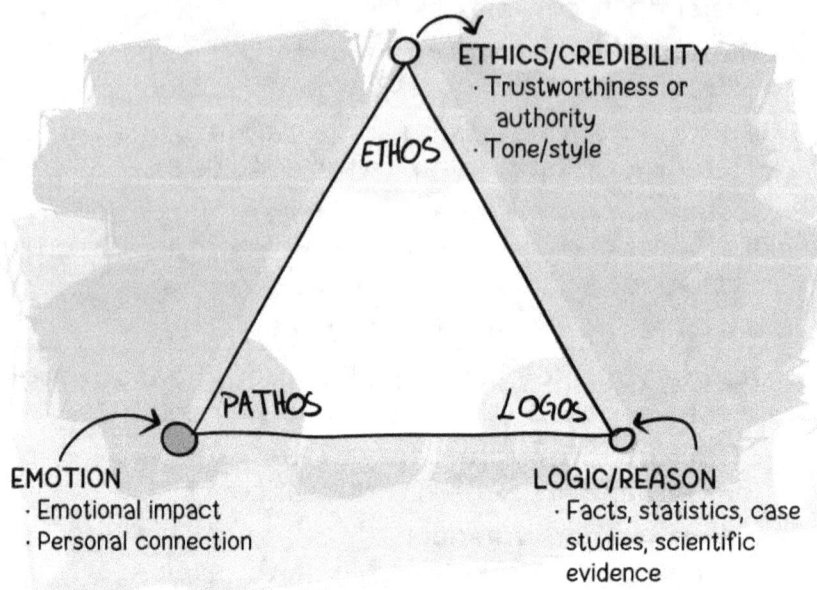

Chapter 68: The Rhetorical Triangle

Balancing Persuasion: The Rhetorical Triangle

The Rhetorical Triangle is a classical framework for understanding and applying the three key elements of effective persuasion: Ethos (credibility), Pathos (emotion), and Logos (logic). This approach, rooted in Aristotle's teachings, remains relevant in modern communication.

For example:

- **Scenario:** A leader motivates their team to adopt a new strategy.
- **Rhetorical Triangle Application:** They establish credibility with their expertise (ethos), appeal to team values (pathos), and present clear data and reasoning (logos).

Balancing these three elements ensures that your message resonates with both the mind and the heart of your audience.

The Three Elements of the Rhetorical Triangle

1. **Ethos (Credibility):** Establish your trustworthiness and authority on the subject.

   Example: "As someone with 10 years of experience in this field, I've seen these strategies succeed."

2. **Pathos (Emotion):** Appeal to your audience's emotions, values, and beliefs.

   Example: "This strategy will help us build a brighter future for our families and communities."

3. **Logos (Logic):** Use data, facts, and logical reasoning to support your argument.

   Example: "Research shows a 25% increase in efficiency with this approach."

Applications of the Rhetorical Triangle

1. **In Public Speaking:**
   - Combine credibility, emotion, and logic to engage and inspire audiences.

2. **In Marketing:**
   - Build trust in your brand (ethos), connect emotionally with customers (pathos), and highlight product benefits with evidence (logos).

3. **In Conflict Resolution:**
   - Balance empathy with logic and authority to mediate disagreements effectively.

Why the Rhetorical Triangle is Effective

This method helps:

1. **Enhance Persuasion:** Appeals to the audience's intellect, emotions, and trust simultaneously.

2. **Build Credibility:** Establishes you as a reliable and empathetic communicator.

3. **Foster Engagement:** Creates a balanced and compelling argument.

Challenges and Limitations

1. **Overemphasis on One Element:** Focusing too much on one aspect may weaken the overall message.
2. **Cultural Differences:** Some audiences may prioritize logic (logos) over emotion (pathos) or vice versa.
3. **Credibility Risk:** Weak ethos can undermine the entire argument, even if logos and pathos are strong.

For instance, presenting powerful data (logos) without establishing trust (ethos) may leave your audience sceptical.

How to Use the Rhetorical Triangle Effectively

1. **Know Your Audience:** Tailor the balance of ethos, pathos, and logos to their preferences and values.
2. **Strengthen Ethos:** Build credibility through expertise, authenticity, and professionalism.
3. **Blend Pathos and Logos:** Use emotional appeals to complement logical arguments, not replace them.

Exercises

1. **Analyze a Speech:** Choose a famous speech and evaluate how it uses ethos, pathos, and logos. Reflect on its impact.
2. **Practice Balancing Elements:** Write a persuasive argument for a topic of your choice, balancing all three elements.
3. **Reframe an Existing Message:** Take a past communication and adjust it to incorporate ethos, pathos, and logos more effectively.

Closing Thoughts

The Rhetorical Triangle provides a timeless framework for crafting persuasive and impactful messages. By balancing credibility, emotion, and logic, it ensures your communication resonates deeply with your audience.

This technique enhances your ability to persuade, inspire, and connect in diverse settings, from public speaking to everyday conversations.

Chapter 69: Active Listening

Listening with Purpose: Active Listening

Active Listening is the process of fully focusing on, understanding, and responding to what someone is saying. Unlike passive listening, which involves simply hearing words, active listening requires engagement, empathy, and feedback to ensure effective communication.

For example:

- **Scenario:** A manager is conducting a performance review.

- **Active Listening Application:** Instead of interrupting or rushing, they listen attentively, paraphrase key points, and ask clarifying questions.

This method fosters mutual understanding, builds trust, and enhances relationships in both personal and professional settings.

How Active Listening Works

1. **Focus on the Speaker:** Eliminate distractions and give your full attention.

    Example: "Put away your phone and make eye contact while the other person is speaking."

2. **Show Understanding:** Use verbal and nonverbal cues to convey attentiveness.

    Example: Nod, smile, or use phrases like "I see" or "Go on."

3. **Paraphrase and Summarize:** Restate key points to confirm your understanding.

    Example: "So, what you're saying is that you'd like more autonomy in your role?"

4. **Ask Questions:** Clarify ambiguities or dig deeper into the speaker's message.

    Example: "Can you elaborate on what you mean by 'more support from the team'?"

Applications of Active Listening

1. **In Leadership:**
    o   Build trust and rapport with team members by actively listening to their concerns.
2. **In Conflict Resolution:**
    o   Diffuse tension and foster understanding by truly hearing both sides.
3. **In Personal Relationships:**
    o   Strengthen connections by showing empathy and validating feelings.

Why Active Listening is Effective

This method helps:

1. **Enhance Understanding:** Reduces miscommunication and clarifies intent.
2. **Build Trust:** Demonstrates respect and empathy, strengthening relationships.

3. **Encourage Open Dialogue:** Makes others feel heard and valued, fostering collaboration.

Challenges and Limitations

1. **Time-Intensive:** Fully engaging in conversations can be demanding, especially in busy environments.
2. **Emotional Effort:** Listening empathetically to emotional topics may be mentally draining.
3. **Cultural Differences:** Listening styles and expectations may vary across cultures.

For instance, in some cultures, silence during a conversation signifies respect, while in others, it may be perceived as disengagement.

How to Practice Active Listening Effectively

1. **Be Present:** Remove distractions and focus solely on the speaker.
2. **Manage Emotions:** Stay calm and composed, even during challenging conversations.
3. **Respond Thoughtfully:** Avoid interrupting or offering solutions prematurely; prioritize understanding first.

Exercises

1. **Reflect on a Recent Conversation:** Analyze a discussion where you practiced active listening. What worked well, and what could you improve?
2. **Role-Play Active Listening:** Partner with someone to simulate a conversation where you actively listen and provide feedback.
3. **Use a Journal:** After a conversation, jot down the speaker's key points to reinforce understanding and identify areas for growth.

Closing Thoughts

Active Listening is a cornerstone of effective communication. By being fully present and empathetic, you can navigate conversations with greater clarity, respect, and impact. This skill is essential for building trust, resolving conflicts, and enhancing relationships.

Chapter 70: Mirroring and Paraphrasing

Reflecting Understanding: Mirroring and Paraphrasing

Mirroring and Paraphrasing are techniques used to demonstrate understanding and build rapport during conversations. By reflecting the speaker's words or gestures and summarizing their key points, you create a sense of connection and validation.

For example:

- **Scenario:** A friend shares concerns about their workload.

- **Mirroring and Paraphrasing Application:** You nod, maintain similar body language, and say, "It sounds like you're feeling overwhelmed with the amount of work you have."

These techniques are especially useful in conflict resolution, counseling, and team communication.

How Mirroring and Paraphrasing Work

1. **Mirroring:**
   - Imitate the speaker's tone, pace, and gestures subtly to create a sense of alignment.
   - Example: If the speaker is leaning forward and speaking softly, do the same.

2. **Paraphrasing:**
   - Restate the speaker's message in your own words to confirm understanding.
   - Example: "So, you're saying you'd like more support from your colleagues to manage deadlines?"

3. **Combine Both:**
   - Use mirroring to build connection and paraphrasing to clarify and validate the speaker's message.

Applications of Mirroring and Paraphrasing

1. **In Customer Service:**
   - Reflect customer concerns to show empathy and ensure you understand their needs.

2. **In Mediation:**
   - Use paraphrasing to clarify each party's perspective and foster mutual understanding.

3. **In Personal Relationships:**
   - Strengthen bonds by validating feelings and demonstrating attentiveness.

Why Mirroring and Paraphrasing Are Effective

These techniques help:

1. **Build Rapport:** Create a sense of connection and trust.
2. **Enhance Clarity:** Reduce misunderstandings and ensure alignment.
3. **Foster Empathy:** Show that you value and respect the speaker's perspective.

Challenges and Limitations

1. **Overuse of Mirroring:** Excessive imitation may come across as insincere or awkward.
2. **Paraphrasing Errors:** Misinterpreting or oversimplifying the speaker's message can cause frustration.
3. **Cultural Sensitivities:** Mirroring gestures or tone may not be appropriate in all cultural contexts.

For instance, in some cultures, maintaining direct eye contact or mimicking body language might be seen as intrusive.

How to Use Mirroring and Paraphrasing Effectively

1. **Be Subtle with Mirroring:** Avoid mimicking too obviously; focus on natural alignment.
2. **Paraphrase Thoughtfully:** Capture the essence of the speaker's message without altering its meaning.
3. **Seek Confirmation:** Ask the speaker if your paraphrase accurately reflects their intent.

Exercises

1. **Mirror in a Conversation:** Practice subtly mirroring someone's tone and gestures during a casual discussion. Reflect on how it affects the interaction.
2. **Paraphrase Feedback:** After listening to someone, paraphrase their key points and ask for confirmation. Adjust as needed.
3. **Role-Play:** Simulate a conflict resolution scenario where you use both techniques to foster understanding and agreement.

Closing Thoughts

Mirroring and Paraphrasing are powerful tools for building trust, enhancing communication, and fostering empathy. By reflecting and clarifying messages, you ensure that others feel heard, valued, and understood.

Chapter 71: Using Analogies Effectively

Making the Complex Relatable: Using Analogies Effectively

An analogy is a comparison between two concepts to clarify or explain the unfamiliar using something familiar. Analogies are powerful tools for simplifying complex ideas, sparking understanding, and engaging audiences.

For example:

- **Scenario:** A teacher explains the flow of electricity.
- **Analogy Application:** They compare it to water flowing through a pipe, making the abstract concept relatable.

When used effectively, analogies can bridge gaps in understanding, making your message more compelling and memorable.

How Analogies Work

1. **Identify the Concept:** Pinpoint the idea you want to explain or clarify.

   Example: "How does a blockchain work?"

2. **Find a Familiar Comparison:** Choose a relatable analogy that mirrors the key features of your concept.

   Example: "A blockchain is like a digital ledger where each transaction is recorded, similar to pages in a checkbook."

3. **Highlight Key Similarities:** Focus on the parallels that simplify understanding without oversimplifying.

4. **Test the Analogy:** Ensure the comparison resonates with your audience and doesn't introduce confusion.

Applications of Analogies

1. **In Education:**
   - Explain abstract or technical concepts by comparing them to everyday experiences.

2. **In Business Presentations:**
   - Use analogies to make data or strategies more accessible to stakeholders.

3. **In Personal Communication:**
   - Clarify your perspective during conversations by relating ideas to shared experiences.

Why Analogies Are Effective

This method helps:

1. **Simplify Complexity:** Breaks down abstract ideas into relatable components.

2. **Enhance Engagement:** Captures attention by connecting with familiar concepts.

3. **Foster Retention:** Makes messages more memorable by linking them to existing knowledge.

Challenges and Limitations

1. **Risk of Oversimplification:** Simplifying too much may distort the original concept.
2. **Cultural Context:** Analogies reliant on specific cultural references may not resonate universally.
3. **Potential Confusion:** Poorly chosen analogies can mislead or confuse the audience.

For instance, comparing cloud computing to a physical cloud may misrepresent the technical realities of the concept.

How to Use Analogies Effectively

1. **Know Your Audience:** Tailor analogies to their experiences, interests, and cultural background.
   Example: "What comparisons would feel familiar to this group?"
2. **Keep it Relevant:** Ensure the analogy aligns with the concept's key characteristics.
   Example: "Does this comparison accurately reflect the main features?"
3. **Explain the Transition:** Clarify how the analogy relates to the original idea.

Exercises

1. **Create an Analogy:** Choose a complex concept and develop an analogy to explain it. Test it with someone unfamiliar with the topic.
2. **Analyze a Famous Analogy:** Study an analogy used in a speech, book, or article. What makes it effective or ineffective?
3. **Reframe a Concept:** Take a technical or abstract idea and develop two or three analogies for different audiences.

Closing Thoughts

Analogies are bridges between the familiar and the unfamiliar, transforming complexity into clarity. By leveraging relatable comparisons, you can communicate more effectively, engage your audience, and leave a lasting impression.

Mastering this skill enables you to explain ideas with greater impact, making your message accessible and memorable across diverse contexts.

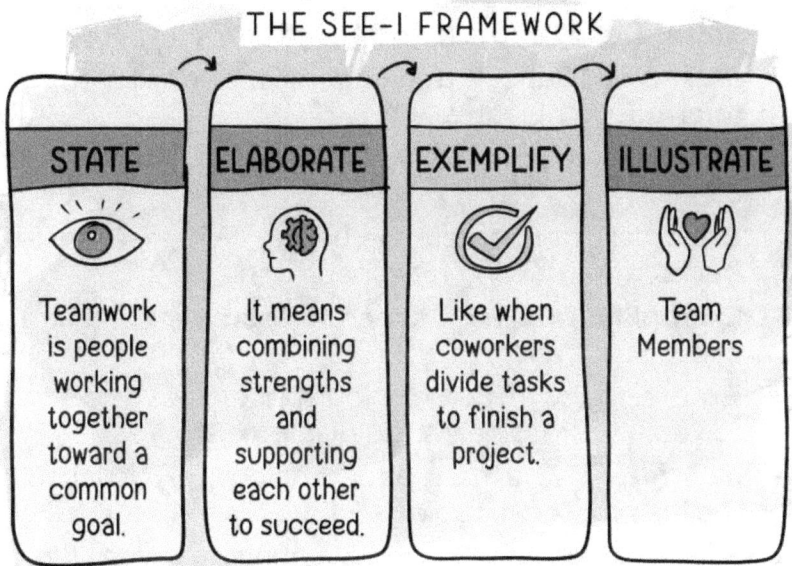

STATE	ELABORATE	EXEMPLIFY	ILLUSTRATE
Teamwork is people working together toward a common goal.	It means combining strengths and supporting each other to succeed.	Like when coworkers divide tasks to finish a project.	Team Members

Chapter 72: The SEE-I Framework (State, Elaborate, Exemplify, Illustrate)

Clarifying Ideas with Structure: The SEE-I Framework

The SEE-I Framework is a method for explaining ideas clearly and thoroughly. It involves four steps: State the idea, Elaborate on it, provide an Example, and Illustrate it with a metaphor, analogy, or diagram.

For example:

- **Scenario:** A trainer explains the concept of teamwork.
- **SEE-I Application:** They state its definition, elaborate on its importance, provide an example of a successful team, and illustrate it as gears working together in a machine.

This framework ensures clarity and engagement, making complex ideas more accessible and relatable.

How the SEE-I Framework Works

1. **State:** Clearly and succinctly define the idea or concept.

   Example: "Critical thinking is the ability to analyze information objectively."

2. **Elaborate:** Expand on the idea with additional details or context.

   Example: "It involves evaluating evidence, identifying biases, and drawing reasoned conclusions."

3. **Exemplify:** Provide a concrete example to illustrate the concept in action.

   Example: "For instance, a journalist uses critical thinking to verify sources before publishing a story."

4. **Illustrate:** Use a metaphor, analogy, or visual to make the idea more relatable.

   Example: "Think of critical thinking as a filter that separates fact from fiction, like a sieve separating sand from rocks."

Applications of the SEE-I Framework

1. **In Teaching:**
   - Explain abstract concepts in a structured, engaging way for students.

2. **In Business Communication:**
   - Present ideas, proposals, or strategies with clarity and impact.

3. **In Personal Development:**
   - Reflect on and articulate your understanding of key concepts or values.

Why the SEE-I Framework is Effective

This method helps:

1. **Enhance Clarity:** Breaks down complex ideas into manageable components.

2. **Foster Engagement:** Combines structure with creativity to maintain interest.

3. **Promote Retention:** Reinforces understanding through repetition and illustration.

Challenges and Limitations

1. **Time-Intensive:** Providing elaboration, examples, and illustrations may require significant effort.
2. **Relevance of Examples:** Poorly chosen examples or illustrations can confuse rather than clarify.
3. **Over-Structuring:** Strict adherence to the framework might limit spontaneity or flexibility.

For instance, forcing an illustration where it isn't needed may distract from the core idea.

How to Use the SEE-I Framework Effectively

1. **Adapt to Context:** Tailor the framework to the audience's needs and the complexity of the topic.
2. **Choose Relatable Examples:** Ensure examples and illustrations resonate with your audience.
3. **Practice Brevity:** Keep each step concise to maintain focus and flow.

Exercises

1. **Apply SEE-I to a Concept:** Choose an idea and explain it using all four steps of the framework. Share it with someone and seek feedback.
2. **Analyze SEE-I in Action:** Review a lecture or article and identify where the framework is implicitly or explicitly applied.
3. **Create a Training Module:** Design a short lesson or presentation using SEE-I to explain a topic of your choice.

Closing Thoughts

The SEE-I Framework is a powerful tool for breaking down ideas into clear, engaging, and accessible explanations. By combining structure with creativity, it ensures your message is understood and remembered.

Mastering this framework equips you to communicate effectively in education, business, and everyday conversations, making your ideas resonate with any audience.

Chapter 73: Building Common Ground

Finding Unity: Building Common Ground

Building common ground involves identifying shared values, goals, or experiences that bridge differences and foster collaboration. By focusing on what unites rather than divides, this approach strengthens relationships and resolves conflicts more effectively.

For example:

- **Scenario:** A manager mediates a disagreement between two team members.

- **Common Ground Application:** They emphasize the shared goal of delivering a successful project, redirecting attention away from personal grievances.

This technique is critical in negotiation, conflict resolution, and team-building, creating a foundation for trust and cooperation.

How to Build Common Ground

1. **Identify Shared Values:** Look for beliefs, goals, or interests that both parties prioritize.

   Example: "We all want this project to succeed."

2. **Acknowledge Differences:** Respect and validate differing perspectives while steering the focus toward commonalities.

   Example: "I understand we have different approaches, but we agree on the importance of customer satisfaction."

3. **Use Inclusive Language:** Frame statements to emphasize collaboration and unity.

   Example: "How can we work together to achieve this goal?"

4. **Focus on Mutual Benefits:** Highlight outcomes that benefit everyone involved.

   Example: "Resolving this issue will help us meet our deadlines and improve team morale."

Applications of Building Common Ground

1. **In Negotiations:**
   - Establish a basis for compromise by focusing on shared interests.

2. **In Conflict Resolution:**
   - Redirect disagreements toward mutual goals or values.

3. **In Leadership:**
   - Foster team cohesion by emphasizing collective objectives.

Why Building Common Ground is Effective

This method helps:

1. **Foster Collaboration:** Encourages cooperation by emphasizing shared goals.

2. **Defuse Tensions:** Shifts focus away from disagreements toward unity.

3. **Build Trust:** Demonstrates respect and understanding, strengthening relationships.

Challenges and Limitations

1. **Deep Divisions:** Finding shared values can be difficult in polarized situations.
2. **Superficial Agreement:** Focusing solely on commonalities may ignore underlying issues.
3. **Resistance to Collaboration:** Some individuals may prioritize winning over finding unity.

For instance, in high-stakes negotiations, parties might resist acknowledging shared goals if it weakens their bargaining position.

How to Build Common Ground Effectively

1. **Start Small:** Focus on minor shared interests before tackling larger issues.
2. **Ask Open-Ended Questions:** Encourage dialogue to uncover common values.

   Example: "What's most important to you in this situation?"
3. **Balance Unity and Differences:** Address disagreements while emphasizing alignment.

Exercises

1. **Identify Common Ground:** Think of a recent disagreement and identify shared values or goals. Reflect on how they could have influenced the outcome.
2. **Facilitate a Team Exercise:** Lead a group activity that highlights shared interests or objectives, such as brainstorming a vision statement.
3. **Reframe a Conflict:** Choose a past conflict and rewrite it with an emphasis on building common ground.

Closing Thoughts

Building common ground is a vital skill for navigating conflicts, fostering collaboration, and strengthening relationships. By focusing on shared values and goals, you can bridge divides and create a foundation for mutual respect and cooperation.

This technique empowers you to connect with others meaningfully, transforming challenges into opportunities for unity and growth.

Chapter 74: Structuring Evidence with Logic

Making Arguments Solid: Structuring Evidence with Logic

Structuring evidence with logic ensures that your arguments are persuasive, clear, and credible. By organizing data, examples, and reasoning in a cohesive manner, you build a foundation that supports your conclusions effectively.

For example:

- **Scenario:** A team pitches a new marketing strategy.
- **Structuring Evidence Application:** They present market research, case studies, and projected outcomes in a logical progression that supports their proposal.

This approach is essential in business, academia, and any context where persuasion relies on clear reasoning.

How to Structure Evidence Logically

1. **Start with a Clear Claim:** Clearly articulate your main argument or thesis.

   Example: "Investing in digital marketing will increase customer engagement and revenue."

2. **Provide Supporting Evidence:** Use data, examples, or expert opinions to substantiate your claim.

   Example: "Our market analysis shows a 30% growth in online engagement for competitors using similar strategies."

3. **Connect Evidence to the Claim:** Explain how each piece of evidence supports your argument.

   Example: "This demonstrates that digital marketing aligns with current customer behavior trends."

4. **Address Counterarguments:** Anticipate objections and refute them with evidence.

   Example: "While initial costs are higher, the long-term ROI outweighs the investment."

Applications of Structuring Evidence

1. **In Business Proposals:**
   - o Present compelling arguments for projects, investments, or strategies.

2. **In Academic Writing:**
   - o Organize essays or research papers to support a thesis with logical reasoning.

3. **In Everyday Debates:**
   - o Persuade others in discussions by presenting clear, evidence-based arguments.

Why Structuring Evidence is Effective

This method helps:

1. **Enhance Persuasiveness:** Builds credibility by linking claims to reliable evidence.

2. **Clarify Arguments:** Organizes information logically, making it easier to follow.

3. **Address Skepticism:** Anticipates objections and reinforces the strength of your case.

Challenges and Limitations

1. **Overloading with Data:** Excessive evidence can overwhelm or confuse the audience.
2. **Logical Fallacies:** Poor connections between evidence and claims can weaken arguments.
3. **Bias in Evidence Selection:** Cherry-picking data may undermine credibility.

For instance, using selective statistics to support an argument while ignoring contradictory data might damage trust.

How to Structure Evidence Effectively

1. **Prioritize Quality Over Quantity:** Focus on the most compelling and relevant evidence.
2. **Use Clear Transitions:** Guide the audience through your reasoning with phrases like "This shows that…" or "As a result, we can conclude…"
3. **Balance Evidence Types:** Combine quantitative data with qualitative examples for a well-rounded argument.

Exercises

1. **Analyze an Argument:** Choose an opinion piece or presentation and evaluate how evidence is structured. Identify strengths and weaknesses.
2. **Build Your Argument:** Choose a topic and organize your evidence to support a clear claim. Share it with someone for feedback.
3. **Refine an Existing Argument:** Take a past debate or discussion and restructure your evidence for greater clarity and impact.

Closing Thoughts

Structuring evidence with logic is a cornerstone of persuasive communication. By presenting data, examples, and reasoning in a cohesive framework, you ensure that your arguments are credible, compelling, and impactful.

Chapter 75: Avoiding Loaded Questions

Asking the Right Way: Avoiding Loaded Questions

A loaded question is one that contains a hidden assumption or bias, often designed to corner the respondent into a specific answer. Avoiding loaded questions ensures fairness and neutrality in communication, fostering open dialogue and trust.

For example:

- **Scenario:** A manager asks, "Why did you let this project fail?"

- **Loaded Question Issue:** This assumes the employee is at fault without considering other factors.

Rephrasing loaded questions into neutral ones promotes productive conversations, collaboration, and mutual understanding.

How to Identify and Avoid Loaded Questions

1. **Recognize Hidden Assumptions:** Analyze whether the question presumes something unproven or biased.

   Example: "When will you fix your bad attitude?" assumes the person has a bad attitude.

2. **Rephrase for Neutrality:** Rewrite the question to focus on facts or open exploration.

   Example: "How do you feel about this project's outcome?"

3. **Clarify Intent:** Ensure the question's purpose is constructive, not accusatory.

   Example: Instead of "Why are you always late?" ask, "Is there something preventing you from arriving on time?"

4. **Focus on Solutions:** Frame questions to encourage problem-solving or understanding.

   Example: "What can we do to ensure the project succeeds next time?"

Applications of Avoiding Loaded Questions

1. **In Leadership:**
   - Foster trust and accountability by asking fair, unbiased questions.

2. **In Conflict Resolution:**
   - De-escalate tensions by avoiding accusatory or confrontational phrasing.

3. **In Journalism:**
   - Maintain neutrality and objectivity when interviewing or reporting.

Why Avoiding Loaded Questions is Effective

This method helps:

1. **Encourage Honest Responses:** Removes pressure or defensiveness from the conversation.

2. **Promote Fairness:** Ensures questions are unbiased and focused on understanding.

3. **Build Trust:** Demonstrates respect and openness in communication.

Challenges and Limitations

1. **Unintentional Bias:** Hidden assumptions may slip into questions unconsciously.
2. **Balancing Neutrality:** Overly vague questions may fail to elicit meaningful answers.
3. **Time Constraints:** Reframing questions thoughtfully can require extra effort in fast-paced settings.

For instance, during a heated debate, rephrasing a loaded question on the spot may be challenging but essential for maintaining dialogue.

How to Practice Avoiding Loaded Questions

1. **Pause and Reflect:** Before asking a question, consider whether it contains implicit assumptions.
2. **Seek Feedback:** Practice with colleagues or friends to identify and correct biases in your questions.
3. **Focus on Open-Ended Formats:** Use "What" or "How" questions to encourage exploration rather than confrontation.

Exercises

1. **Rewrite Loaded Questions:** Take five examples of loaded questions and rephrase them into neutral, constructive formats.
2. **Analyze a Conversation:** Reflect on a past discussion where loaded questions may have been used. How did they impact the interaction?
3. **Role-Play:** Practice asking neutral, open-ended questions in a mock debate or negotiation scenario.

Closing Thoughts

Avoiding loaded questions is a key skill for fostering open, respectful, and productive communication. By eliminating hidden assumptions and focusing on neutrality, you create an environment where honest dialogue and collaboration can thrive.

This technique enhances your ability to navigate conflicts, lead teams, and build trust in both personal and professional relationships.

Chapter 76: Recognizing Emotional Triggers

Navigating Sensitivity: Recognizing Emotional Triggers

Emotional triggers are words, phrases, or topics that provoke strong emotional reactions, often rooted in personal experiences or beliefs. Recognizing and managing these triggers ensures that conversations remain constructive and respectful.

For example:

- **Scenario:** A colleague reacts defensively during a feedback session.
- **Emotional Trigger Issue:** The feedback unintentionally touched on a sensitive topic.

Understanding emotional triggers can help prevent misunderstandings, diffuse conflicts, and nurture positive relationships.

How to Recognize Emotional Triggers

1. **Reflect on Personal Reactions:** Identify words or topics that provoke strong emotions in yourself.

    Example: "Why do I feel frustrated when discussing deadlines?"

2. **Observe Nonverbal Cues:** Watch for signs of discomfort or tension, such as crossed arms, raised voices, or abrupt tone shifts.

3. **Ask Open Questions:** Encourage the other person to share their perspective or concerns.

    Example: "You seem upset—can you tell me what's on your mind?"

4. **Acknowledge Sensitivities:** Validate feelings and address concerns without judgment.

    Example: "I understand that this topic is challenging for you."

Applications of Recognizing Emotional Triggers

1. **In Leadership:**
    o   Navigate difficult conversations with empathy and awareness.

2. **In Conflict Resolution:**
    o   Identify and address the underlying emotions driving disagreements.

3. **In Personal Relationships:**
    o   Foster deeper connections by understanding and respecting sensitivities.

Why Recognizing Emotional Triggers is Effective

This method helps:

1. **Improve Communication:** Reduces misunderstandings and emotional escalation.

2. **Strengthen Relationships:** Demonstrates empathy and respect for others' experiences.

3. **Encourage Self-Awareness:** Promotes emotional intelligence in navigating sensitive topics.

Challenges and Limitations

1. **Subtle Signals:** Nonverbal cues may be difficult to interpret accurately.
2. **Managing Personal Bias:** Avoid projecting your own assumptions onto others' emotions.
3. **Navigating Complex Triggers:** Deeply rooted triggers may require time and trust to address fully.

For instance, unresolved trauma may result in triggers that are not immediately apparent or easy to discuss.

How to Manage Emotional Triggers Effectively

1. **Stay Calm:** Maintain composure and avoid reacting impulsively.
2. **Practice Empathy:** Seek to understand the root of the emotion rather than dismissing it.
3. **Reframe the Conversation:** Shift the focus to shared goals or solutions when a trigger arises.

Exercises

1. **Reflect on Your Triggers:** Write about a situation where you felt emotionally triggered. What caused it, and how could you manage it differently?
2. **Analyze a Past Interaction:** Think of a conversation where emotions ran high. How could recognizing triggers have changed the outcome?
3. **Practice with a Partner:** Role-play a challenging discussion, focusing on identifying and addressing potential triggers.

Closing Thoughts

Recognizing emotional triggers is essential for fostering understanding, empathy, and constructive dialogue. By identifying and addressing sensitivities, you can navigate difficult conversations with greater confidence and care.

Chapter 77: Simplifying Complex Ideas

Breaking Down Complexity: Simplifying Complex Ideas

Simplifying complex ideas involves breaking them into smaller, more manageable components or using clear, relatable language to ensure understanding. This skill is essential when communicating intricate concepts to diverse audiences.

For example:

- **Scenario:** A data analyst presents findings to a non-technical team.
- **Simplification Application:** Instead of using jargon, they explain trends and insights with relatable examples and visuals.

Simplifying doesn't mean oversimplifying; it's about making the message accessible without losing its essence.

How to Simplify Complex Ideas

1. **Identify the Core Message:** Focus on the main point or takeaway you want to communicate.

   Example: "What is the one thing your audience should remember?"

2. **Break It Into Steps:** Divide the concept into smaller, logical segments.

   Example: "Step 1: What is the problem? Step 2: How does the solution work?"

3. **Use Analogies and Examples:** Relate the concept to something familiar.

   Example: "Think of blockchain as a digital ledger, like balancing a checkbook online."

4. **Visualize the Idea:** Use diagrams, charts, or metaphors to represent the concept visually.

Applications of Simplifying Complex Ideas

1. **In Education:**
   - o Teach difficult subjects in a way that resonates with students at different levels.

2. **In Business Communication:**
   - o Explain strategies, data, or technical solutions to stakeholders with varying expertise.

3. **In Everyday Interactions:**
   - o Clarify your thoughts or perspectives when discussing nuanced topics with others.

Why Simplifying Complex Ideas is Effective

This method helps:

1. **Enhance Clarity:** Ensures your audience grasps the message without confusion.

2. **Improve Engagement:** Keeps listeners interested by avoiding overwhelming details.

3. **Foster Retention:** Simplified ideas are easier to remember and act upon.

Challenges and Limitations

1. **Risk of Oversimplification:** Stripping too much detail may compromise accuracy.
2. **Audience Diversity:** Different levels of expertise may require varying degrees of simplification.
3. **Time Constraints:** Simplifying complex concepts effectively requires preparation and creativity.

For instance, reducing a medical explanation too much could leave out critical information that affects understanding.

How to Simplify Effectively

1. **Know Your Audience:** Tailor your explanation to their background and needs.

   Example: "What terms or examples will resonate with this group?"

2. **Focus on Key Points:** Prioritize the most critical aspects of the idea.

   Example: "What is the simplest way to convey the message without losing meaning?"

3. **Use Visuals and Stories:** Supplement explanations with images or narratives that reinforce understanding.

Exercises

1. **Simplify a Concept:** Take a complex idea you're familiar with and explain it to someone with no prior knowledge of the topic.
2. **Reframe a Presentation:** Choose a past presentation and simplify its key points for a general audience. Reflect on the changes.
3. **Create a Visual Aid:** Develop a chart, diagram, or infographic to represent a complicated concept in a straightforward way.

Closing Thoughts

Simplifying complex ideas is a critical skill for effective communication. By breaking down information and using relatable language, you ensure that your audience understands and retains your message.

This skill enhances your ability to connect, persuade, and educate in any context, from professional presentations to everyday conversations.

Chapter 78: Using Data to Bolster Arguments

Backing Arguments with Evidence: Using Data to Bolster Arguments

Data adds credibility and strength to your arguments by providing factual evidence to support your claims. When used effectively, data can make your message more persuasive, impactful, and trustworthy.

For example:

- **Scenario:** A non-profit advocates for increased funding.
- **Data Application:** They use statistics on program outcomes to demonstrate the impact of their work.

Data-driven arguments are particularly valuable in fields such as business, policy, education, and marketing, where evidence-based decision-making is essential.

How to Use Data Effectively

1. **Choose Relevant Data:** Select statistics, trends, or metrics directly related to your argument.

   Example: "What data points best illustrate the problem or solution?"

2. **Present Data Clearly:** Use charts, graphs, or tables to make information accessible.

   Example: "This bar graph shows a 20% increase in customer retention after implementing the new strategy."

3. **Explain the Connection:** Link data directly to your argument or conclusion.

   Example: "These numbers highlight why our proposed solution is both effective and necessary."

4. **Anticipate Questions:** Be prepared to explain the source, methodology, and context of the data.

Applications of Using Data

1. **In Business:**
   - Support strategies, proposals, or decisions with performance metrics and market analysis.

2. **In Education:**
   - Use data to highlight learning trends, gaps, or achievements in the classroom.

3. **In Advocacy:**
   - Persuade stakeholders or the public by presenting data on social, economic, or environmental issues.

Why Using Data is Effective

This method helps:

1. **Enhance Credibility:** Demonstrates that your arguments are grounded in evidence.

2. **Clarify Complex Issues:** Transforms abstract ideas into tangible insights.

3. **Persuade More Effectively:** Appeals to logic and rationality, reinforcing your message.

Challenges and Limitations

1. **Misinterpretation Risk:** Poorly presented data can confuse or mislead the audience.
2. **Overloading with Information:** Too much data may overwhelm or distract from the main message.
3. **Bias in Data Selection:** Cherry-picking favorable data points can harm credibility.

For example, selectively highlighting only positive survey results while ignoring negative feedback might appear deceptive.

How to Use Data Effectively

1. **Focus on Quality:** Use credible, well-sourced, and up-to-date data.
2. **Simplify Presentation:** Highlight key insights rather than overwhelming your audience with every detail.
3. **Combine with Narrative:** Frame data within a compelling story to enhance emotional and logical appeal.

Exercises

1. **Analyze a Report:** Choose a data-driven report and evaluate how effectively it supports its conclusions. Identify strengths and areas for improvement.
2. **Build a Data Argument:** Select a topic and gather relevant data to create a persuasive argument. Present it to a peer for feedback.
3. **Create a Visual Summary:** Develop a chart or infographic that highlights key data points for a specific argument.

Closing Thoughts

Data is a powerful tool for enhancing the persuasiveness and credibility of your arguments. By selecting relevant information and presenting it clearly, you can support your claims with evidence that resonates with your audience.

This skill is indispensable in today's information-driven world, helping you make compelling cases across professional, academic, and personal contexts.

Chapter 79: The Rule of Three in Persuasion

Power in Simplicity: The Rule of Three in Persuasion

The Rule of Three is a principle suggesting that ideas presented in groups of three are more impactful, memorable, and persuasive. By leveraging this natural preference for triads, communicators can simplify complex messages and enhance their effectiveness.

For example:

- **Scenario:** A marketer presents a product.
- **Rule of Three Application:** They highlight three key benefits: affordability, durability, and ease of use.

This method is widely used in speeches, storytelling, marketing, and education to create concise and engaging messages.

How to Apply the Rule of Three

1. **Identify the Key Points:** Select three main ideas or takeaways you want your audience to remember.

   Example: "What are the three most important benefits of this proposal?"

2. **Organize for Impact:** Arrange your points logically, building toward the most compelling one.

   Example: "Start with affordability, then highlight durability, and finish with ease of use."

3. **Reinforce with Repetition:** Use triads throughout your message for consistency and emphasis.

   Example: "We need innovation, collaboration, and determination to succeed."

Applications of the Rule of Three

1. **In Speeches:**
   - Deliver impactful messages with triads like "life, liberty, and the pursuit of happiness."

2. **In Marketing:**
   - Highlight three product features or benefits in advertisements or presentations.

3. **In Teaching:**
   - Simplify lessons by organizing content into three key concepts or steps.

Why the Rule of Three is Effective

This method helps:

1. **Enhance Clarity:** Focuses attention on the most critical points.

2. **Improve Retention:** Capitalizes on the brain's preference for triads, making information easier to remember.

3. **Create Impact:** Simplifies complexity while maintaining depth and engagement.

Challenges and Limitations

1. **Oversimplification:** Complex topics may require more than three points for adequate explanation.
2. **Repetition Risk:** Overusing triads can make communication feel formulaic or predictable.
3. **Inappropriate Contexts:** Certain situations may require a more detailed or flexible approach.

For example, a technical report may demand more than three key takeaways to convey comprehensive information.

How to Use the Rule of Three Effectively

1. **Prioritize Key Messages:** Focus on the three most important or impactful ideas.
2. **Adapt to the Audience:** Ensure your triad resonates with their needs and expectations.
3. **Balance Depth and Simplicity:** Use the rule as a guideline, not a constraint, when complexity demands more detail.

Exercises

1. **Craft a Triad:** Choose a topic and organize your key points into a three-part structure. Present it to someone for feedback.
2. **Analyze a Famous Speech:** Identify how the Rule of Three is applied in speeches or slogans. Reflect on its effectiveness.
3. **Reframe a Complex Message:** Simplify a detailed argument or explanation into three key takeaways.

Closing Thoughts

The Rule of Three is a timeless technique for crafting memorable, persuasive, and impactful messages. By organizing ideas into triads, you can enhance clarity, engage your audience, and ensure your key points are retained.

This method is a versatile tool for effective communication, whether you're presenting a speech, crafting a marketing pitch, or teaching a concept.

Chapter 80: The Importance of Visual Aids

Making Ideas Visible: The Importance of Visual Aids

Visual aids — such as charts, graphs, images, and diagrams — enhance communication by making ideas tangible, engaging, and easier to understand. They complement verbal or written content, helping audiences process and retain information more effectively.

For example:

- **Scenario:** A scientist presents research findings.
- **Visual Aid Application:** They use a graph to show the correlation between two variables, simplifying complex data into an easily understood visual.

In today's fast-paced, information-driven world, well-designed visual aids are indispensable for clear and persuasive communication.

How to Use Visual Aids Effectively

1. **Choose the Right Aid:** Select visuals that align with your content and audience.

   Example: Use graphs for data, diagrams for processes, and images for concepts.

2. **Simplify the Design:** Keep visuals clean and uncluttered, focusing on key points.

   Example: Highlight one trend in a graph rather than overloading it with multiple datasets.

3. **Integrate Seamlessly:** Use visuals to complement, not replace, your verbal or written message.

   Example: Explain the chart's significance rather than just showing it.

4. **Test for Clarity:** Ensure your visuals are easily interpretable by your audience.

Applications of Visual Aids

1. **In Presentations:**
   - Use slides with charts, images, or videos to engage and inform the audience.

2. **In Education:**
   - Incorporate diagrams, infographics, or animations to clarify lessons.

3. **In Reports and Proposals:**
   - Include graphs and tables to support arguments and provide evidence.

Why Visual Aids Are Effective

This method helps:

1. **Enhance Engagement:** Captures attention with appealing and relevant visuals.

2. **Clarify Information:** Simplifies complex concepts or data into digestible formats.

3. **Improve Retention:** Makes content more memorable by appealing to visual learning styles.

Challenges and Limitations

1. **Overuse of Visuals:** Excessive or irrelevant visuals can distract rather than enhance.
2. **Technical Issues:** Poor-quality images or software glitches may disrupt communication.
3. **Cultural Sensitivities:** Images or symbols may carry different meanings across cultures.

For instance, using color-coded graphs in regions with different color associations might confuse the audience.

How to Use Visual Aids Effectively

1. **Focus on Quality:** Use high-resolution, professional visuals that align with your message.
2. **Balance Content and Visuals:** Ensure visuals support your narrative without overshadowing it.
3. **Practice with Visuals:** Familiarize yourself with presenting alongside your chosen aids to avoid reliance or distraction.

Exercises

1. **Create a Visual Aid:** Design a graph, diagram, or infographic to represent a topic of your choice. Share it with someone for feedback.
2. **Analyze a Presentation:** Review a presentation that uses visuals. Identify what works well and what could be improved.
3. **Reframe a Report:** Take a text-heavy report and incorporate visual aids to enhance clarity and engagement.

Closing Thoughts

Visual aids are powerful tools for enhancing communication, making ideas more engaging, and ensuring information is understood and retained. When used effectively, they complement your message and elevate its impact.

This skill is essential in professional, academic, and personal contexts, empowering you to connect with audiences through clarity, creativity, and precision.

Part IV: Mastery

Section: Logical Thinking in Complex Systems

Complex systems are characterized by interconnected components, dynamic interactions, and emergent behaviors. Understanding these systems requires a shift from linear thinking to a more holistic and analytical approach. In this section, we'll explore tools and frameworks that help navigate complexity, identify leverage points, and anticipate unintended consequences.

Chapter 81: Systems Thinking

Seeing the Bigger Picture: Systems Thinking

Systems Thinking is a framework for understanding complex systems by analyzing the relationships and interactions between their components. Instead of isolating parts, it emphasizes the whole system, identifying patterns, feedback loops, and interdependencies.

For example:

- **Scenario:** A city addresses traffic congestion.
- **Systems Thinking Application:** They analyze how road design, public transportation, and urban planning influence traffic flow rather than focusing solely on building new roads.

This approach is essential for tackling multifaceted problems in fields such as ecology, economics, and organizational management.

How Systems Thinking Works

1. **Define the System:** Identify the boundaries, components, and purpose of the system.

   Example: "What elements make up the healthcare system, and how do they interact?"

2. **Analyze Interconnections:** Map relationships and feedback loops within the system.

   Example: "How do policy changes affect patient outcomes and resource allocation?"

3. **Identify Patterns and Trends:** Look for recurring behaviors or emerging dynamics.

   Example: "Why does patient demand spike during certain times of the year?"

4. **Anticipate Outcomes:** Consider how changes to one component might affect the whole system.

   Example: "What are the unintended consequences of reducing hospital staffing?"

Applications of Systems Thinking

1. **In Environmental Management:**
   - Address climate change by analyzing the interconnected effects of energy use, deforestation, and policy.

2. **In Business Strategy:**
   - Improve organizational efficiency by understanding how departments and processes interact.

3. **In Education:**
   - Teach students to analyze historical events or social issues as part of larger systems.

Why Systems Thinking is Effective

This method helps:

1. **Enhance Understanding:** Provides a holistic view of complex issues.

2. **Anticipate Consequences:** Identifies potential ripple effects and unintended outcomes.

3. **Promote Collaboration:** Encourages stakeholders to work together by understanding shared interconnections.

Challenges and Limitations

1. **Complexity Overload:** Large systems can be overwhelming to analyze and model.
2. **Data Requirements:** Requires comprehensive and accurate data to map interactions effectively.
3. **Time-Intensive:** Mapping and analyzing systems can take significant time and effort.

For instance, addressing supply chain inefficiencies may require analyzing global logistics, local policies, and market dynamics simultaneously.

How to Use Systems Thinking Effectively

1. **Start Small:** Focus on a manageable subsystem or component before expanding the analysis.
2. **Collaborate Across Disciplines:** Include diverse perspectives to capture all relevant interconnections.
3. **Use Visual Tools:** Create diagrams or models to represent relationships and feedback loops.

Exercises

1. **Map a System:** Choose a complex issue and map its components, interconnections, and feedback loops.
2. **Analyze a Pattern:** Reflect on a recurring challenge in your work or life. How does Systems Thinking explain it?
3. **Apply Systems Thinking:** Practice applying Systems Thinking to a real-world problem, such as improving workplace efficiency or addressing community issues. Evaluate how focusing on interconnections influences your solutions.

Closing Thoughts

Systems Thinking offers a powerful lens for understanding complexity, uncovering hidden dynamics, and making decisions that consider long-term impacts. By shifting from isolated analysis to holistic thinking, you can address challenges with greater depth and foresight, transforming problems into opportunities for sustainable solutions.

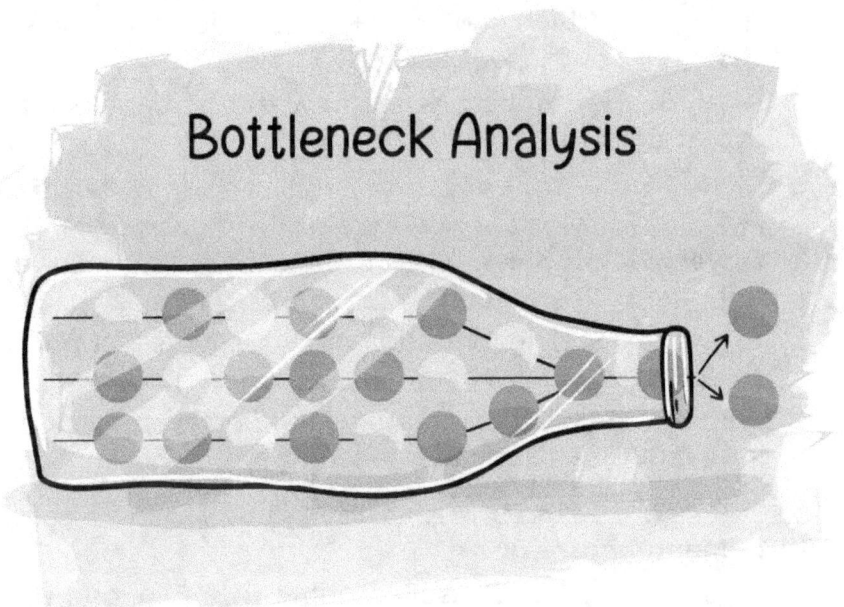
Bottleneck Analysis

Chapter 82: Bottleneck Analysis

Clearing the Path: Bottleneck Analysis

Bottleneck Analysis focuses on identifying and resolving the constraints that slow down or limit the performance of a system. By addressing these critical points, you can optimize efficiency, reduce delays, and improve outcomes.

For example:

- **Scenario:** A manufacturing plant experiences delays in production.
- **Bottleneck Analysis Application:** The team discovers that outdated machinery in one department is slowing down the entire workflow and replaces it.

This method is widely used in project management, supply chain optimization, and operational efficiency initiatives.

How Bottleneck Analysis Works

1. **Identify the Bottleneck:** Pinpoint the process, resource, or component causing delays or inefficiencies.

Example: "Which step in our production line takes the most time or causes backups?"

2. **Analyze the Impact:** Assess how the bottleneck affects overall performance and outcomes.

   Example: "How much additional cost or delay is this bottleneck causing?"

3. **Develop Solutions:** Explore strategies to resolve or mitigate the constraint.

   Example: "Should we add more resources, streamline the process, or eliminate unnecessary steps?"

4. **Monitor Results:** Evaluate the effectiveness of your intervention and adjust as needed.

Applications of Bottleneck Analysis

1. **In Manufacturing:**
   - Identify and resolve inefficiencies in production lines.

2. **In Project Management:**
   - Address delays caused by resource shortages or process inefficiencies.

3. **In Customer Service:**
   - Reduce wait times by identifying and addressing points of congestion in service delivery.

Why Bottleneck Analysis is Effective

This method helps:

1. **Optimize Efficiency:** Eliminates the primary sources of delay or waste.

2. **Improve Resource Allocation:** Focuses efforts on the areas with the greatest impact.

3. **Enhance Outcomes:** Resolving bottlenecks can significantly improve overall performance.

Challenges and Limitations

1. **Identifying Root Causes:** Symptoms may mask the true source of the problem.

2. **Temporary Solutions:** Addressing one bottleneck may reveal new constraints elsewhere.

3. **Balancing Costs:** Solutions may require significant investment or trade-offs.

For instance, hiring more staff to resolve a bottleneck may increase operational costs, requiring careful cost-benefit analysis.

How to Use Bottleneck Analysis Effectively

1. **Gather Data:** Use metrics and observations to identify bottlenecks objectively.
2. **Prioritize Critical Constraints:** Focus on bottlenecks with the greatest impact on overall performance.
3. **Iterate Solutions:** Continuously monitor and adapt strategies as new challenges emerge.

Exercises

1. **Identify a Bottleneck:** Reflect on a process in your work or daily life. What's slowing it down, and how can you address it?
2. **Analyze a System:** Choose a real-world example, such as traffic congestion or supply chain delays, and conduct a bottleneck analysis.
3. **Design a Solution:** Propose and test strategies for resolving a bottleneck in a hypothetical or real scenario.

Closing Thoughts

Bottleneck Analysis is a vital tool for improving efficiency and maximizing system performance. By identifying and addressing critical constraints, you can clear the path to better outcomes and smoother operations.

This method equips you to navigate challenges with focus and precision, ensuring that resources are used effectively to achieve your goals.

Chapter 83: Identifying Leverage Points

Strategic Impact: Identifying Leverage Points

A leverage point is a place within a system where a small change can produce a significant impact. Identifying these points allows decision-makers to prioritize efforts and resources for maximum effectiveness.

For example:

- **Scenario:** A school district wants to improve student performance.
- **Leverage Point Application:** They discover that teacher training has a more significant effect on student outcomes than increased funding for facilities and focus resources accordingly.

Understanding leverage points is essential for addressing complex problems in a targeted and efficient way.

How to Identify Leverage Points

1. **Map the System:** Understand the components, interactions, and feedback loops within the system.

   Example: "How do policies, resources, and stakeholders interact in this system?"

2. **Analyze Causal Relationships:** Identify areas where changes have ripple effects across the system.

   Example: "What happens when we change resource allocation?"

3. **Evaluate Potential Impact:** Prioritize leverage points based on their potential for meaningful and lasting change.

   Example: "Will this intervention improve the system as a whole or just one part?"

4. **Implement and Monitor:** Test interventions at leverage points and monitor their outcomes.

Applications of Identifying Leverage Points

1. **In Business Strategy:**
   o Identify critical processes or decisions that drive profitability and growth.

2. **In Public Policy:**
   o Focus on interventions, such as education or healthcare access, that have broad societal benefits.

3. **In Personal Development:**
   o Target habits or behaviors that create the most significant positive changes in life.

Why Identifying Leverage Points is Effective

This method helps:

1. **Maximize Efficiency:** Focuses on actions with the highest return on investment.

2. **Promote Systemic Change:** Addresses root causes rather than symptoms.

3. **Enhance Decision-Making:** Simplifies complex problems by highlighting high-impact solutions.

Challenges and Limitations

1. **Complexity in Systems:** Leverage points may be hidden or difficult to pinpoint in intricate systems.
2. **Resistance to Change:** Stakeholders may oppose interventions, even at identified leverage points.
3. **Unintended Consequences:** Changes at leverage points can produce unexpected outcomes elsewhere.

For instance, reducing class sizes might improve teacher-student interactions but increase demand for qualified educators, straining resources.

How to Identify Leverage Points Effectively

1. **Involve Stakeholders:** Collaborate with those who understand the system to identify key areas of influence.
2. **Focus on Feedback Loops:** Target points where changes reinforce positive outcomes or disrupt negative cycles.
3. **Test Incrementally:** Implement small changes and measure their effects before scaling interventions.

Exercises

1. **Map a System:** Choose a system you're familiar with and identify possible leverage points. Reflect on their potential impact.
2. **Analyze Past Successes:** Think of a successful intervention you've seen or experienced. What leverage point was addressed?
3. **Propose a Solution:** Identify a leverage point in a hypothetical or real-world problem and design an intervention.

Closing Thoughts

Identifying leverage points is a powerful strategy for driving meaningful change in complex systems. By focusing on areas with the greatest potential impact, you can achieve transformative results with minimal resources.

This method equips you to address challenges strategically and efficiently, turning complexity into opportunity.

Chapter 84: Emergent Behavior Analysis

Unpredictable Patterns: Emergent Behavior Analysis

Emergent behavior occurs when interactions among individual components of a system produce outcomes that cannot be predicted by analyzing the components alone. Analyzing these behaviors is crucial for understanding and managing complex systems.

For example:

- **Scenario:** An online platform experiences viral trends.
- **Emergent Behavior Analysis Application:** The team studies how individual user interactions contribute to collective phenomena like trends or misinformation.

Emergent behaviors are common in ecosystems, social networks, markets, and other systems where collective dynamics arise from decentralized interactions.

How to Analyze Emergent Behavior

1. **Observe the System:** Identify patterns or phenomena that arise unexpectedly.

    Example: "What trends or behaviors are emerging in this social media platform?"

2. **Understand Local Interactions:** Examine how individual components or agents influence one another.

    Example: "How do user likes, shares, and comments amplify specific content?"

3. **Model the Dynamics:** Use simulations, models, or data analysis to explore how emergent behaviors develop.

    Example: "What happens when we tweak the algorithm that ranks content?"

4. **Adapt Interventions:** Develop strategies to guide or mitigate emergent behaviors.

Applications of Emergent Behavior Analysis

1. **In Ecosystems:**
    o   Understand how individual species interactions create balanced or disrupted ecosystems.

2. **In Economics:**
    o   Analyze how individual market behaviors lead to trends like booms or crashes.

3. **In Technology:**
    o   Study the collective behavior of users in online platforms or AI-driven systems.

Why Emergent Behavior Analysis is Effective

This method helps:

1. **Reveal Hidden Dynamics:** Uncovers patterns that are invisible when focusing on individual components.

2. **Predict System Behavior:** Anticipates collective outcomes in complex environments.

3. **Inform Interventions:** Guides strategies to shape or respond to emergent phenomena.

Challenges and Limitations

1. **Unpredictability:** Emergent behaviors can be difficult or impossible to foresee.
2. **Modeling Complexity:** Simulating large-scale interactions requires advanced tools and expertise.
3. **Resistance to Control:** Emergent behaviors may be resistant to top-down interventions.

For instance, efforts to curb misinformation online may inadvertently amplify it if users resist perceived censorship.

How to Analyze Emergent Behavior Effectively

1. **Embrace Complexity:** Accept that some emergent behaviors may defy simple explanations.
2. **Collaborate Across Disciplines:** Work with experts in relevant fields to analyze and interpret dynamics.
3. **Monitor Continuously:** Regularly observe and adapt to evolving behaviors within the system.

Exercises

1. **Observe Emergent Patterns:** Choose a system, like traffic flow or online trends, and identify emergent behaviors.
2. **Analyze Collective Dynamics:** Reflect on a past situation where emergent behavior influenced outcomes. What were the underlying interactions?
3. **Design a Simulation:** Use basic tools or software to simulate a system and observe how small changes affect emergent patterns.

Closing Thoughts

Emergent behavior analysis is a vital tool for understanding the unpredictable dynamics of complex systems. By focusing on collective outcomes and their underlying interactions, you can navigate uncertainty and develop strategies that align with the system's natural tendencies.

Chapter 85: Scenario Mapping

Preparing for Possibilities: Scenario Mapping

Scenario Mapping is a strategic planning technique that explores possible future outcomes based on current trends and uncertainties. By mapping out various scenarios, decision-makers can anticipate challenges, identify opportunities, and plan for diverse possibilities.

For example:

- **Scenario:** A tech company evaluates market expansion.
- **Scenario Mapping Application:** They map outcomes based on variables like competition, customer demand, and regulatory changes, preparing for best-case, worst-case, and neutral scenarios.

This method is widely used in business strategy, risk management, and policy development to navigate uncertainty effectively.

How Scenario Mapping Works

1. **Define Key Variables:** Identify the factors that could significantly influence outcomes.

   Example: "How will economic conditions, consumer behavior, and technological advancements shape the future?"

2. **Develop Scenarios:** Create narratives or outlines for possible futures based on variations in the key variables.

   Example: "Scenario A: High demand and low competition. Scenario B: Low demand and high competition."

3. **Assess Implications:** Analyze how each scenario impacts your goals, strategies, and resources.

   Example: "What resources are needed to thrive in Scenario A versus Scenario B?"

4. **Plan for Flexibility:** Develop strategies that are adaptable across multiple scenarios.

Applications of Scenario Mapping

1. **In Business Strategy:**
   o Plan for market fluctuations, competitor actions, and technological shifts.

2. **In Public Policy:**
   o Anticipate the effects of regulations, social trends, or environmental changes.

3. **In Personal Planning:**
   o Map potential outcomes of major life decisions, like career changes or relocations.

Why Scenario Mapping is Effective

This method helps:

1. **Enhance Preparedness:** Anticipates challenges and reduces surprises.

2. **Promote Strategic Flexibility:** Encourages adaptive thinking and contingency planning.

3. **Foster Innovation:** Sparks creative solutions by exploring diverse possibilities.

Challenges and Limitations

1. **Uncertainty in Variables:** Unpredictable factors can lead to incomplete or inaccurate scenarios.
2. **Analysis Paralysis:** Too many scenarios may overwhelm decision-making.
3. **Overemphasis on Extremes:** Focusing only on best- or worst-case scenarios might neglect moderate possibilities.

For instance, overpreparing for an unlikely catastrophe might waste resources better spent on probable outcomes.

How to Use Scenario Mapping Effectively

1. **Prioritize Variables:** Focus on the factors most likely to influence outcomes significantly.
2. **Balance Scenarios:** Include a range of possibilities, from optimistic to pessimistic to neutral.
3. **Engage Stakeholders:** Involve diverse perspectives to capture a broader range of scenarios.

Exercises

1. **Map a Decision:** Choose a decision you're facing and develop three scenarios based on key uncertainties. Reflect on how this shapes your strategy.
2. **Analyze Past Events:** Think of a past situation where scenario mapping could have helped. What variables and outcomes would you have considered?
3. **Facilitate a Group Exercise:** Work with a team to map scenarios for a shared challenge or opportunity.

Closing Thoughts

Scenario Mapping is a powerful tool for navigating uncertainty and preparing for diverse possibilities. By envisioning potential futures, you can make more informed decisions, anticipate risks, and seize opportunities with confidence.

This method enhances your ability to think strategically, adapt to change, and plan effectively in dynamic environments.

Chapter 86: The Butterfly Effect Awareness

Small Actions, Big Effects: The Butterfly Effect Awareness

The Butterfly Effect is a concept from chaos theory describing how small changes in initial conditions can lead to vastly different outcomes in complex systems. Being aware of this phenomenon helps decision-makers recognize the potential ripple effects of their actions.

For example:

- **Scenario:** A city revises its public transportation routes.
- **Butterfly Effect Awareness Application:** Planners consider how minor route changes might influence traffic patterns, local businesses, and commuter habits.

This awareness is particularly relevant in fields such as urban planning, environmental science, and economics, where systems are highly interconnected.

How the Butterfly Effect Works

1. **Understand Initial Conditions:** Recognize the starting point of a system or decision.

   Example: "What small factors could influence this system over time?"

2. **Anticipate Ripple Effects:** Analyze how small changes might propagate through the system.

   Example: "How will a small policy adjustment affect related sectors or stakeholders?"

3. **Plan for Uncertainty:** Accept that not all outcomes can be predicted but consider possible trajectories.

   Example: "What contingency plans can address unexpected consequences?"

4. **Monitor Outcomes:** Track the effects of decisions over time and adjust as needed.

Applications of the Butterfly Effect Awareness

1. **In Environmental Policy:**
   - Assess how small ecological changes can impact ecosystems globally.

2. **In Technology Development:**
   - Evaluate how minor design decisions might influence user behavior and system performance.

3. **In Personal Choices:**
   - Reflect on how small habits or decisions can compound into significant life changes.

Why Butterfly Effect Awareness is Effective

This method helps:

1. **Promote Thoughtful Decisions:** Encourages careful consideration of potential long-term impacts.

2. **Foster Adaptability:** Prepares for unexpected consequences in dynamic systems.

3. **Highlight Interconnectivity:** Reveals how small actions can influence larger outcomes.

Challenges and Limitations

1. **Uncertainty in Predictions:** Small changes don't always lead to significant effects.
2. **Analysis Complexity:** Tracing ripple effects in large systems can be highly complex.
3. **Paralysis by Fear:** Overemphasis on potential consequences may hinder action.

For example, delaying decisions out of fear of unintended ripple effects might prevent necessary progress.

How to Apply Butterfly Effect Awareness Effectively

1. **Think Systemically:** Consider how actions interact with broader systems.
2. **Start with Small Tests:** Experiment with minor changes before implementing large-scale interventions.
3. **Adapt Continuously:** Monitor results and adjust strategies as new ripple effects emerge.

Exercises

1. **Reflect on a Small Action:** Think of a past decision or action that had unexpected consequences. What lessons can you learn?
2. **Map Ripple Effects:** Choose a current decision and brainstorm possible outcomes based on the Butterfly Effect.
3. **Test in a System:** Introduce a small change in a controlled system and observe how it influences the whole.

Closing Thoughts

The Butterfly Effect reminds us that even the smallest actions can have profound and far-reaching consequences. By considering potential ripple effects, you can navigate complex systems more thoughtfully and prepare for a wide range of outcomes.

This awareness enhances your ability to act with foresight and adaptability, empowering you to make impactful decisions in an interconnected world.

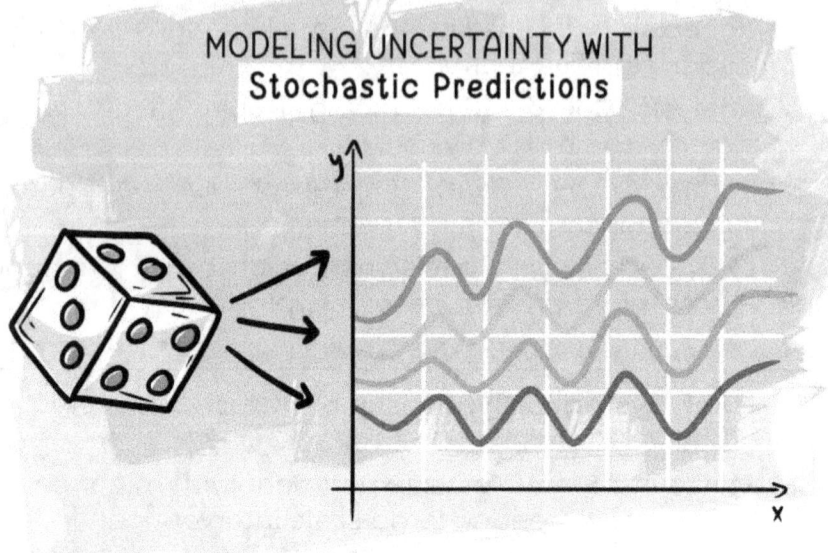

MODELING UNCERTAINTY WITH
Stochastic Predictions

Chapter 87: Stochastic Modeling

Modeling Uncertainty: Stochastic Modeling

Stochastic Modeling is a mathematical approach to predict and analyze outcomes that involve randomness or uncertainty. Unlike deterministic models, which assume fixed inputs and outputs, stochastic models incorporate variability to reflect real-world complexities.

For example:

- **Scenario:** A financial analyst projects future stock prices.
- **Stochastic Modeling Application:** They use probabilistic models to account for market fluctuations, economic changes, and investor behavior.

This technique is widely used in finance, engineering, healthcare, and environmental science to make informed decisions under uncertainty.

How Stochastic Modeling Works

1. **Define the System:** Identify the variables and processes influenced by randomness.

   Example: "What factors affect patient wait times in a hospital?"

2. **Incorporate Probabilities:** Assign probabilities to potential outcomes or events.

   Example: "What's the likelihood of an emergency increasing wait times?"

3. **Run Simulations:** Use computational tools to simulate multiple scenarios and outcomes.

   Example: "How do patient arrivals vary over time, and what's the impact on staffing needs?"

4. **Analyze Results:** Evaluate patterns, trends, and probabilities to inform decisions.

Applications of Stochastic Modeling

1. **In Finance:**
   - Forecast investment returns, risk assessments, or market trends.

2. **In Healthcare:**
   - Predict disease progression or optimize resource allocation for patient care.

3. **In Environmental Science:**
   - Model climate change impacts, such as temperature fluctuations or sea level rise.

Why Stochastic Modeling is Effective

This method helps:

1. **Account for Uncertainty:** Reflects real-world variability in predictions.

2. **Enhance Decision-Making:** Provides probabilistic insights to guide strategies.

3. **Support Risk Management:** Identifies potential risks and their likelihoods.

Challenges and Limitations

1. **Complexity in Implementation:** Developing and interpreting models requires expertise and computational resources.

2. **Data Dependency:** Reliable predictions depend on accurate and comprehensive input data.

3. **Uncertainty in Outputs:** Probabilistic results may not provide definitive answers.

For instance, predicting rainfall patterns using stochastic models may guide planning but can't guarantee specific outcomes.

How to Use Stochastic Modeling Effectively

1. **Start with Simple Models:** Begin with basic probabilistic assumptions before adding complexity.

2. **Validate with Data:** Test models against historical or real-world data to ensure accuracy.

3. **Combine with Other Tools:** Use stochastic modeling alongside deterministic approaches for a balanced analysis.

Exercises

1. **Build a Simple Model:** Choose a real-world problem and develop a basic stochastic model to predict outcomes.

2. **Analyze Variability:** Reflect on a decision or system influenced by randomness. How could stochastic modeling improve predictions?

3. **Simulate Scenarios:** Use software tools to run stochastic simulations for a project or decision, and analyze the results.

Closing Thoughts

Stochastic modeling is a powerful technique for navigating uncertainty and making data-driven decisions in dynamic environments. By incorporating randomness and variability, you can develop more accurate and realistic predictions.

This method equips you to tackle complex problems with confidence, ensuring that your strategies are robust and adaptable in the face of uncertainty.

FEEDBACK LOOP ANALYSIS

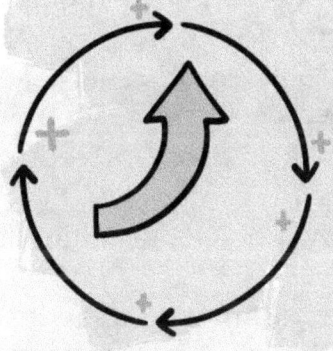

Reinforcing Loop

Balancing Loop

Chapter 88: Feedback Loop Analysis

Understanding Cycles: Feedback Loop Analysis

Feedback Loop Analysis examines how actions within a system produce feedback that influences future behaviors. Feedback loops can either amplify (positive loops) or stabilize (negative loops) outcomes, shaping the dynamics of the system over time.

For example:

- **Scenario:** A business monitors customer reviews and sales.
- **Feedback Loop Analysis Application:** Positive reviews attract more customers (reinforcing loop), while stock shortages reduce satisfaction (balancing loop).

This method is essential for understanding and managing dynamic systems in economics, biology, technology, and organizational management.

How Feedback Loop Analysis Works

1. **Identify the Loops:** Map the actions, responses, and feedback within the system.

   Example: "What actions generate reinforcing or balancing feedback in this process?"

2. **Distinguish Loop Types:** Determine whether loops amplify or stabilize system behavior.

   Example: "Does this feedback increase or reduce the original action?"

3. **Analyze Interactions:** Study how loops interact and influence each other.

   Example: "How do customer satisfaction and supply chain dynamics interact?"

4. **Adjust Strategies:** Leverage or mitigate feedback loops to align with your goals.

Applications of Feedback Loop Analysis

1. **In Economics:**
   - Analyze market trends driven by supply-demand cycles or speculative behaviors.

2. **In Healthcare:**
   - Study how feedback between treatment effectiveness and patient behavior shapes outcomes.

3. **In Business:**
   - Optimize operations by balancing feedback in workflows.

Why Feedback Loop Analysis is Effective

This method helps:

1. **Reveal System Dynamics:** Highlights the cyclical nature of interactions within systems.

2. **Anticipate Outcomes:** Predicts long-term effects of actions and interventions.

3. **Enhance Decision-Making:** Provides insights into managing or leveraging feedback.

Challenges and Limitations

1. **Complex Interactions:** Systems with multiple loops may be difficult to map and interpret.
2. **Unintended Effects:** Interventions targeting one loop may disrupt others.
3. **Data Requirements:** Accurate analysis requires reliable data on system behaviors.

For instance, efforts to improve customer satisfaction may unintentionally increase costs, disrupting profitability.

How to Analyze Feedback Loops Effectively

1. **Map the System:** Create diagrams to visualize loops and their interactions.
2. **Focus on Key Loops:** Prioritize loops with the greatest impact on system performance.
3. **Test Interventions:** Experiment with small changes to understand their effects on feedback dynamics.

Exercises

1. **Map Feedback in a System:** Choose a process or system you're familiar with and map its feedback loops. Reflect on how they shape outcomes.
2. **Analyze Reinforcing Loops:** Think of a situation where positive feedback amplified results. How could you manage or leverage this loop?
3. **Design a Balancing Strategy:** Identify a system with a destabilizing loop and propose interventions to stabilize it.

Closing Thoughts

Feedback Loop Analysis provides deep insights into the cyclical dynamics of complex systems. By understanding how actions and responses shape each other, you can anticipate outcomes, manage risks, and optimize performance.

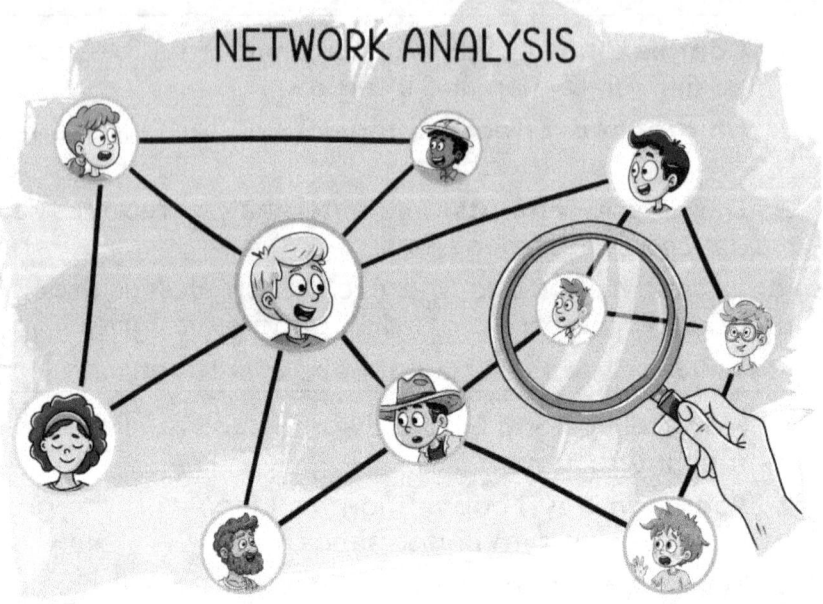

Chapter 89: Network Analysis

Mapping Connections: Network Analysis

Network Analysis is the study of relationships and interactions within a system, represented as nodes (individual entities) and edges (connections between them). This method uncovers patterns, identifies key influencers, and reveals the flow of information, resources, or influence.

For example:

- **Scenario:** A company wants to optimize communication within its teams.
- **Network Analysis Application:** They map the organizational network, identifying bottlenecks or underutilized connections to improve collaboration.

This technique is widely used in social sciences, logistics, technology, and biology to analyze and optimize complex systems.

How Network Analysis Works

1. **Define the Network:** Identify the nodes (entities) and edges (connections) relevant to your system.

   Example: "Who are the stakeholders, and how do they interact?"

2. **Map the Relationships:** Visualize the network using diagrams or software tools.

   Example: "What does the organizational communication network look like?"

3. **Analyze Metrics:** Assess features like centrality (importance of nodes), density (connection tightness), and flow (resource or information movement).

   Example: "Which team member is the most connected and acts as a bridge between departments?"

4. **Identify Opportunities:** Use insights to improve efficiency, strengthen connections, or address vulnerabilities.

Applications of Network Analysis

1. **In Social Networks:**
   o Study the spread of information, influence, or trends in online platforms.

2. **In Supply Chains:**
   o Optimize the flow of goods and resources by analyzing logistical networks.

3. **In Healthcare:**
   o Map disease transmission pathways to develop effective containment strategies.

Why Network Analysis is Effective

This method helps:

1. **Reveal Hidden Patterns:** Uncovers structures and dynamics not visible through linear analysis.

2. **Identify Key Players:** Pinpoints influential nodes or critical connections within the network.

3. **Optimize Systems:** Improves efficiency, communication, or resource allocation.

Challenges and Limitations

1. **Data Complexity:** Large networks may require extensive data collection and computational resources.
2. **Dynamic Changes:** Networks evolve over time, making static analysis less reliable.
3. **Unintended Consequences:** Intervening in one part of the network may disrupt others.

For instance, removing a central node in a supply chain could cause widespread inefficiencies.

How to Use Network Analysis Effectively

1. **Focus on Objectives:** Clearly define what you aim to achieve with the analysis.
2. **Use Visualization Tools:** Leverage software to map and interpret complex networks.
3. **Test Interventions:** Simulate changes within the network to predict outcomes before implementation.

Exercises

1. **Map a Personal Network:** Analyze your own professional or social network. Identify key connections and areas for improvement.
2. **Study a Public Network:** Choose a public network, like a social media platform or public transit system, and map its structure.
3. **Analyze an Organization:** Reflect on a team or organization you know. How could network analysis improve its communication or efficiency?

Closing Thoughts

Network Analysis is a powerful tool for understanding and optimizing connections within complex systems. By mapping and analyzing relationships, you can uncover hidden dynamics, identify key influencers, and make informed decisions to enhance efficiency and impact.

This method equips you to navigate interconnected systems with clarity, ensuring that your strategies are both effective and sustainable.

Chapter 90: Chaos Theory in Decision-Making

Embracing Uncertainty: Chaos Theory in Decision-Making

Chaos Theory explores how small differences in initial conditions can lead to vastly different outcomes in dynamic systems. Applying this concept to decision-making emphasizes the need for adaptability, flexibility, and awareness of unintended consequences in complex and unpredictable environments.

For example:

- **Scenario:** A company launches a new product.
- **Chaos Theory Application:** They prepare for unexpected market reactions, such as viral trends or unforeseen competition, by building adaptive strategies.

Chaos Theory is particularly useful in fields such as weather forecasting, economics, and organizational strategy, where uncertainty and complexity are inherent.

How Chaos Theory Applies to Decision-Making

1. **Acknowledge Unpredictability:** Accept that not all outcomes can be controlled or predicted.

   Example: "How might small market changes create unexpected impacts on our sales?"

2. **Focus on Patterns:** Look for recurring dynamics or trends within the system.

   Example: "What cyclical behaviors influence our customer base?"

3. **Prepare for Flexibility:** Develop strategies that can adapt to a range of potential scenarios.

   Example: "How can we pivot quickly if our initial strategy encounters resistance?"

4. **Learn from Feedback:** Continuously monitor outcomes and adjust strategies accordingly.

Applications of Chaos Theory in Decision-Making

1. **In Business:**
   - Navigate volatile markets or industries with adaptive strategies.

2. **In Environmental Science:**
   - Study and address the unpredictable impacts of climate change on ecosystems.

3. **In Personal Growth:**
   - Embrace uncertainty in life decisions and focus on adaptability and resilience.

Why Chaos Theory is Effective

This method helps:

1. **Promote Flexibility:** Encourages adaptive thinking in uncertain and dynamic contexts.

2. **Enhance Resilience:** Prepares for unexpected challenges and opportunities.

3. **Foster Long-Term Success:** Focuses on sustainability and learning rather than rigid plans.

Challenges and Limitations

1. **Complexity in Analysis:** Understanding chaotic systems requires advanced tools and expertise.
2. **Overwhelming Uncertainty:** Emphasizing unpredictability may hinder confidence in decision-making.
3. **Difficulty in Forecasting:** Long-term predictions in chaotic systems are often unreliable.

For instance, predicting long-term weather patterns with precision is challenging due to the chaotic nature of atmospheric systems.

How to Apply Chaos Theory Effectively

1. **Start with Small Steps:** Focus on incremental changes and monitor their effects.
2. **Embrace Iteration:** Use trial and error to refine strategies and learn from outcomes.
3. **Build Resilience:** Develop systems and strategies that can absorb shocks and adapt to change.

Exercises

1. **Reflect on Past Decisions:** Think of a decision where small changes led to significant outcomes. What can you learn from this?
2. **Analyze a Chaotic System:** Choose a system, like traffic flow or stock markets, and explore its unpredictable dynamics.
3. **Prepare for Flexibility:** Develop a flexible plan for a current project or decision, considering potential uncertainties.

Closing Thoughts

Chaos Theory teaches us to embrace uncertainty and focus on adaptability in decision-making. By understanding the unpredictable dynamics of complex systems, you can develop strategies that are resilient, flexible, and aligned with long-term success.

This method empowers you to navigate challenges with confidence, turning uncertainty into an opportunity for innovation and growth.

Section: Navigating Uncertainty and Ambiguity

In a world where uncertainty and ambiguity are constant, the ability to make sound decisions becomes a critical skill. This final section equips you with tools and frameworks for navigating the unknown, balancing risks and rewards, and adapting to unforeseen circumstances.

Chapter 91: Probability Trees

Breaking Down Uncertainty: Probability Trees

Probability Trees are visual tools that map possible outcomes of a decision or event, assigning probabilities to each branch. By organizing complex scenarios into a structured diagram, this method helps decision-makers calculate expected values and make informed choices.

For example:

- **Scenario:** A company considers launching a new product.
- **Probability Tree Application:** They evaluate potential market responses—high demand, moderate demand, or low demand—and assign probabilities to each scenario to guide investment decisions.

How Probability Trees Work

1. **Define the Decision:** Identify the starting point and the possible outcomes.

   Example: "Should we launch the product now or wait for more market research?"

2. **Map Possible Outcomes:** Create branches for each potential result or decision.

   Example: "High sales, moderate sales, or low sales."

3. **Assign Probabilities:** Estimate the likelihood of each outcome based on data or expert judgment.

   Example: "60% chance of moderate sales, 30% chance of high sales, 10% chance of low sales."

4. **Calculate Expected Values:** Multiply probabilities by the value of each outcome to guide decisions.

Applications of Probability Trees

1. **In Business Strategy:**
   - Assess risks and rewards of investments or product launches.

2. **In Medical Decision-Making:**
   - Evaluate treatment options based on patient outcomes and probabilities.

3. **In Personal Finance:**
   - Analyze potential outcomes of investment or saving strategies.

Why Probability Trees Are Effective

This method helps:

1. **Visualize Complexity:** Breaks down multifaceted decisions into clear, manageable components.

2. **Quantify Risk:** Assigns measurable probabilities to outcomes for data-driven decisions.

3. **Clarify Decision Paths:** Identifies the most rational choice based on expected values.

Challenges and Limitations

1. **Uncertain Probabilities:** Estimating probabilities may rely on assumptions or incomplete data.
2. **Complexity in Large Systems:** Trees can become unwieldy with too many branches or layers.
3. **Overemphasis on Quantification:** Focusing solely on probabilities may overlook qualitative factors.

For instance, a product launch decision might also depend on brand perception, which isn't easily quantified.

How to Use Probability Trees Effectively

1. **Start Simple:** Focus on the most significant outcomes and decisions to avoid overcomplication.
2. **Validate Probabilities:** Base probability estimates on reliable data or expert opinions.
3. **Combine with Other Methods:** Use probability trees alongside qualitative analysis for a balanced approach.

Exercises

1. **Map a Decision:** Choose a decision with multiple outcomes and create a probability tree. Reflect on how this clarifies your options.
2. **Analyze a Past Event:** Reconstruct a previous decision using a probability tree. What insights can you gain in hindsight?
3. **Test Expected Values:** Apply probability trees to calculate expected values for a hypothetical scenario, such as a new project or investment.

Closing Thoughts

Probability Trees are powerful tools for navigating uncertainty, breaking down complex decisions, and making data-driven choices. By visualizing outcomes and assigning probabilities, you can approach challenges with clarity and confidence.

Chapter 92: The Maximin/Minimax Principle

Balancing Risks and Rewards: The Maximin/Minimax Principle

The Maximin/Minimax Principle is a decision-making strategy used in uncertain or competitive scenarios. The Maximin approach focuses on maximizing the minimum possible gain, ensuring a safety-first mindset. The Minimax approach minimizes the maximum potential loss, emphasizing risk reduction.

For example:

- **Scenario:** A company is deciding between a conservative investment with lower risks or a higher-risk venture with potentially higher returns.

- **Maximin Application:** They choose the conservative option to ensure steady, minimum gains.

- **Minimax Application:** They avoid the venture most likely to incur significant losses, even if it means sacrificing higher potential returns.

How the Maximin/Minimax Principle Works

1. **Identify Possible Outcomes:** List all potential results for each decision or strategy.

   Example: "What are the gains or losses associated with each investment option?"

2. **Evaluate Worst-Case Scenarios:** Assess the minimum gains and maximum losses for each choice.

   Example: "If the market declines, what's the worst-case outcome for each option?"

3. **Choose a Strategy:** Select the Maximin approach (maximize minimum gain) or Minimax approach (minimize maximum loss) based on your priorities.

   Example: "Do we value safety over opportunity, or vice versa?"

4. **Consider Trade-Offs:** Balance the benefits of security with the potential for higher rewards.

Applications of the Maximin/Minimax Principle

1. **In Financial Planning:**
   o Choose investment strategies based on risk tolerance and market conditions.

2. **In Negotiations:**
   o Minimize potential losses while ensuring acceptable gains.

3. **In Personal Decision-Making:**
   o Approach life choices, like career changes or relocations, with risk-conscious strategies.

Why the Maximin/Minimax Principle is Effective

This method helps:

1. **Enhance Risk Awareness:** Forces consideration of worst-case scenarios and their impact.

2. **Promote Strategic Thinking:** Encourages decisions that align with risk tolerance and goals.

3. **Provide a Framework:** Offers a structured approach to decision-making in uncertain environments.

Challenges and Limitations

1. **Overly Conservative Decisions:** Focusing on minimizing losses may limit opportunities for higher gains.
2. **Incomplete Information:** Assessing all possible outcomes accurately may not always be feasible.
3. **Subjective Judgments:** Deciding between Maximin and Minimax often depends on individual risk preferences.

For instance, choosing a low-risk investment may seem safe but could result in lower returns compared to a well-researched higher-risk option.

How to Use the Maximin/Minimax Principle Effectively

1. **Align with Objectives:** Choose the approach that best matches your risk tolerance and long-term goals.
2. **Combine with Data:** Use reliable data to estimate outcomes and validate decisions.
3. **Revisit Regularly:** Reassess strategies as conditions or priorities change.

Exercises

1. **Apply to a Decision:** Think of a current or past decision involving uncertainty. Map out worst-case scenarios and apply the Maximin/Minimax Principle.
2. **Compare Strategies:** Choose a hypothetical scenario, like a job offer or investment choice, and evaluate it using both Maximin and Minimax approaches.
3. **Reflect on Risk Tolerance:** Analyze your own preferences for risk and safety in decision-making. How does this influence your choices?

Closing Thoughts

The Maximin/Minimax Principle is a valuable framework for balancing risks and rewards in uncertain situations. By focusing on worst-case scenarios, you can make decisions that align with your values, goals, and risk tolerance.

This method enhances your ability to navigate uncertainty with clarity and confidence, empowering you to make thoughtful and strategic choices.

Chapter 93: Utility Theory

Maximizing Satisfaction: Utility Theory

Utility Theory is a decision-making framework that evaluates options based on their ability to maximize satisfaction, value, or benefit for the decision-maker. It emphasizes weighing outcomes against personal preferences, goals, or priorities.

For example:

- **Scenario:** A person chooses between two job offers—one with a higher salary but longer hours, and another with a lower salary but better work-life balance.
- **Utility Theory Application:** They consider which option provides greater overall satisfaction, balancing financial benefits with personal well-being.

How Utility Theory Works

1. **Define Utility:** Determine what "satisfaction" or "value" means in the context of the decision.

   Example: "Is utility based on financial gain, personal happiness, or social impact?"

2. **Quantify Preferences:** Assign utility values to each option based on how well it meets your priorities.

   Example: "Option A scores 8/10 for salary and 5/10 for work-life balance, while Option B scores 6/10 and 9/10, respectively."

3. **Evaluate Trade-Offs:** Compare utility scores across options to identify the best choice.

   Example: "Which option has the highest total utility when combining all factors?"

4. **Make a Decision:** Choose the option that maximizes utility within your constraints.

Applications of Utility Theory

1. **In Business:**
   - Optimize strategies or investments by evaluating their expected utility for stakeholders.

2. **In Healthcare:**
   - Balance risks and benefits of treatments to maximize patient outcomes.

3. **In Personal Choices:**
   - Prioritize options, such as vacation destinations or major purchases, based on overall satisfaction.

Why Utility Theory is Effective

This method helps:

1. **Clarify Priorities:** Encourages explicit consideration of what matters most.

2. **Quantify Decisions:** Provides a structured approach to evaluate and compare options.

3. **Maximize Benefits:** Ensures choices align with long-term goals and values.

Challenges and Limitations

1. **Subjectivity:** Utility values are based on personal preferences, which may change over time.

2. **Complex Trade-Offs:** Balancing competing factors can be difficult and time-consuming.

3. **Uncertainty in Outcomes:** Predicted utility may not always align with actual experiences.

For instance, a high-paying job might seem like the best choice but could lead to dissatisfaction if work-life balance suffers.

How to Apply Utility Theory Effectively

1. **Reflect on Goals:** Clearly define what "utility" means to you in each decision.
2. **Involve Stakeholders:** Consider the preferences and priorities of others affected by the decision.
3. **Test Assumptions:** Revisit utility assessments to ensure they remain accurate and relevant.

Exercises

1. **Evaluate a Past Decision:** Choose a decision where you balanced competing priorities. How would Utility Theory have clarified your choice?
2. **Quantify Preferences:** Apply Utility Theory to a hypothetical scenario, such as choosing between two purchases or career paths.
3. **Create a Utility Table:** List options, assign utility scores to each factor, and calculate totals to identify the best choice.

Closing Thoughts

Utility Theory provides a structured approach to decision-making that aligns choices with personal or organizational priorities. By evaluating options based on their ability to maximize satisfaction or value, you can make more thoughtful and intentional decisions.

This method enhances your ability to weigh trade-offs, clarify goals, and achieve outcomes that truly matter in both simple and complex scenarios.

Chapter 94: Signal Detection Theory

Separating Signal from Noise: Signal Detection Theory

Signal Detection Theory (SDT) is a framework for understanding how decisions are made in uncertain conditions, particularly when distinguishing meaningful signals from background noise. It is widely applied in fields like communication, medicine, and technology, where discerning important information is critical.

For example:

- **Scenario:** A doctor examines test results for signs of disease.

- **Signal Detection Application:** They balance the risk of false positives (overdiagnosis) against false negatives (missed diagnosis) to make accurate decisions.

How Signal Detection Theory Works

1. **Define the Signal:** Identify what you are trying to detect or recognize amidst noise.

   Example: "Is there a meaningful pattern in this data?"

2. **Set Criteria for Detection:** Decide the threshold for determining whether a signal is present.

   Example: "What level of test result indicates a likely diagnosis?"

3. **Weigh Trade-Offs:** Balance the consequences of false positives (detecting a signal when none exists) and false negatives (missing a true signal).

   Example: "What are the risks of overdiagnosis versus underdiagnosis?"

4. **Incorporate Probabilities:** Use data to refine detection criteria and improve accuracy.

Applications of Signal Detection Theory

1. **In Medicine:**
   - Diagnose diseases based on test results and patient symptoms.

2. **In Technology:**
   - Detect cyber threats or system malfunctions in IT networks.

3. **In Communication:**
   - Identify key messages or trends in large volumes of information.

Why Signal Detection Theory is Effective

This method helps:

1. **Enhance Accuracy:** Reduces errors by balancing detection thresholds.

2. **Improve Decision-Making:** Provides a structured approach for uncertain or noisy conditions.

3. **Optimize Resource Use:** Focuses attention and resources on the most meaningful signals.

Challenges and Limitations

1. **Uncertain Criteria:** Setting the right detection threshold requires reliable data and judgment.
2. **Balancing Trade-Offs:** Minimizing false positives can increase false negatives, and vice versa.
3. **Complex Noise:** High levels of noise can obscure even strong signals, complicating detection.

For instance, in financial markets, detecting a trend (signal) amidst daily fluctuations (noise) can be challenging without robust analysis.

How to Use Signal Detection Theory Effectively

1. **Define Objectives:** Clearly identify the signal you are trying to detect and its importance.
2. **Refine Criteria:** Continuously adjust detection thresholds based on feedback and outcomes.
3. **Leverage Data:** Use statistical models or machine learning tools to enhance detection accuracy.

Exercises

1. **Analyze Detection Trade-Offs:** Reflect on a past decision where you had to balance false positives and negatives. How could SDT have improved your approach?
2. **Test Detection Criteria:** Apply SDT to a hypothetical scenario, such as identifying trends in a dataset or diagnosing a condition.
3. **Simulate a Noisy Environment:** Create a scenario with distracting noise and practice identifying meaningful signals.

Closing Thoughts

Signal Detection Theory provides a valuable framework for decision-making in uncertain and noisy conditions. By balancing detection criteria and weighing trade-offs, you can improve accuracy and effectiveness in identifying meaningful signals.

This method equips you to make thoughtful decisions in fields ranging from medicine to technology, ensuring that critical signals are recognized and acted upon amidst the noise.

Chapter 95: Decision-Making Under Ambiguity

Navigating the Unknown: Decision-Making Under Ambiguity

Decision-Making Under Ambiguity involves making choices when outcomes, probabilities, or even the criteria for success are unclear. This requires balancing intuition, adaptability, and critical thinking to navigate uncertainty effectively.

For example:

- **Scenario:** A start-up decides whether to enter a market with limited data on consumer preferences.
- **Decision-Making Application:** They rely on a combination of market research, expert judgment, and iterative testing to minimize risks.

How to Approach Decision-Making Under Ambiguity

1. **Clarify Goals:** Define what success looks like, even if other factors are uncertain.

   Example: "What are the key objectives for entering this market?"

2. **Gather What Data You Can:** Use available information to guide initial decisions, while acknowledging gaps.

   Example: "What trends or benchmarks can inform our approach?"

3. **Embrace Iteration:** Take small, calculated steps and adjust as new information emerges.

   Example: "What pilot project can we run to test this strategy?"

4. **Balance Intuition and Analysis:** Leverage past experience and analytical tools to make informed choices.

Applications of Decision-Making Under Ambiguity

1. **In Start-ups:**
   o Launch new products or services in uncertain markets.

2. **In Crisis Management:**
   o Respond to emergencies or disasters with incomplete information.

3. **In Career Planning:**
   o Make life choices, such as career changes, with unclear outcomes.

Why Decision-Making Under Ambiguity is Effective

This method helps:

1. **Promote Flexibility:** Encourages adaptability as conditions change or new data emerges.

2. **Reduce Paralysis:** Provides a framework for action despite uncertainty.

3. **Build Resilience:** Develops confidence and skills to navigate unpredictable situations.

Challenges and Limitations

1. **Lack of Information:** Decisions may be based on incomplete or unreliable data.
2. **Inherent Risks:** Ambiguity increases the potential for unforeseen outcomes.
3. **Emotional Stress:** Navigating uncertainty can be mentally and emotionally taxing.

For instance, entering a new market without clear data on consumer preferences risks both financial loss and reputational damage.

How to Make Decisions Under Ambiguity Effectively

1. **Focus on Core Values:** Align decisions with your principles and long-term goals.
2. **Test Small Steps:** Minimize risks by experimenting with smaller-scale actions before full implementation.
3. **Reassess Regularly:** Continuously review outcomes and adapt strategies as clarity improves.

Exercises

1. **Reflect on Ambiguous Decisions:** Think of a time when you had to make a decision without full information. How did you approach it, and what did you learn?
2. **Simulate Uncertainty:** Create a hypothetical scenario with ambiguous outcomes and practice making decisions.
3. **Apply to a Current Challenge:** Identify a situation with ambiguity in your life or work. Develop a plan for navigating it using small, iterative steps.

Closing Thoughts

Decision-Making Under Ambiguity is a critical skill for navigating an uncertain and fast-changing world. By embracing flexibility, balancing intuition with analysis, and iterating thoughtfully, you can act decisively even when clarity is lacking.

This approach enhances your resilience, adaptability, and confidence, ensuring you can navigate the unknown with clarity and purpose.

Chapter 96: Applying Monte Carlo Simulations

Simulating the Future: Applying Monte Carlo Simulations

Monte Carlo Simulations use randomness and repeated trials to model complex systems and predict a range of possible outcomes. By exploring the variability of inputs, this method provides insights into uncertainty and helps guide decision-making in dynamic environments.

For example:

- **Scenario:** A project manager estimates a project's completion time.
- **Monte Carlo Simulation Application:** They simulate the project timeline hundreds of times with varying task durations to predict the most likely completion date.

How Monte Carlo Simulations Work

1. **Define the Problem:** Identify the decision or system to be modeled.

   Example: "What is the potential range of returns for this investment portfolio?"

2. **Determine Variables:** Select the uncertain factors and assign probability distributions.

   Example: "What are the likely ranges for market growth rates or inflation?"

3. **Run Simulations:** Use software or tools to perform thousands of random iterations, each producing a potential outcome.

   Example: "What does the portfolio's value look like across 10,000 simulated scenarios?"

4. **Analyze Results:** Assess the distribution of outcomes to inform decisions.

Applications of Monte Carlo Simulations

1. **In Finance:**
   - Forecast investment risks, returns, and market volatility.

2. **In Project Management:**
   - Predict project completion times and budget variations.

3. **In Engineering:**
   - Model system reliability or performance under varying conditions.

Why Monte Carlo Simulations Are Effective

This method helps:

1. **Capture Variability:** Reflects the full range of possible outcomes, not just averages.

2. **Quantify Risks:** Provides probabilistic insights to guide risk management.

3. **Enhance Decision-Making:** Informs strategies with data-driven predictions.

Challenges and Limitations

1. **Data Quality:** Reliable results depend on accurate input data and probability distributions.
2. **Computational Intensity:** Simulations can be resource-intensive for complex systems.
3. **Interpretation of Results:** Understanding and applying probabilistic outcomes require expertise.

For instance, predicting a project's timeline requires accurate estimates of task durations and dependencies to avoid misleading conclusions.

How to Use Monte Carlo Simulations Effectively

1. **Define Clear Goals:** Clearly outline what you want the simulation to predict or analyze.
2. **Validate Inputs:** Use reliable data and realistic probability distributions for accuracy.
3. **Combine with Expert Judgment:** Supplement simulation results with domain expertise for better decisions.

Exercises

1. **Simulate a Simple Scenario:** Use a Monte Carlo tool or spreadsheet to model a basic problem, such as forecasting expenses with varying costs.
2. **Analyze Simulation Results:** Reflect on how the range of outcomes influences your decision-making.
3. **Apply to a Real Decision:** Identify a current project or decision that could benefit from Monte Carlo Simulations. Develop and test a model.

Closing Thoughts

Monte Carlo Simulations are invaluable for modeling uncertainty, exploring variability, and predicting outcomes in complex systems. By embracing probabilistic thinking, you can make more informed, data-driven decisions in the face of uncertainty.

This method enhances your ability to plan strategically, mitigate risks, and adapt effectively to dynamic environments.

Chapter 97: Black Swan Event Analysis

Preparing for the Unthinkable: Black Swan Event Analysis

A Black Swan Event is a rare, unpredictable occurrence with significant consequences, often misunderstood until after it happens. Black Swan Event Analysis involves identifying vulnerabilities, preparing for the unexpected, and building resilience against low-probability but high-impact events.

For example:

- **Scenario:** A business evaluates its supply chain.
- **Black Swan Analysis Application:** They assess risks from rare events, such as a global pandemic or natural disaster, and develop contingency plans.

How Black Swan Event Analysis Works

1. **Identify Vulnerabilities:** Assess areas of your system or strategy susceptible to extreme disruptions.

Example: "What critical dependencies would fail in a rare but severe crisis?"

2. **Evaluate Potential Impacts:** Consider the magnitude of damage a Black Swan Event could cause.

   Example: "How would a sudden economic collapse affect our business?"

3. **Develop Contingencies:** Build robust systems and strategies to mitigate risks or recover quickly.

   Example: "What backup suppliers or resources can we secure?"

4. **Cultivate Resilience:** Foster adaptability and flexibility to respond effectively to unforeseen events.

Applications of Black Swan Event Analysis

1. **In Business Continuity:**
   - Prepare for supply chain disruptions, market crashes, or cybersecurity threats.

2. **In Public Policy:**
   - Plan for rare events like pandemics, natural disasters, or geopolitical conflicts.

3. **In Personal Finance:**
   - Build emergency funds or diversify investments to weather economic shocks.

Why Black Swan Event Analysis is Effective

This method helps:

1. **Increase Awareness:** Highlights risks often overlooked due to their rarity.

2. **Promote Preparedness:** Encourages proactive measures to mitigate high-impact events.

3. **Build Resilience:** Strengthens systems and strategies to recover from crises.

Challenges and Limitations

1. **Unpredictability:** By definition, Black Swan Events are difficult to foresee or quantify.

2. **Overinvestment in Rare Risks:** Excessive focus on rare events might neglect more likely challenges.

3. **Psychological Resistance:** Humans often downplay or ignore risks perceived as improbable.

For instance, businesses may dismiss the likelihood of a pandemic, leaving them unprepared when one occurs.

How to Analyze Black Swan Events Effectively

1. **Think Beyond the Likely:** Consider low-probability, high-impact risks in addition to common challenges.

2. **Test Scenarios:** Simulate responses to hypothetical Black Swan Events to identify weaknesses.

3. **Balance Resources:** Allocate efforts proportionally, addressing both rare and probable risks.

Exercises

1. **Reflect on Past Events:** Analyze a historical Black Swan Event. How could better preparation have mitigated its impact?

2. **Identify Vulnerabilities:** Assess a system or strategy you're involved with. What rare risks could disrupt it?

3. **Develop a Contingency Plan:** Create a plan for a hypothetical Black Swan Event in your work or life.

Closing Thoughts

Black Swan Event Analysis equips you to navigate the unexpected, mitigate extreme risks, and build resilience in uncertain environments. By preparing for rare but impactful occurrences, you can safeguard systems, strategies, and goals against even the most unpredictable challenges.

This approach enhances your ability to thrive in a volatile and interconnected world, turning uncertainty into an opportunity for proactive growth.

Chapter 98: Heuristic-Based Iteration

Learning Through Approximation: Heuristic-Based Iteration

Heuristic-Based Iteration involves using simple, rule-of-thumb strategies (heuristics) to tackle complex problems in a step-by-step, iterative process. Rather than aiming for perfection immediately, this method focuses on continuous improvement and adapting to feedback.

For example:

- **Scenario:** A product development team tests a new app feature.

- **Heuristic-Based Iteration Application:** They release a prototype, gather user feedback, and refine the feature in successive iterations based on insights.

This approach is particularly useful in dynamic environments where solutions evolve over time.

How Heuristic-Based Iteration Works

1. **Define the Goal:** Clearly articulate what you aim to achieve or solve.

   Example: "How can we improve customer engagement on the app?"

2. **Choose a Heuristic:** Use a guiding principle or rule of thumb to start solving the problem.

   Example: "Start by addressing the most common user complaints."

3. **Test and Evaluate:** Implement a solution, observe the outcomes, and gather feedback.

   Example: "How did users respond to the new feature?"

4. **Refine and Iterate:** Use insights to adjust your approach and repeat the process.

Applications of Heuristic-Based Iteration

1. **In Product Development:**
   - Improve designs or features through iterative prototyping and testing.
2. **In Education:**
   - Adapt teaching methods based on student performance and feedback.
3. **In Personal Growth:**
   - Refine habits or skills through trial and error and consistent practice.

Why Heuristic-Based Iteration is Effective

This method helps:

1. **Promote Flexibility:** Encourages adaptation and responsiveness to feedback.
2. **Accelerate Learning:** Focuses on actionable insights rather than overanalysis.
3. **Reduce Perfectionism:** Emphasizes progress and continuous improvement over flawless execution.

Challenges and Limitations

1. **Incomplete Solutions:** Early iterations may not fully solve the problem.
2. **Feedback Dependence:** Requires reliable input to guide refinements.
3. **Risk of Overfitting:** Overly narrow focus on feedback may limit broader innovation.

For instance, refining a feature based only on vocal user feedback might overlook the needs of silent majority users.

How to Use Heuristic-Based Iteration Effectively

1. **Start with Simple Steps:** Begin with the most straightforward heuristic to generate momentum.
2. **Prioritize Feedback:** Actively seek diverse input to guide adjustments.
3. **Balance Exploration and Refinement:** Avoid getting stuck in minor refinements; explore new ideas when necessary.

Exercises

1. **Reflect on an Iterative Process:** Think of a situation where you used trial and error. How could heuristics have improved the process?
2. **Simulate a Challenge:** Apply heuristic-based iteration to a hypothetical problem, like designing a better workspace.
3. **Identify a Heuristic:** Choose a personal or professional challenge and develop a rule of thumb to guide iterative improvements.

Closing Thoughts

Heuristic-Based Iteration transforms complexity into manageable steps, fostering adaptability and continuous growth. By combining simple strategies with iterative learning, you can solve problems effectively and refine solutions over time.

This method enhances your ability to navigate uncertainty, innovate with confidence, and achieve sustainable success in evolving environments.

Balancing Action and Risk

Chapter 99: The Precautionary Principle Revisited

When in Doubt, Proceed with Care: The Precautionary Principle Revisited

The Precautionary Principle advises caution in decision-making when potential risks are significant but uncertain. It emphasizes acting conservatively to avoid harm, particularly in scenarios with high stakes or limited knowledge.

For example:

- **Scenario:** A city considers adopting a new pesticide.
- **Precautionary Principle Application:** They conduct extensive testing to ensure environmental safety before widespread use.

This principle is particularly relevant in environmental policy, public health, and technological innovation, where the stakes of unintended consequences are high.

How the Precautionary Principle Works

1. **Identify Uncertain Risks:** Assess situations where potential harm is significant but poorly understood.

   Example: "What are the unknown long-term effects of this new technology?"

2. **Evaluate Alternatives:** Consider safer or more conservative approaches to achieve your goals.

   Example: "Can we reduce pesticide use by adopting organic farming practices?"

3. **Apply Caution:** Delay action or implement safeguards until risks are better understood.

   Example: "What safety measures can minimize potential harm?"

4. **Monitor and Adapt:** Continuously review new data and adjust strategies as knowledge improves.

Applications of the Precautionary Principle

1. **In Environmental Policy:**
   - Protect ecosystems by limiting potentially harmful industrial practices.

2. **In Medicine:**
   - Avoid widespread use of untested treatments or interventions.

3. **In Technology:**
   - Assess the societal impact of innovations like AI or biotechnology before full deployment.

Why the Precautionary Principle is Effective

This method helps:

1. **Minimize Risks:** Reduces the likelihood of irreversible harm.

2. **Promote Responsible Innovation:** Encourages ethical and sustainable development.

3. **Foster Public Trust:** Demonstrates commitment to safety and well-being.

Challenges and Limitations

1. **Paralysis by Analysis:** Excessive caution can delay beneficial innovations.
2. **Unclear Risks:** Identifying potential harm may be speculative or subjective.
3. **Balancing Trade-Offs:** Overemphasis on caution might overlook immediate benefits.

For instance, delaying renewable energy projects for extensive impact assessments might exacerbate climate challenges.

How to Apply the Precautionary Principle Effectively

1. **Prioritize High-Stakes Risks:** Focus on areas where harm could be severe or irreversible.
2. **Balance Caution with Progress:** Combine precaution with innovation to avoid stalling beneficial developments.
3. **Adapt to Evidence:** Adjust strategies as risks become clearer and better understood.

Exercises

1. **Reflect on a Risky Decision:** Think of a time when you faced uncertainty. How could the Precautionary Principle have influenced your decision?
2. **Apply to a Hypothetical Challenge:** Develop a cautious approach for adopting a new technology or policy.
3. **Evaluate Trade-Offs:** Identify a current project or decision where balancing caution and progress is critical.

Closing Thoughts

The Precautionary Principle is a guide for navigating high-risk, uncertain situations with care and foresight. By prioritizing safety and ethical responsibility, you can protect against potential harm while fostering sustainable growth.

This principle empowers you to balance caution with innovation, ensuring that progress aligns with long-term well-being and integrity.

Chapter 100: Cognitive Flexibility in Uncertainty

Adapting to the Unknown: Cognitive Flexibility in Uncertainty

Cognitive Flexibility is the ability to shift perspectives, adapt to new information, and revise strategies in response to changing circumstances. It is a cornerstone of effective decision-making in uncertain and ambiguous situations, where rigid thinking often leads to missed opportunities or poor outcomes.

For example:

- **Scenario:** A business leader faces sudden market disruption.
- **Cognitive Flexibility Application:** They quickly pivot their strategy, leveraging emerging trends to turn challenges into opportunities.

This skill is vital for thriving in dynamic environments, from personal challenges to global crises.

How Cognitive Flexibility Works

1. **Recognize Change:** Stay attuned to shifting circumstances and emerging information.

   Example: "What new factors are influencing this situation?"

2. **Reframe Perspectives:** Look at challenges or problems from multiple angles.

   Example: "How does this obstacle create new opportunities?"

3. **Adapt Strategies:** Adjust plans or goals based on updated insights.

   Example: "What changes can we make to stay aligned with current conditions?"

4. **Embrace Learning:** View setbacks or uncertainty as opportunities for growth and innovation.

Applications of Cognitive Flexibility

1. **In Leadership:**
   - Navigate organizational changes, market disruptions, or crises with agility.

2. **In Personal Growth:**
   - Adjust to life changes, such as career shifts or unexpected challenges, with resilience.

3. **In Education:**
   - Tailor teaching strategies to diverse learning needs or evolving curricula.

Why Cognitive Flexibility is Effective

This method helps:

1. **Enhance Adaptability:** Encourages responsiveness to new challenges and opportunities.

2. **Improve Problem-Solving:** Fosters creativity and innovation by exploring multiple solutions.

3. **Build Resilience:** Strengthens the ability to thrive in uncertain or high-pressure situations.

Challenges and Limitations

1. **Overwhelm from Options:** Too many perspectives or solutions may delay decision-making.
2. **Resistance to Change:** Personal or organizational biases may hinder adaptability.
3. **Lack of Confidence:** Frequent changes may create uncertainty or a lack of direction.

For instance, constantly revising strategies without a clear vision might confuse teams or dilute focus.

How to Cultivate Cognitive Flexibility

1. **Practice Perspective-Taking:** Regularly challenge yourself to see situations from different viewpoints.

   Example: "How would a customer, competitor, or stakeholder view this problem?"
2. **Embrace Uncertainty:** Accept that not all answers are immediate or clear, and remain open to experimentation.

   Example: "What can we try that hasn't been attempted before?"
3. **Encourage Collaborative Thinking:** Seek diverse input to expand your understanding and options.

   Example: "What insights can team members from different backgrounds bring to this challenge?"

Exercises

1. **Reframe a Problem:** Choose a current challenge and identify three alternative perspectives or solutions.
2. **Simulate Adaptability:** Create a hypothetical scenario with sudden changes and practice adjusting strategies in real-time.
3. **Reflect on Past Adaptations:** Think of a situation where you successfully pivoted in response to change. What made that approach effective?

Closing Thoughts

Cognitive Flexibility is the ultimate skill for navigating the uncertainties of a dynamic world. By staying adaptable, open-minded, and resilient, you can turn challenges into opportunities and thrive amidst change.

This skill is essential for personal and professional success, empowering you to embrace uncertainty as a catalyst for growth, creativity, and innovation.

Conclusion: Building a Life Rooted in Logic

Over the course of this book, we've explored 100 methods designed to sharpen your logical thinking, dismantle confusion, and illuminate the path toward clear and effective decision-making. These methods span a wide range of disciplines, from recognizing cognitive biases and evaluating evidence to mastering communication and navigating uncertainty. Each chapter offered tools you can apply in your daily life to solve problems, analyze situations, and make decisions that align with your goals and values.

Logical thinking isn't just a skill — it's a practice. It's something you cultivate daily, like a muscle that grows stronger with use. Whether you're navigating workplace challenges, making important life choices, or seeking to understand the world around you, logic is your compass. By applying these methods, you can approach every situation with clarity and confidence, transforming complexity into opportunity.

Cultivate Logical Thinking Daily

Now, the challenge lies in making logical thinking a habit. Start small — practice a method from this book each day, whether it's applying Occam's Razor to a tricky decision, reframing an argument for clarity, or using a heuristic to iterate toward a solution. The more you integrate these techniques into your thought process, the more naturally they'll become part of how you think, communicate, and act.

Logical thinking isn't about removing emotion or creativity; it's about enhancing them. It allows you to blend intuition with reason, balancing heart and mind in your approach to life. Embrace this journey not as a rigid framework, but as a way to unlock your potential and navigate the world with purpose and insight.

Closing Thoughts

This book is not the end of your journey — it's a beginning. As you move forward, continue to question, analyze, and refine your thinking.

The power of logical thinking lies in its universality. It applies to every field, every challenge, and every opportunity.

Go forward with confidence, curiosity, and the courage to think deeply. The future is yours to shape — one thoughtful decision at a time.

Appendix A: Quick Guide to the Chapters

This appendix provides a concise overview of the 100 methods explored in this book. Use it as a quick reference to revisit key concepts, tools, and techniques for sharpening your logical thinking and decision-making skills.

Part I: Foundations

Focus: Fundamental tools and principles of logical reasoning.

Section: Building Blocks of Logic

1. Occam's Razor: Simplify solutions by focusing on the fewest assumptions.

2. The Principle of Charity: Interpret arguments in their strongest, fairest form.

3. Falsifiability: Ensure claims can be tested and disproven.

4. Syllogisms: Use structured arguments to deduce logical conclusions.

5. Deductive Reasoning: Draw specific conclusions from general premises.

6. Inductive Reasoning: Infer general rules from specific observations.

7. Abductive Reasoning: Find the most likely explanation for observed phenomena.

8. Modus Ponens: Apply "If A, then B" to validate logical statements.

9. Modus Tollens: Disprove statements by negating their outcomes.

10. Reductio ad Absurdum: Demonstrate falsehood by showing contradictions.

Section: Recognizing and Avoiding Fallacies

11. Spotting Strawman Arguments: Avoid misrepresenting opposing views.

12. Recognizing Ad Hominem Attacks: Focus on arguments, not personal attacks.

13. Avoiding Post Hoc Reasoning: Separate correlation from causation.

14. Identifying Circular Arguments: Avoid conclusions that rely on their own premise.

15. Detecting False Dilemmas: Recognize when multiple options are ignored.

16. Understanding Appeal to Authority Fallacies: Validate claims beyond expert opinion.

17. The Gambler's Fallacy: Avoid assuming patterns in random events.

18. Slippery Slope Analysis: Analyze exaggerated claims of inevitable outcomes.

19. Avoiding Hasty Generalizations: Base conclusions on sufficient evidence.

20. Distinguishing Correlation from Causation: Avoid mistaking coincidence for causality.

Part II: Advanced Logical Tools

Focus: Practical frameworks and strategies for complex reasoning.

Section: Problem-Solving Frameworks

21. The 5 Whys: Uncover root causes by asking iterative "why" questions.

22. Ishikawa (Fishbone) Diagrams: Visualize causes of problems to address root issues.

23. Root Cause Analysis: Identify and eliminate underlying problems.

24. The Socratic Method: Use questions to stimulate critical thinking.

25. SWOT Analysis: Assess strengths, weaknesses, opportunities, and threats.

26. First Principles Thinking: Break down problems into foundational truths.

27. Reverse Engineering: Work backward to understand processes or problems.

28. Hypothesis Testing: Validate ideas through experimentation and observation.

29. Bayesian Thinking: Update probabilities as new information becomes available.

30. Counterfactual Reasoning: Explore "what if" scenarios to evaluate alternatives.

31. Analogical Reasoning: Use comparisons to find patterns and insights.

32. Pareto Analysis: Focus on the vital few causes of most outcomes.

33. Ladder of Inference: Trace reasoning steps to avoid flawed conclusions.

34. Heuristic Analysis: Use mental shortcuts for quick, effective problem-solving.

35. The Eisenhower Matrix: Prioritize tasks based on urgency and importance.

Section: Cognitive Bias Mitigation

36. Recognizing Anchoring Bias: Avoid being overly influenced by initial information.

37. Overcoming Confirmation Bias: Seek evidence that challenges your beliefs.

38. Mitigating Availability Heuristics: Base decisions on data, not immediate examples.

39. Combatting the Dunning-Kruger Effect: Recognize the limits of your knowledge.

40. Avoiding Framing Effects: Present information neutrally to avoid skewed perceptions.

41. Understanding the Halo Effect: Separate single traits from overall evaluations.

42. Reframing with Devil's Advocacy: Challenge ideas to ensure robustness.

43. Premortem Analysis: Anticipate and address potential failures before they occur.

44. Overcoming Status Quo Bias: Evaluate decisions objectively, not based on inertia.

45. Appreciating Base Rates: Use statistical context to inform judgments.

46. Debiasing with Probabilistic Thinking: Incorporate probabilities into decisions.

47. Overcoming Loss Aversion: Focus on long-term gains, not short-term losses.

48. Distinguishing Intuition from Analysis: Balance gut feelings with logical reasoning.

49. Applying the Illusion of Transparency Test: Clarify ideas others might misinterpret.

50. The Outside View Technique: Use external perspectives to avoid overconfidence.

Part III: Practical Applications

Focus: Applying logical methods to real-world contexts.

Section: Decision-Making Techniques

51. Weighted Decision Matrix: Compare options using weighted criteria.

52. Expected Value Calculation: Evaluate decisions based on likely outcomes.

53. Decision Trees: Map decision pathways and their potential consequences.

54. Scenario Planning: Prepare for multiple future possibilities.

55. The Delphi Method: Use expert consensus for complex decisions.

56. Multi-Criteria Decision Analysis (MCDA): Evaluate decisions with multiple factors.

57. Cost-Benefit Analysis: Compare benefits and costs for informed choices.

58. The Precautionary Principle: Act cautiously in high-risk situations.

59. The Monte Carlo Method: Model uncertainty using probabilistic simulations.

60. Risk Assessment Matrices: Prioritize risks based on likelihood and impact.

61. Sensitivity Analysis: Explore how changes affect outcomes.

62. Adaptive Thinking: Adjust strategies dynamically in changing conditions.

63. The OODA Loop (Observe, Orient, Decide, Act): Make decisions quickly and effectively.

64. The Six Thinking Hats: Use diverse perspectives for balanced decisions.

65. Weighted Trade-Off Grids: Balance trade-offs to optimize decisions.

Section: Enhancing Communication and Persuasion

66. Reframing Arguments for Clarity: Present ideas more effectively.

67. The Pyramid Principle: Structure communication logically from top to bottom.

68. The Rhetorical Triangle: Balance ethos, logos, and pathos for persuasion.

69. Active Listening: Build understanding through attentive engagement.

70. Mirroring and Paraphrasing: Validate and clarify others' perspectives.

71. Using Analogies Effectively: Simplify concepts with relatable comparisons.

72. The SEE-I Framework: State, Elaborate, Exemplify, and Illustrate ideas clearly.

73. Building Common Ground: Connect with others to foster agreement.

74. Structuring Evidence with Logic: Organize facts to strengthen arguments.

75. Avoiding Loaded Questions: Ensure neutrality in phrasing.

76. Recognizing Emotional Triggers: Manage emotions in discussions.

77. Simplifying Complex Ideas: Break down intricate concepts for clarity.

78. Using Data to Bolster Arguments: Strengthen cases with evidence.

79. The Rule of Three in Persuasion: Use triads to create memorable messages.

80. The Importance of Visual Aids: Enhance communication with engaging visuals.

Part IV: Mastery

Focus: Expert-level strategies for navigating uncertainty, complexity, and ambiguity.

Section: Logical Thinking in Complex Systems

81. Systems Thinking: Analyze systems holistically to uncover patterns.

82. Bottleneck Analysis: Identify and resolve constraints limiting performance.

83. Identifying Leverage Points: Focus on areas where small changes yield big results.

84. Emergent Behavior Analysis: Understand outcomes arising from interactions.

85. Scenario Mapping: Explore potential futures to prepare effectively.

86. The Butterfly Effect Awareness: Recognize small actions with big consequences.

87. Stochastic Modeling: Use probabilistic models to analyze variability.

88. Feedback Loop Analysis: Study how actions and outcomes influence each other.

89. Network Analysis: Map and optimize relationships within systems.

90. Chaos Theory in Decision-Making: Navigate unpredictable dynamics.

Section: Navigating Uncertainty and Ambiguity

91. Probability Trees: Map outcomes and calculate probabilities.

92. The Maximin/Minimax Principle: Balance risks and rewards in decision-making.

93. Utility Theory: Optimize satisfaction based on priorities and preferences.

94. Signal Detection Theory: Distinguish signals from noise in uncertain data.

95. Decision-Making Under Ambiguity: Act effectively despite unclear conditions.

96. Applying Monte Carlo Simulations: Model uncertainty using repeated trials.

97. Black Swan Event Analysis: Prepare for rare, high-impact events.

98. Heuristic-Based Iteration: Solve problems through trial and improvement.

99. The Precautionary Principle Revisited: Act cautiously in the face of unknown risks.

100. Cognitive Flexibility in Uncertainty: Adapt thinking to thrive in change.

Appendix B: Chapter Categories and Listings

This appendix organizes the chapters into their respective categories, offering a clear structure to navigate the topics covered in the book. Use this guide to locate chapters based on your specific interests or areas of focus.

Part I: Foundations

Focus: Fundamental tools and principles of logical reasoning.

Section: Building Blocks of Logic

- Occam's Razor
- The Principle of Charity
- Falsifiability
- Syllogisms
- Deductive Reasoning
- Inductive Reasoning
- Abductive Reasoning
- Modus Ponens
- Modus Tollens
- Reductio ad Absurdum

Section: Recognizing and Avoiding Fallacies

- Spotting Strawman Arguments
- Recognizing Ad Hominem Attacks
- Avoiding Post Hoc Reasoning
- Identifying Circular Arguments

- Detecting False Dilemmas
- Understanding Appeal to Authority Fallacies
- The Gambler's Fallacy
- Slippery Slope Analysis
- Avoiding Hasty Generalizations
- Distinguishing Correlation from Causation

Part II: Advanced Logical Tools

Focus: Practical frameworks and strategies for complex reasoning.

Section: Problem-Solving Frameworks

- The 5 Whys
- Ishikawa (Fishbone) Diagrams
- Root Cause Analysis
- The Socratic Method
- SWOT Analysis
- First Principles Thinking
- Reverse Engineering
- Hypothesis Testing
- Bayesian Thinking
- Counterfactual Reasoning
- Analogical Reasoning
- Pareto Analysis
- Ladder of Inference
- Heuristic Analysis
- The Eisenhower Matrix

Section: Cognitive Bias Mitigation

- Recognizing Anchoring Bias
- Overcoming Confirmation Bias
- Mitigating Availability Heuristics
- Combatting the Dunning-Kruger Effect
- Avoiding Framing Effects
- Understanding the Halo Effect

- Reframing with Devil's Advocacy
- Premortem Analysis
- Overcoming Status Quo Bias
- Appreciating Base Rates
- Debiasing with Probabilistic Thinking
- Overcoming Loss Aversion
- Distinguishing Intuition from Analysis
- Applying the Illusion of Transparency Test
- The Outside View Technique

Part III: Practical Applications

Focus: Applying logical methods to real-world contexts.

Section: Decision-Making Techniques

- Weighted Decision Matrix
- Expected Value Calculation
- Decision Trees
- Scenario Planning
- The Delphi Method
- Multi-Criteria Decision Analysis (MCDA)
- Cost-Benefit Analysis
- The Precautionary Principle
- The Monte Carlo Method
- Risk Assessment Matrices
- Sensitivity Analysis
- Adaptive Thinking
- The OODA Loop (Observe, Orient, Decide, Act)
- The Six Thinking Hats
- Weighted Trade-off Grids

Section: Enhancing Communication and Persuasion

- Reframing Arguments for Clarity
- The Pyramid Principle
- The Rhetorical Triangle
- Active Listening

- Mirroring and Paraphrasing
- Using Analogies Effectively
- The SEE-I Framework (State, Elaborate, Exemplify, Illustrate)
- Building Common Ground
- Structuring Evidence with Logic
- Avoiding Loaded Questions
- Recognizing Emotional Triggers
- Simplifying Complex Ideas
- Using Data to Bolster Arguments
- The Rule of Three in Persuasion
- The Importance of Visual Aids

Part IV: Mastery

Focus: Expert-level strategies for navigating uncertainty, complexity, and ambiguity.

Section: Logical Thinking in Complex Systems
- Systems Thinking
- Bottleneck Analysis
- Identifying Leverage Points
- Emergent Behavior Analysis
- Scenario Mapping
- The Butterfly Effect Awareness
- Stochastic Modeling
- Feedback Loop Analysis
- Network Analysis
- Chaos Theory in Decision-Making

Section: Navigating Uncertainty and Ambiguity
- Probability Trees
- The Maximin/Minimax Principle
- Utility Theory
- Signal Detection Theory
- Decision-Making Under Ambiguity

- Applying Monte Carlo Simulations
- Black Swan Event Analysis
- Heuristic-Based Iteration
- The Precautionary Principle Revisited
- Cognitive Flexibility in Uncertainty

Appendix C: Practice Scenarios

This appendix provides practical scenarios designed to help you apply the logical methods from the book. Each exercise includes a description of the scenario, the situation's details, and a challenge highlighting the relevant methods you can use to solve it. Use these scenarios individually or in group discussions to deepen your understanding and practice your skills.

Scenario 1: Business Decision

Situation:

A company is debating whether to launch a new product in a highly competitive market. The decision involves balancing potential profits, brand positioning, and market risks.

Challenge:

Use **SWOT Analysis** to evaluate strengths, weaknesses, opportunities, and threats, and apply the **Decision Tree Method** to map potential outcomes and their consequences.

Scenario 2: Policy Debate

Situation:

A city council is considering implementing a congestion charge to reduce traffic and pollution, but there's strong opposition from local businesses.

Challenge:

Apply the **Principle of Charity** to fairly analyze both sides of the argument, and use **Cost-Benefit Analysis** to assess the economic and social impacts of the policy.

Scenario 3: Financial Planning

Situation:

An individual is choosing between two investment options: a low-risk, steady-return bond and a high-risk, potentially high-reward stock.

Challenge:

Use the **Maximin/Minimax Principle** to evaluate the risks and rewards, and incorporate **Expected Value Calculation** to quantify potential financial outcomes.

Scenario 4: Healthcare Dilemma

Situation:

A doctor must decide between two treatment plans for a critically ill patient: one aggressive and riskier, the other safer but slower to act.

Challenge:

Apply **Utility Theory** to weigh the benefits and risks of each treatment and use **Bayesian Thinking** to update probabilities as new patient data becomes available.

Scenario 5: Negotiation Challenge

Situation:

Two companies negotiating a partnership face tension after one side presents an exaggerated scenario to strengthen its position.

Challenge:

Use **Spotting Strawman Arguments** to identify misrepresentations and apply **Reframing with Devil's Advocacy** to ensure the discussion remains constructive.

Scenario 6: Personal Career Choice

Situation:

A recent graduate is deciding between a high-paying corporate job with stability and a lower-paying start-up role with significant growth potential.

Challenge:

Use the **Eisenhower Matrix** to prioritize personal and professional values and apply the **Weighted Decision Matrix** to evaluate options across multiple criteria.

Scenario 7: Marketing Strategy

Situation:

A marketing team must choose between focusing their efforts on a social media campaign or an email marketing strategy.

Challenge:

Apply the **5 Whys** to uncover the root goals of the campaign and use **Hypothesis Testing** to predict which strategy aligns better with their objectives.

Scenario 8: Community Issue

Situation:

A neighborhood group is deciding how to address rising crime rates. They're debating whether to improve lighting, increase patrols, or start community outreach programs.

Challenge:

Use **Systems Thinking** to analyze how various factors contribute to crime and apply **Bottleneck Analysis** to identify the most effective intervention points.

Scenario 9: Global Issue

Situation:

A non-profit organization aims to combat climate change but must prioritize limited resources across multiple projects, such as renewable energy initiatives and reforestation programs.

Challenge:

Apply the **Precautionary Principle** to minimize environmental risks and use **Scenario Planning** to prepare for future climate-related uncertainties.

Scenario 10: Educational Reform

Situation:

A school district is evaluating whether to transition from traditional teaching methods to project-based learning to improve student engagement and critical thinking skills.

Challenge:

Use the **Socratic Method** to foster discussions among stakeholders and apply **First Principles Thinking** to assess the core benefits and challenges of the proposed change.

Scenario 11: Conflict Resolution

Situation:

Two co-workers have conflicting ideas about the direction of a major project, creating tension in team meetings.

Challenge:

Use **Active Listening** to understand both sides and apply **Building Common Ground** to find a mutually beneficial solution.

Scenario 12: Start-up Risk

Situation:

A tech start-up is preparing to launch a new product but is concerned about uncertain market demand and the financial risks of failure.

Challenge:

Use **Monte Carlo Simulations** to model potential market outcomes and apply **Signal Detection Theory** to identify meaningful trends in early customer feedback.

Scenario 13: Consumer Decision

Situation:

A family is deciding whether to buy or rent a home, weighing financial considerations, flexibility, and long-term goals.

Challenge:

Apply **Cost-Benefit Analysis** to compare the financial implications of buying versus renting and use **Sensitivity**

Analysis to explore how different scenarios (e.g., interest rate changes) might affect the decision.

Scenario 14: Crisis Management

Situation:

A company is dealing with a public relations crisis after a controversial statement went viral, causing backlash from customers.

Challenge:

Apply **Premortem Analysis** to anticipate potential missteps in the response strategy and use **Cognitive Flexibility** to adjust messaging as the situation evolves.

Scenario 15: Innovative Design

Situation:

An engineering team is tasked with creating a more efficient and sustainable solar panel to meet growing energy demands.

Challenge:

Use **Reverse Engineering** to study successful designs from competitors and apply **Feedback Loop Analysis** to refine the prototype during testing.

How to Use These Scenarios

These scenarios are designed to provide hands-on opportunities to apply logical methods and frameworks in diverse situations. Start by identifying which methods are most relevant to the scenario, then work through the problem systematically, applying the techniques from the chapters.

Revisit these scenarios regularly, practice different methods for the same scenario, and explore how alternative approaches can lead to different insights.

Appendix D: Checklist for Your Logical Thinking Guide

This checklist serves as a quick reference to enhance your logical thinking skills and ensure you approach problems, decisions, and challenges systematically. Use it to assess your process, refine your methods, and improve your outcomes.

1. Clarifying the Problem

- Have you clearly defined the problem or question you're addressing?
- Are you separating symptoms from root causes?
- Do you understand the context and scope of the issue?

2. Gathering Relevant Information

- Have you collected all available data and evidence?
- Are your sources credible and unbiased?
- Have you cross-checked the information for accuracy?

3. Evaluating Assumptions

- What assumptions are you making in your analysis?
- Are these assumptions based on evidence or bias?
- Can your assumptions be tested or challenged?

4. Identifying Key Variables

- What factors have the most significant impact on the issue?
- Are you prioritizing the most critical variables?

- Have you identified any dependencies or correlations?

5. Choosing the Right Method

- Have you selected a logical method that fits the problem?
- Are you familiar with how to apply this method effectively?
- Have you considered alternative methods for a different perspective?

6. Structuring Arguments

- Is your argument clear, logical, and evidence-based?
- Have you addressed counterarguments or alternative viewpoints?
- Are you avoiding logical fallacies in your reasoning?

7. Mitigating Bias

- Are you aware of potential cognitive biases influencing your thinking?
- Have you actively sought perspectives that challenge your assumptions?
- Are you using tools like probabilistic thinking to reduce bias?

8. Evaluating Risks and Rewards

- Have you identified potential risks and their likelihood?
- Are you balancing risks with potential rewards?
- Have you considered long-term impacts as well as short-term effects?

9. Simplifying Complexity

- Have you broken down complex problems into smaller parts?
- Are you focusing on the most impactful elements first?
- Have you avoided overcomplicating the issue unnecessarily?

10. Testing Hypotheses

- Are your hypotheses testable and falsifiable?
- Have you planned experiments or collected data to validate them?
- Are you prepared to revise your hypothesis if evidence contradicts it?

11. Using Visual Tools

- Have you used diagrams, flowcharts, or matrices to organize your thinking?
- Do your visuals clarify relationships and patterns in the data?
- Are your visual aids easy to understand and interpret?

12. Planning for Uncertainty

- Have you considered multiple scenarios and their outcomes?
- Are you building flexibility into your plans to adapt to change?
- Have you prepared for low-probability, high-impact events?

13. Engaging Stakeholders

- Have you consulted others with relevant expertise or perspectives?
- Are you presenting your reasoning in a clear and structured way?
- Have you addressed stakeholder concerns or objections?

14. Communicating Effectively

- Are you tailoring your message to your audience?
- Have you provided clear evidence to support your conclusions?
- Are you listening actively and responding to feedback constructively?

15. Reviewing and Refining

- Have you revisited your process to identify areas for improvement?
- Are you learning from past successes and mistakes?
- Are you regularly practicing and refining your logical thinking skills?

Pro Tip: The Key to Consistency

Logical thinking isn't about achieving perfection — it's about maintaining consistency. Use this checklist as a guide to ensure you stay on track, but remember to remain flexible. Each situation is unique, and the ability to adapt your methods is as important as mastering them. Regularly reflect on your thought processes, incorporate feedback, and embrace a mindset of continuous improvement. Logical thinking is a journey — use this checklist to guide your way forward.

Here's another book by Quinn Voss that you might like